1/17/18

To Diane

Thank you

for your generous support

[illegible]

The Black Book of the American Left

The Black Book of the American Left

The Collected Conservative Writings of David Horowitz

Volume III

The Great Betrayal

Second Thoughts Books
Los Angeles

First American edition published in 2013 by Second Thoughts Books.

Manufactured in the United States and printed on acid-free paper. The paper used in this publication meets the minimum requirements of ANSI/NISO Z39.48 1992 (R 1997) *(Permanence of Paper)*.

Book design and production by Catherine Campaigne; copy-edited by David Landau; research provided by Mike Bauer.

FIRST AMERICAN EDITION

LIBRARY OF CONGRESS CATALOGING-IN-PUBLICATION DATA

Horowitz, David, 1939–
The black book of the American left : the collected conservative writings of David Horowitz / by David Horowitz.
volumes cm.
Includes bibliographical references and index.
ISBN 978-1-886442-96-2 (hardback)
1. Social movements—United States—History. 2. Radicalism—United States. 3. Anti-Americanism—United States. 4. Horowitz, David, 1939– Political and social views. I. Title.
HX86.H788 2013
335.00973 2013000496

10 9 8 7 6 5 4 3 2 1

Contents

INTRODUCTION TO VOLUME III

The Great Betrayal

The Great Betrayal is the third volume of my collected writings that make up *The Black Book of the American Left.* Its chapters focus on events beginning with the Islamic attacks of 9/11 and culminating in the Iraq War. They describe what can now be seen as a tragic turn in our nation's history that has already profoundly and adversely affected its future.

The effort to remove the Saddam regime in Iraq by force was initially supported by both major political parties. But in only the third month of fighting the Democratic Party turned against the war it had authorized for reasons unrelated to events on the battlefield or changes in policy. This political division over the war fractured the home front with crippling implications for the war effort itself and, beyond that, America's efforts to curtail the terrorist activities of other regimes in the Middle East, most pointedly Syria and Iran. The internal divisions were greater than any the nation had experienced since the Civil War, and the betrayal by the Democrats of a war policy they had supported was without precedent in the history of America's wars overseas.

The internal divisions at the end of the Vietnam War were not at all commensurate with those over Iraq. The 1972 McGovern presidential campaign, which called for an American retreat from Vietnam, was launched after ten years of fighting with no result, when both parties had already conceded the war could not be won. The conflict between the two major parties was over how to end the war and over what the war had become, not—as in Iraq—over whether the war was illegal and immoral to begin with and should never have been fought. The Democrats' opposition to a war they had authorized, represented a betrayal of the nation and its men and women in arms that has no equivalent in American history.

The domestic divisions over both wars were initiated by a radical left whose agendas went far beyond the conflicts themselves. In the decades that followed their efforts to bring the Vietnam War to an ignoble end, the left had made ever deeper inroads into the Democratic Party until, in 2008, the party nominated a senator from its anti-war ranks who became the 44th president of the United States.[1] Of far greater significance than the successful candidacy of one anti-war spokesman, however, was the path the entire Democratic Party took in first abandoning a war its leaders had approved, and then conducting a five-year campaign against the war while it was still in progress.

I have written two previous books about this defection and its destructive consequences. The first, *Unholy Alliance* (2004), documented the emergence of the post-9/11 anti-war movement, its tacit alliance with the *jihadist* enemy and its malign influence on the Democratic Party's fateful turn.[2] The second, *Party of Defeat* (2008), was written with Ben Johnson and focused on the sabotage of the war effort by leaders of the Democratic Party, by progressive activists and by a left-leaning national media. This chorus of opposition took advantage of American missteps to conduct a no-holds-barred propaganda campaign worthy of an enemy, even going so far as to leak classified information that destroyed vital national security programs and put all Americans at risk.[3] Political opponents of the war attacked the moral character of the commander-in-chief and the mission both parties had endorsed. This assault on America's role in the war dealt a devastating blow to American power and influence from which they have yet to recover.

---

[1]Barack Obama's long-standing roots in the radical left are documented in Stanley Kurtz, *Radical-in-Chief*, Threshold, 2010.

[2]*Unholy Alliance: Radical Islam and the American Left*, Regnery, 2004

[3]*Party of Defeat: How Democrats and Radicals Undermined America's War on Terror Before and After 9/11* (with Ben Johnson), Spence, 2008

It is customary and natural for human beings to identify with the communities they inhabit, and on whose health and security their lives depend. This is the foundation of all patriotic sentiment. But once individuals become possessed by the idea that political power can be "transformative" and create a fundamentally different human environment, they develop an allegiance to the idea itself and to the parties and entities in which they see it embodied. Such individuals come to feel alienated from the societies they live in but are determined to replace, and finally to see their own country as an enemy because it is the enemy of their progressive dreams. This is how generations of leftists came to identify with the Communist adversary and its cold war against the democracies of the West.

When the Communist empire collapsed, I was curious to see whether this progressive reflex would survive the fall. Lacking the real world instantiation of their dreams Soviet Russia had provided, would progressives continue to volunteer as frontier guards for America's enemies, even the most reprehensible among them?[4] The answer was not long in coming.

On November 9, 1989, the Berlin Wall came down, liberating hundreds of millions of captive people from their Soviet prison. The following August, Iraq's sadistic dictator ordered his armies into Kuwait and erased that sovereign nation from the political map. Unlike the Soviet rulers who paid lip service to progressive ideals, Saddam Hussein was a self-identified fascist who did not pretend to advance the cause of "social justice" or liberal values. Even by 20th-century standards, Saddam was an exceptionally cruel and bloody tyrant. But he was also an enemy of the United States, and that proved enough to persuade progressives to lend him a helping hand. When America organized an international coalition to reverse Iraq's aggression, the progressive left opposed the action as though America rather than the Saddam regime were at fault.

---

[4]See the introduction to Volume II in this series for the origins of the term "frontier guards" to describe the behaviors of the international left.

At the time, the only reason there were no large protests against the war over Kuwait was because progressives were freshly demoralized by the Soviet debacle and still in disarray. But their mood changed over the course of the next decade. As the millennium approached, leftists began to regroup, organizing a series of large and violent demonstrations against "globalization," the term with which they re-labeled their old nemesis "international capitalism." When Islamic fanatics attacked New York and Washington in 2001, leaders of the globalization protests re-positioned their agendas to focus on the new American "imperialism" in Afghanistan and then Iraq. Eventually, millions of leftists at home and abroad participated in protests to prevent America and the coalition it led from removing Saddam Hussein. Without overtly supporting the Saddam regime as they had the Kremlin, progressives resumed their role as frontier guards for the enemies of the United States.[5]

The chapters of *The Great Betrayal* consist of articles that were written as the post-9/11 events were unfolding. Because they were written as the events were taking place, the individual chapters are best read in sequence, and are arranged in chronological order for that purpose. I have edited the selections to clean up infelicities that are the price one pays for working on deadlines and in the heat of battle. Some repetitive passages have been excised, while some new passages have been inserted to clarify the historical context for readers coming at these issues for the first time. In making these texts more readable I have refrained from inserting views of the events that I did not hold or express at the time.

---

[5]These developments are described and analyzed in *Unholy Alliance: Radical Islam and the American Left*, Regnery, 2004.

PART I

The War on Terror

(9/11/2001–2/18/2002)

I

Today Is Pearl Harbor

The destruction of the World Trade Center, the attack on the Pentagon, the revelation to all the world that even the White House is vulnerable, should be a wakeup call to Americans. This country is at war, and we are far behind in securing our citizens' safety and preparing for our defense. How was it possible to hijack four commercial airliners from major airports—one of them Dulles International—and to do so within a set time frame? How could obvious targets like the Pentagon and the World Trade Center Towers be so undefended?

We know the answer. America is soft. America is in denial. America is embarrassed at the idea that it has enemies and must protect itself. America has been so eager to cash in on "peace dividends" from the Cold War that it has stripped itself of prudent defenses. Americans are unwilling to recognize that much of the world hates us, and will continue to hate us because we are prosperous, democratic and free.

Today's tragedies must be a wakeup call. It's time for us to remember that the first duty of government is to provide for the common defense. That means it's time to spend the economic surplus on national security now, beginning with a missile-defense system that will prevent even bigger terrorist disasters in the future. It is time to dramatically increase our domestic counter-terrorist and intelligence efforts, and to step up the monitoring of

---

Published on September 11, 2001; http://archive.frontpagemag.com/Printable.aspx?ArtId=21215

all groups who have declared war on the United States. It's time to tighten our security systems, beginning with airport checks, to let the imperative of profiling potential terrorists—Islamic and Palestinian terrorists—outweigh the objections of the ACLU and other leftist groups. It's time for those on the political left to rethink their alliances with anti-American radicals at home and abroad. It's time for the president to identify the monsters who planned this day of infamy, and then to carry out a massive military strike against them and any government who sponsored these acts.

In sum, it is time for a new sobriety in America about what is at stake in the political battles with those who condemn America as an "oppressor" nation and the "root cause" of the attacks on itself. It is time for Americans who love this country to stand up in her defense.

2

Enemies Within

On the morning of the attacks on the World Trade Center and the Pentagon, readers of the *New York Times*—including many who would never be able to read the paper again—opened its pages to be confronted by a color photo showing a middle-aged couple holding hands and affecting a defiant look at the camera. In an irony that could not have been more poignant, the article was headlined, "No Regrets for a Love of Explosives."[1] The couple pictured were Bill Ayers and Bernardine Dohrn, former leaders of the 1960s' Weather Underground, America's first terrorist cult. One of their bombing targets, as it happened, was the Pentagon.

"I don't regret setting bombs," Ayers was quoted in the opening line of *The Times'* profile; "I feel we didn't do enough."[2] In 1969, Ayers and Dohrn led a "war council" in Flint, Michigan whose purpose was to launch a military offensive inside the United States to help Third World revolutionaries conquer and destroy it. Dressed in high-heeled boots and a leather mini-skirt—her signature uniform—Dohrn incited the assembled radicals to join the war against "Amerikkka" and create chaos and destruction in "the

September 17, 2001; http://archive.frontpagemag.com/Printable.aspx?ArtId=24446; http://www.salon.com/2001/09/18/ayers_3/

[1]Dinitia Smith, "No Regrets for a Love of Explosives; In a Memoir of Sorts, a War Protester Talks of Life With the Weathermen," *The New York Times*, September 11, 2001, http://www.nytimes.com/2001/09/11/books/no-regrets-for-love-explosives-memoir-sorts-war-protester-talks-life-with.html

[2]Ibid.

belly of the beast." Her voice rising to a fevered pitch, Dohrn raised three fingers in a "fork salute" to mass-murderer Charles Manson, whom she proposed as a symbol to her troops. Referring to the helpless victims of the so-called Manson family as the "Tate Eight" (after the actress they murdered, Sharon Tate), Dohrn shouted: "Dig it. First they killed those pigs, then they ate dinner in the same room with them, they even shoved a fork into a victim's stomach! Wild!"[3]

Embarrassed today by this memory, but unable to expunge it from the record and unwilling to repudiate the politics that led to her terrorist deeds, Dohrn resorted to the lie direct. "It was a joke," she told the sympathetic *Times* reporter, Dinitia Smith. Dohrn was actually protesting America's own crimes, she said. "We were mocking violence in America. Even in my most inflamed moment I never supported a racist mass murderer."[4] In 1980 I conducted interviews with thirty members of the Weather Underground who were present at the Flint War Council, including most of its leadership. Not one of them thought Dohrn was anything but deadly serious when she uttered her infamous salute.[5] It was a direct incitement, not a satirical aside. As soon as her tribute to Manson was completed, Dohrn was followed to the platform by another Weather leader who ranted, "We're against everything that's 'good and decent' in honky America. We will loot and burn and destroy. We are the incubation of your mothers' nightmares."[6]

It has long been a fashion among media sophisticates to ridicule the late J. Edgar Hoover and the FBI agents who sought to protect Americans from the threats posed by people like Ayers and Dohrn and their "Days of Rage." But Hoover's description of

---

[3]Ibid.

[4]Ibid.

[5]See the account of the Weather Underground written by Peter Collier and me, "Doing It," in *Destructive Generation,* Summit, 1989).

[6]The speaker was John Jacobs, otherwise known as "J. J." Ronald Radosh, "Don't Need a Weatherman," *The Weekly Standard,* October 8, 2001, https://www.weeklystandard.com/Content/Public/Articles/000/000/000/267rdlhy.asp

Bernardine Dohrn as "La Pasionaria of the lunatic left"[7] is far more accurate than anything that can be found in the *New York Times* profile.

Instead of a critique of this malignant pair and their destructive resume, *The Times'* portrait provides a soft-focus promotion for Ayers's newly published *Fugitive Days,* a memoir notable for its dishonesty and its celebration of his malevolent exploits.[8] Ayers's text wallows in familiar Marxist incitements and the homicidal delusions of Sixties radicalism; it includes a loving reprint of an editorial from the old socialist magazine *Alarm!* written by Albert Parsons, one of the violent Haymarket anarchists, whom the Weathermen idolized:

> Dynamite! Of all the good stuff, that is the stuff! Stuff several pounds of this sublime stuff into an inch pipe ... plug up both ends, insert a cap with a fuse attached, place this in the immediate vicinity of a lot of rich loafers who live by the sweat of other people's brows, and light the fuse. A most cheerful and gratifying result will follow. In giving dynamite to the downtrodden millions of the globe, science has done its best work.[9]

In *Fugitive Days,* Ayers has written—and *The Times* has promoted—a text that the bombers of the World Trade Center could have packed in their flight bags, alongside the Koran, as they embarked on their sinister mission. "Memory is a motherf*cker," Ayers warns his readers, in the illiterate style that made him an icon of the New Left. It is as close as he gets to acknowledging that his account leaves World-Trade-Center-size holes in the story of his criminal past. Among them is how Weatherman imploded in the year other Americans were celebrating the bicentennial of their nation, because the devotion of its members to the bibles of

---

[7]Dinitia Smith, op. cit.

[8]Bill Ayers, *Fugitive Days,* Beacon Press, September 10, 2001

[9]Albert Parsons, *Alarm!,* February 21, 1885. *The Alarm* was one of the leading anarchist newspapers in the country during the 1880s. It was edited and published in Chicago. See: http://chicagocrimescenes.blogspot.com/2009/01/arbeiter-zeitung-and-alarm.html

the cause—Lenin, Stalin, Mao—eventually led them into a series of brainwashing rituals and purges that decimated their ranks. None of this is remembered in Ayers's book. Nor is the passage of their closest comrades into the ranks of the May 19th Communist Organization, which murdered three officers, including the first black policeman on the Nyack, NY force, during the infamous robbery of a Brinks armored car in 1981. The point of the omissions is to hide from others (and from Ayers himself) the real-world consequences of the anti-American ideologies that took root in the Sixties and now flourish on college campuses across the country.

Today William Ayers is not merely an author favored by *The New York Times* but a "Distinguished Professor" of Education at the University of Illinois, Chicago.[10] His Lady Macbeth is not merely a lawyer but a member of the American Bar Association's governing elite, as well as the director of Northwestern University's Children and Family Justice Center.[11] These facts reflect a reality about the culture of facile defamation of America, and the instinct to appease her mortal enemies, that confronts us as we struggle to deal with the terrorist attack.

President Bush has correctly defined the repulsive deed that left 3,000 dead as an "act of war." It must be said that this is a very belated recognition of our reality, which was postponed for almost a decade by a Democratic administration infused with the attitudes of self-flagellation and moral equivalence perfectly expressed on the day of the attack by John Lahr, a writer for the Microsoft Internet journal *Slate.* On this day that crushed to death and burned alive 3,000 innocent civilians at their workplaces, John Lahr advised America to "Rush to Thought, Not to Judgment."(!)

> I fear the hysteria in the American character, which splits so easily into good and bad, which rushes to judgment rather than to thought. The terrorists have taken aim at the American government and American capitalism and brought them both—

[10]http://www.discoverthenetworks.org/individualProfile.asp?indid=2169
[11]http://www.discoverthenetworks.org/individualProfile.asp?indid=2190

> symbolically at least—down. America, from the point of view of the terrorists, has been humiliated and brutalized as they feel they have felt humiliated and brutalized by America.[12]

This is the we-feel-your-terrorist-pain appeasement perspective perfectly tuned. The hysteria in the *American* character! A character that permitted fanatical America-haters to bomb the World Trade Center in a test run in 1993 without so much as instituting serious security at its airports lest the American Civil Liberties Union and other members of the appeasement coalition take their government to court to ensure that foreign terrorists, too, enjoy the rights of law-abiding American citizens. Hysterical America, which during the Clinton years forbade its intelligence operatives from using assets who were "human-rights violators" in their efforts to prevent such terrorist attacks. Who in these Middle Eastern thugdoms with any access to authority or power, let alone terrorist networks, is not a *human-rights violator*? Liberal self-hatred masquerading as a concern for human rights was the primary reason that such a complicated and lethal attack could be planned and carried out without coming to the attention of American intelligence agencies. It was more important for the liberals in the Clinton administration to be sensitive to the utopian concerns of the progressive elites, and of the one-world kleptocrats at the UN, than to protect the American people.

America the brutalizer! Osama bin Laden, our terrorist enemy and mass murderer, is not exactly one of the huddled masses targeted by American imperialists. He is a Saudi prince. Omar Abdel Rahman, architect of the first World Trade Center bombing, is a sheik. Brutalization is not what they suffer. They *are* the brutes. Like other radical zealots, they are driven by a religious fanaticism, confident that God is on their side and that those who do not share their faith—Christians, Jews, atheists—are *infidels*, worthy

---

[12]John Lahr, "John Lahr and August Wilson," *Slate*, September 11, 2001, http://www.slate.com/articles/life/the_breakfast_table/features/2001/john_lahr_and_august_wilson/rush_to_thought_not_judgment.html

of destruction. In Palestinian schools in democratic Israel, Palestinian schoolchildren are taught by their Palestinian teachers to chant, "Destroy the heathen Jews." Not those who have actually injured them, but those who are not Muslims. Religious fanaticism will express itself in political—and eventually military—fanaticism, whatever America does. Ask not, Americans, what your country has done to deserve its pain. Ask what has been done to inflict pain on your country and what you can do about it.

In May 1998, three years before the World Trade Center's destruction, Osama bin Laden was interviewed by ABC News reporter John Miller. He explained his war this way:[13]

> John Miller: Mr. bin Laden, you have issued a fatwa [death sentence] calling on all Muslims to kill Americans where they can, when they can. Is that directed at all Americans, just American military, just Americans in Saudi Arabia?
>
> Osama bin Laden: Allah ordered us ... to purify Muslim land of all non-believers.... We are surprised this question is coming from Americans.... American history does not distinguish between civilians and military, and not even women and children. They are the ones who used the bombs against Nagasaki.... *America does not have a religion that will prevent it from destroying all people....* We are sure of Allah's victory and our victory against the Americans and the Jews as promised by the prophet, peace be upon him.... We predict a black day for America and the end of the United States as United States.... (emphasis added)

Is this clear enough? This holy war is not about American *acts.* It is about who we *are.* It is not a war that can be negotiated away. It is them or us.

This is the hour for America to take care of itself, to take steps to defend itself. America must be hard where it has been soft, calculating where it has been sensitive, strong where it has been

---

[13]*Frontline,* May 1998, http://www.pbs.org/wgbh/pages/frontline/shows/binladen/who/interview.html

weak. For Osama bin Laden is impressed with American weakness, the very kind of weakness urged by appeasers like John Lahr.

Rush to thought, not judgment.

> Osama bin Laden: We have seen in the last decade the decline of the American government and the weakness of the American soldier. He is ready to wage cold wars but unprepared to fight hot wars. This was proven in Beirut when the Marines fled after two explosions, showing they can run in less than twenty-four hours. This was then repeated in Somalia. *We are ready for all occasions. We rely on Allah.*[14]

On the day of the World Trade Center's destruction, I appeared on a Fox TV program in San Diego and did my best to steer the discussion towards the steps America must take to defend herself, to carry the war to the enemy camp. But the host would have none of it. While thousands of Americans lay underneath the rubble of the Trade Center, she wanted to discuss the danger of American "hysteria," the "threat" that American prejudice might pose to Muslims in our midst. It did not even occur to her that, if Americans were prejudiced in a way that made this issue pressing, these terrorists would never have been trained as pilots by American companies, housed in American homes, or ignored by American security agents at the airports where they hijacked the airliners in order to convert them into bombs.

Bill Ayers and Bernardine Dohrn are a far more typical academic couple, and their *New York Times* interviewer a far more familiar arbiter of information to the American public, than it is comforting to contemplate. We have already been treated to TV

---

[14]*ABC News* Transcript of 1998 Interview with Osama Bin Laden, May 28, 1998, http://abcnews.go.com/2020/video/osama-bin-laden-interview-1998–13506629; Osama Bin Laden Interview, May 1998, (*ABC News* Video), http://abcnews.go.com/2020/video/osama-bin-laden-interview-1998–13506629; "Usama bin Ladin: 'American Soldiers Are Paper Tigers'," *Middle East Quarterly,* December 1998, pp. 73–79, http://www.meforum.org/435/usama-bin-ladin-american-soldiers-are-paper-tigers

images of college students shifting the blame to American shoulders while the embers of the Trade Center are still warm. Many of us have children or grandchildren in secondary schools who, in this hour of mourning, have been lectured by their teachers on America's sins and on chickens coming home to roost. The political friends of Bill Ayers and Bernardine Dohrn have been busily at work for the last two decades, seeding our educational culture with anti-American poisons that may one day destroy us.

A visit to a well-traveled website "Building Progressive Community" reveals how profoundly America has been rejected, and how passionately its bloodthirsty enemies have been embraced, by significant sections of our population, even as we enter a life-and-death struggle with an enemy that wants to exterminate us:

- Not only have we caused these events with our monstrous foreign policies but also with our complete disregard of our environment causing mortal damage to the Earth (Earth is a living being) and other species that co-exist with us.—Susan Yost, Cumberland, VA
- My heart went out to all the people there as I sat watching, waiting ... and then sadness filled me, sadness that the foreign policy of this country has come back to haunt us; sadness that our government has been so arrogant that a lesson like this occurred; ... It is U.S. policies of terror in other countries that have brought this down on us. —Matthew A Peckham, Eugene, OR
- Our corporate entities not only run this country but have decimated many other small countries in ways we cannot even fathom.... This is a wake up call, America. It is time to change our ways. —Rich Cianflone, Colorado
- We are reaping what we have sown. We will now have the dreaded opportunity to live in the same fear that our financial policies and military assistance have inflicted on others. — Harold Parkey, Fort Worth, TX
- For 56 years, Washington has successfully conducted mass murders.... —William Mandel, Oakland, California (Mandel is

a lifelong Communist and taxpayer-funded public radio commentator.)

- The United States conducts itself as a terrorist organization throughout the world. —Lance Del Goebel, Manhattan, IL
- U.S. foreign policy has come home to roost today ... we are reaping what we have sown. —Glynn Ash[15]

America, the Great Satan.

Actually, these comments are merely cribbed from bin Laden's friend, Saddam Hussein, whose response to the Trade Center attacks was as follows: "Notwithstanding the conflicting human feelings about what happened in America yesterday, America is reaping the thorns sown by its rulers in the world. Those thorns have not only bloodied the feet and the hearts of many, but also the eyes of people shedding tears on their dead whose souls have been reaped by America."[16] Saddam then invoked a litany of misdeeds that could have come from a primer written by Noam Chomsky, Howard Zinn or any number of familiar anti-American leftists: "There is no place that does not have a symbolic monument that shows America's criminal acts against these victims, whether in Japan that was the first to be seared by the nuclear destruction weapons boasted by America, or Vietnam, Iraq ... or the criminal acts the US is now perpetrating by supporting the criminal racist Zionism against our heroic Palestinian people...."[17]

This is the banal excuse of common criminals—the devil made me do it. "I don't think you can understand a single thing we did," explained the pampered bomber Ayers to *The New York Times,* "without understanding the violence of the Vietnam War."[18]

---

[15]http://www.commondreams.org/

[16]Robert Draper, *Dead Certain: The Presidency of George W. Bush,* Free Press, 2008, p. 172

[17]David Horowitz, *How to Beat the Democrats and Other Subversive Ideas,* Spence, 2002, p. 191

[18]Dinitia Smith, op. cit.

I interviewed Ayers ten years ago, in a kindergarten classroom in uptown Manhattan where he was employed to shape the minds of inner-city children. Dressed in bib overalls with golden curls rolling below his ears, Ayers reviewed his activities as a terrorist for my tape recorder. When he was done, he broke into a broad, Jack Horner grin and summed up his experience: "Guilty as hell. Free as a bird. America is a great country."[19]

In my experience, what drives most radicals are passions of resentment, envy and inner rage. Bill Ayers is a scion of wealth. His father was head of Detroit's giant utility Commonwealth Edison, in line for a cabinet position in the Nixon administration before his son ruined it by going on a rampage that to this day he cannot explain to any reasonable person's satisfaction (which is why he has to conceal so much). It could be said of Bill Ayers that he was consumed by angers so terrible they led him to destroy his father's career. But in the ten hours I interviewed him I saw none of it. What I saw was a shallowness beyond conception. All the Weather leaders I interviewed shared a similar vacuity. They were living inside a utopian fantasy, a separate reality, and had no idea of what they had done. Nor any way to measure it. Appreciating the nation into which they had been born, recognizing the great gifts of freedom and opportunity their parents and communities had given them, distinguishing between right and wrong—it was all above their mental and moral ceilings.

In the days ahead, this is only one—but a very important one—of the dangers we face.

---

[19]David Horowitz, op. cit.

3

A Congressional Dissent

Representative Barbara Lee, Democrat of Berkeley and Oakland, was the only member of Congress who refused to defend her country under attack. The *Los Angeles Times* describes Barbara Lee as a "liberal" and compares her to "anti-war" dissenters of the past, most notably Jeanette Rankin, who cast the lone vote in the U.S. Congress against America's entry into the Second World War. Rankin said after Pearl Harbor, "As a woman I can't go to war, and I refuse to send anyone else."

Barbara Lee is not an anti-war activist, she is a communist (small "c") who supports America's enemies and has actively collaborated with them in their war against her country. I first met Barbara Lee when she was working in city politics in Oakland. Our meeting took place in the penthouse headquarters of Huey Newton, the self-styled "Minister of Defense" for the Black Panther Party. Newton was a political gangster at war with America, and Barbara Lee was his undercover agent in local government.

Lee later became a staffer in the office of Democratic congressman Ron Dellums. In this capacity, she committed an act of betrayal that cannot be called treason only because she was never prosecuted for it. At the time, Ron Dellums was the head of the House subcommittee on Military Installations. In that capacity, he had top security clearance and was engaged in a one-man cam-

---

September 19, 2001; http://archive.frontpagemag.com/Printable.aspx?ArtId=21218

paign to thwart U.S. policy towards the Communist dictatorship of Grenada.

U.S. security officials had identified the Communist dictatorship as a threat because of the presence of large numbers of Soviet-bloc advisors and their ongoing construction of an airport that could be used for Soviet military planes. As the ranking Democrat on the House Armed Services Committee, Dellums arranged a trip to Grenada to conduct his own fact-finding tour. On his return, he testified before the House subcommittee on Inter-American Affairs that "based on my personal observations, discussion and analysis of the new international airport under construction in Grenada, it is my conclusion that this project is specifically now and has always been for the purpose of economic development and is not for military use.... It is my thought that it is absurd, patronizing and totally unwarranted for the United States Government to charge that this airport poses a military threat to the United States' national security."[1]

What legislators did not know at the time was that Dellums had previously submitted his report on the airport to the Communist dictator of Grenada for his prior approval, with an offer to make any changes that the dictator or his military advisers might ask. In other words, Dellums acted as an agent of the Communist enemy in abetting his hostile designs against the United States. His emissary in this act of betrayal was Barbara Lee.

We know this from government documents retrieved by U.S. Marines after Grenada was liberated by U.S. forces. One document was a love-letter from Dellums's chief of staff, Carlottia Scott (recent political-issues director of the Democratic National Committee), to the Grenadian dictator himself, Maurice Bishop. In the letter Carlottia Scott wrote: "Ron [Dellums] has become truly committed to Grenada, and has some positive political thinking to

---

[1]*The Grenada Papers,* edited by Paul Seabury and Walter A. McDougall, Institute for Contemporary Studies, 1984, Ch. V, *Propaganda and Public Relations Work in The United States.* Cf. also Peter Collier and David Horowitz, *Destructive Generation,* Summit, 1989), pp. 188–189

share with you.... He's really hooked on you and Grenada and doesn't want anything to happen to building the Revolution and making it strong. He really admires you as a person and even more so as a leader with courage and foresight, principles and integrity.... The only other person that I know of that he expresses such admiration for is Fidel."[2]

Another document liberated by the Marines contained the minutes of a Politburo meeting attended by the Communist dictator and his military command. "Barbara Lee is here presently and has brought with her a report on the international airport that was done by Ron Dellums. They have requested that we look at the document and suggest any changes we deem necessary. They will be willing to make the changes."

If this is not treason, what is?

[2]Ibid.

4

How the Left Undermined America's Security Before 9/11

While the nation was having a good laugh at the expense of Florida's hanging chads and butterfly ballots, Mohammed Atta and Marwan al Shehhi were there, in Florida, learning to drive commercial jetliners [and ram them into the World Trade Center towers]. It will take a novelist to paint that broad canvas properly. It will take some deep political thinking to understand how the lackadaisical attitude toward government and the world helped leave the country so unready for the horror that Atta and Shehhi were preparing.

—Michael Oreskes, *New York Times,* October 21, 2001

The September 11 attacks on the Pentagon and the World Trade Center marked the end of one American era and the beginning of another. As did Pearl Harbor, the September tragedy awakened Americans from insular slumbers and made them aware of a world they could not afford to ignore. Like Franklin Roosevelt, George W. Bush condemned the attacks as acts of war and mobilized a nation to action. It was a dramatic departure from the policy of his predecessor, Bill Clinton, who in characteristic self-absorption had downgraded a series of similar assaults—including onc on the World Trade Center itself—officially regarding them as criminal matters that involved individuals alone.

February 18, 2002, http://archive.frontpagemag.com/Printable.aspx?ArtId=21318

But the differences between the September 11 attacks and Pearl Harbor were also striking. The latter was a military base situated on an island 3,000 miles distant from the American mainland. New York is America's greatest population center, the portal through which immigrant generations of all colors and ethnicities have come in search of a better life. The World Trade Center is the Wall Street hub of the economy they enter; its victims were targeted for participating in the most productive, tolerant and generous society human beings have created. In responding to the attacks, the president himself took note of this: "America was targeted for attack," he told Congress on September 20, "because we're the brightest beacon for freedom and opportunity in the world. And no one will keep that light from shining."

In contrast to Pearl Harbor, the assault on the World Trade Center was hardly a "sneak attack" that American intelligence agencies had little idea was coming. Its Twin Towers had already been bombed eight years earlier, and by the same enemy. The terrorists themselves were already familiar to government operatives, their aggressions frequent enough that several government commissions had been appointed to investigate them. Each had reached the same conclusion. It was not a matter of *whether* the United States was going to be the target of a major terrorist assault; it was a matter of *when.*[1]

In fact, the al-Qaeda terrorists responsible for the September 11 attacks had first engaged U.S. troops as early as 1993, when the Clinton administration deployed U.S. military forces to Somalia.

---

[1]Judith Miller, "A Nation Challenged; the Response; Planning for Terror but Failing to Act," *The New York Times,* December 30, 2001, http://www.nytimes.com/2001/12/30/us/a-nation-challenged-the-response-planning-for-terror-but-failing-to-act.html?pagewanted=all; "If you understood al-Qaeda," Robert Bryant, deputy director of the FBI, told *The Times,* "you knew something was going to happen. You knew they were going to hit us, but you didn't know where. It just made me sick on September 11. I cried when those towers came down." In fact, investigators had almost guessed where the enemy would strike. The report of the National Commission on Terrorism, published in 2000, had a picture of the Twin Towers in the cross-hairs on its cover.

Their purpose was humanitarian: to feed the starving citizens of that Muslim land. But when they arrived, America's goodwill ambassadors were ambushed by al-Qaeda forces. In a 15-hour battle in Mogadishu, 18 Americans were killed and 80 wounded. One dead U.S. soldier was dragged through the streets in an act calculated to humiliate his comrades and his country. The Americans' offense was not that they had brought food to the hungry. Their crime was who they *were*—"unbelievers," emissaries of "the Great Satan," in the political religion of the enemy they now faccd.

The defeat in Mogadishu was a blow not only to American charity but to American power and prestige. Nonetheless, under the leadership of America's commander-in-chief, Bill Clinton, there was no military response to the humiliation. The greatest superpower that the world had ever seen did nothing. It accepted defeat.

The War

On February 26, 1993, eight months prior to the Mogadishu attack, al-Qaeda terrorists had struck the World Trade Center for the first time. Their truck-bomb made a crater six stories deep, killed six people and injured more than a thousand. The planners' intention had been to cause one tower to topple the other and kill tens of thousands of innocent people. It was not only the first major terrorist act ever to take place on U.S. soil but—in the judgment of a definitive account of the event—"the most ambitious terrorist attack ever attempted, anywhere, ever."[2]

Six Palestinian and Egyptian conspirators responsible for the attack were tried in civil courts and got life sentences like common criminals, but its mastermind escaped. He was identified as Ramzi Ahmed Yousef, an Iraqi Intelligence agent. This was a clear indication to authorities that the atrocity was no mere criminal

---

[2]Laurie Mylroie, *Study of Revenge: Saddam Hussein's Unfinished War Against America,* American Enterprise Institute, 2000, p. 1

event, and that it involved more than individual terrorists; it involved hostile terrorist states.

Yet here, too, the Clinton administration's response was to absorb the injury and accept defeat. The president did not even visit the bomb-crater or tend to the victims. Instead, America's commander-in-chief warned against "overreaction." In doing so, he telegraphed a clear message to his nation's enemies: We are unsure of purpose and unsteady of hand; we are self-indulgent and soft; we will not take risks to defend ourselves; we are vulnerable.

Among the terrorist groups that supported the al-Qaeda terrorists was Yasser Arafat's Palestine Liberation Organization. The PLO had created the first terrorist training camps, invented suicide bombings and been the chief propaganda machine behind the idea that terrorist armies were really missionaries for "social justice." Yet, among foreign leaders, Arafat was Clinton's most frequent White House guest. Far from treating Arafat as an enemy of civilized order and an international pariah, the Clinton administration was busily cultivating him as a "partner for peace." For many Washington liberals, terrorism was not the instrument of political fanatics and evil men; it was the product of social conditions—poverty, racism and oppression—for which the Western democracies, particularly America and Israel, were to blame.

The idea that terrorism is rooted in social conditions whose primary source is the United States is, in fact, an organizing theme of the contemporary political left. "Where is the acknowledgment that this [9/11] was not a 'cowardly' attack on 'civilization' or 'liberty' or 'humanity' or 'the free world,'" declared the writer Susan Sontag, speaking for the left, "but an attack on the world's self-proclaimed superpower, undertaken as a consequence of specific American alliances and actions? How many citizens are aware of the ongoing American bombing of Iraq?"[3] Was Sontag unaware

[3]Susan Sontag, *The New Yorker,* September 24, 2001, http://www.newyorker.com/archive/2001/09/24/010924ta_talk_wtc (the comments were posted online on September 17).

that Iraq was behind the first World Trade Center attack? That Iraq had attempted to swallow Kuwait and was a regional aggressor and sponsor of terror? That Iraq had violated the terms of its peace by expelling the UN arms inspectors who were there to prevent it from developing chemical, biological and nuclear weapons? Was she unaware that Iraq was a sponsor of international terror and posed an ongoing threat to others, including the country in which she lived? Was she not aware that Iraq, having broken the 1991 Gulf War truce, was technically at war with the United States?

During the Clinton years, the idea that America was the root cause of global distress had become an all-too-familiar refrain among left-wing elites. It had particular resonance in the institutions that shaped American culture and government policies—universities, the mainstream media and the Oval Office, now occupied by Democrats. In March 1998, two months after Monica Lewinsky became a White House thorn and a household name, Clinton embarked on a presidential hand-wringing expedition to Africa. With a large delegation of African-American leaders in tow, the president made a pilgrimage to Uganda to apologize for the crime of American slavery. The apology was offered despite the fact that no slaves had ever been imported to America from Uganda or any East African state; that slavery in Africa preceded any American involvement by a thousand years; that America and Britain were the two powers responsible for ending the slave trade; and that America had abolished slavery a hundred years before—at great human cost—while slavery persisted in Africa, without African protest, to the present day.

Four months after Clinton left Uganda, al-Qaeda terrorists blew up the U.S. embassies in Kenya and Tanzania.

"Root Causes"

Clinton's continuing ambivalence about America's role in the world was highlighted in the wake of September 11, when he suggested that America actually bore some responsibility for the attacks on itself. In November 2001, even as the new Bush administration was launching America's military response, the former president made a speech in which he admonished citizens who were descended "from various European lineages" that they were "not blameless,"[4] and that America's past involvement in slavery should humble them as they confronted their attackers. Characteristically, the president took no responsibility for his own failure to protect Americans from the attacks.[5]

The idea that there are "root causes" behind campaigns to murder innocent men, women and children, or to terrorize civilian populations, was examined shortly after the Trade Center events by a writer in *The New York Times.* Columnist Edward Rothstein observed that, while there was much hand-wringing and many *mea culpas* on the left after September 11, no one had invoked "root causes" to defend Timothy McVeigh after he blew up the Oklahoma City Federal Building in 1995, killing 187 people.[6] "No

---

[4]The speech was made at Georgetown University on November 7, 2001. See the discussion below.

[5]Andrew Sullivan, *One Last Morrism,* January 11, 2002, http://dish.andrewsullivan.com/2002/01/page/4/; "Given my latest piece on Clinton's record on terrorism, I asked Dick Morris if he thought Clinton would be worried right now about what September 11 was doing to his legacy. Could Clinton be remorseful? Or angry? Or reflective? Morris's answer took a while, since he hasn't spoken to Clinton in years. Here's a short version of his answer: 'The thing about Bill Clinton is that he never, ever, ever, ever, EVER, ever, ever, ever, ever, ever, EVER, blames himself.'"

[6]Christopher Hitchens, "Strangers in a Strange Land," *The Atlantic,* December 2001, http://www.theatlantic.com/magazine/archive/2001/12/stranger-in-a-strange-land/302349/; "October 6, the day immediately preceding the first U.S. counterstroke against the Taliban and Osama bin Laden, found me on a panel at the New York Film Festival. The discussion, on the art of political cinema, had been arranged many months before. But as the chairman announced, the events of September 11 would now provide the atmospheric conditioning for our deliberations. I thus sat on a stage with Oliver Stone, who spoke with feeling about something he termed 'the revolt of September 11,' and with bell hooks, who informed a well-filled auditorium of the Lincoln Center that those who had experienced Spike Lee's movie about the bombing of a Birmingham, Alabama, church in 1963 would understand that 'state terrorism' was nothing new in America.... I would surmise that audience approval of Stone's and hooks's propositions was something near fifty-fifty.

one suggested that this act had its 'root causes' in an injustice that needed to be rectified to prevent further terrorism."[7] The silence was maintained even though McVeigh and his collaborators "asserted that their ideas of rights and liberty were being violated and that the only recourse was terror."[8]

The reason no one invoked "root causes" to explain the Oklahoma City bombing was simply that Timothy McVeigh was not a leftist. Nor did he claim to be acting in behalf of "social justice"—the historically proven code for totalitarian causes. In his address to Congress that defined America's response to September 11, President Bush observed: "We have seen their kind before. They are the heirs of all the murderous ideologies of the 20th century. By sacrificing human life to serve their radical visions, by abandoning every value except the will to power, they follow in the path of fascism, Nazism and totalitarianism."

Like Islamic radicalism, the totalitarian doctrines of communism and fascism are fundamentalist creeds. "The fundamentalist does not believe [his] ideas have any limits or boundaries,... [therefore] the goals of fundamentalist terror are not to eliminate injustice but to eliminate opposition."[9] That is why the humanitarian nature of America's mission to Mogadishu made no difference to America's al-Qaeda foe. The terrorists' goal was not to alleviate hunger. It was to eliminate America. It was to conquer "the Great Satan."

Clapping and hissing are feeble and fickle indicators, true. At different times, in combating both Stone and hooks, I got my own fair share of each. But let's say that three weeks after a mass murder had devastated the downtown district, and at a moment when the miasma from the site could still be felt and smelled, a ticket-buying audience of liberal New Yorkers awarded blame more or less evenhandedly between the members of al-Qaeda and the directors of U.S. foreign policy."

[7]Edward Rothstein, "Exploring the Flaws in the Notion of the 'Root Causes' of Terror," *The New York Times*, November 17, 2001, http://www.nytimes.com/2001/11/17/arts/17CONN.html

[8]The anti-American crank Gore Vidal, writing in *Vanity Fair*, was an exception.

[9]Rothstein, op. cit.

Totalitarians and fundamentalists share a conviction that is religious and political at the same time. Their mission is social redemption through the power of the state. Through political and military power, they intend to create a new world in their own image. This revolutionary transformation encompasses all individuals and requires the control of all aspects of human life:

"Like fundamentalist terror, totalitarian terror leaves no aspect of life exempt from the battle being waged. The state is felt to be the apotheosis of political and natural law, and it strives to extend that law over all humanity.... No injustices, separately or together, necessarily lead to totalitarianism and no mitigation of injustice, however defined, will eliminate its unwavering beliefs, absolutist control and unbounded ambitions."[10]

In 1998, Osama bin Laden explained his war aims to ABC News: "Allah ordered us in this religion to purify Muslim land of all non-believers."[11] As *The New Republic*'s Peter Beinart commented, bin Laden is not a crusader for social justice but "an ethnic cleanser on a scale far greater than the Hutus and the Serbs, a scale that has only one true Twentieth Century parallel."

In the 1990s, America mobilized its military power to go to the rescue of Muslims in the Balkans who were being ethnically cleansed by Serbian communists. This counted for nothing in al-Qaeda's calculations, any more than did America's support for Muslim peasants in Afghanistan fighting for their freedom against the Red Army invaders in the 1980s. The war being waged by radical Islam is not about what America has done, but about what

---

[10]Rothstein, ibid. Cf. my discussion of these issues in *The Politics of Bad Faith,* Free Press, 1998

[11]John Miller, op. cit. For the camera—and the credulous—bin Laden also mentioned other "causes" such as the bombing of Nagasaki. Since the left's attacks on America have almost become a conventional wisdom, it is perhaps necessary to remind some that the Japanese imperialists were the aggressors in World War II, and had invaded China and Southeast Asia with methods that violated international norms, including some of the worst atrocities in the history of warfare. Since the Japanese are not Muslims, bin Laden's expression of concern merely underscored his hypocrisy in mentioning them.

America is. As bin Laden told the world on October 7, the day America began its military response, the war is between those of the faith and those outside the faith; between those who submit to the believers' law and those who, as infidels, do not.[12]

While the Clinton Administration Slept

After the first World Trade Center attack, President Clinton vowed there would be vengeance. But, as with so many of his presidential pronouncements, the strong words were not accompanied by deeds. Nor were they followed by measures necessary to defend the country against the next series of Islamist attacks. After their Mogadishu victory and the 1993 World Trade Center bombing, unsuccessful attempts were made by al-Qaeda groups to blow up the Lincoln and Holland Tunnels and other populated targets, including a massive terrorist incident timed to coincide with the millennium celebrations of January 2000. Another scheme to hijack commercial airliners and use them as bombs, like those used on September 11, was thwarted in the Philippines in 1995. The architect of this effort was the Iraqi intelligence agent Ramzi Yousef.

The following year, 1996, a terrorist attack on the Khobar Towers, a U.S. military barracks in Saudi Arabia, killed 19 American soldiers. The White House response was limp, and the case (in the words of FBI director Louis B. Freeh) "remains unresolved."[13] Two years later, in 1998, al-Qaeda agents blew up the U.S. embassies in Kenya and Tanzania, killing 245 people and injuring 5,000. One CIA official told a reporter: "Two at once is not twice as hard. It is a hundred times as hard."[14] On October 12, 2000 the warship USS

---

[12]"Bin Laden's Warning," October 7, 2001, http://news.bbc.co.uk/2/hi/south_asia/1585636.stm

[13]Susan Page, "Why Clinton Failed To Stop Bin Laden," *USA Today*, November 12, 2001, http://usatoday30.usatoday.com/news/attack/2001/11/12/clinton-usatcov.htm

[14]Thomas Powers, "The Trouble With The CIA," *The New York Review of Books*, January 17, 2002, http://www.nybooks.com/articles/archives/2002/jan/17/the-trouble-with-the-cia/?pagination=false

Cole was bombed while re-fueling in Yemen, yet another Islamic country aligned with the terrorist enemy.[15] Seventeen U.S. sailors were killed and 39 injured.

These were all acts of war, yet the president and his cabinet refused to recognize them as such.[16]

Why the Clinton Administration Slept

Clinton's second-term national security advisor, Sandy Berger, described the official White House position towards these attacks as "a little bit like a Whack-A-Mole game at the circus. They bop up and you whack 'em down, and if they bop up again, you bop 'em back down again."[17] Like the administration he represented, the national security advisor lacked a requisite appreciation of the problem. Iraq's dictator was unimpressed by sporadic U.S. strikes against his regime. He remained defiant, expelling UN weapons inspectors, firing at U.S. warplanes and continuing to build his arsenal of mass destruction. But "the Administration held no clear and consistent view of the Iraqi threat and how it intended to address it,"[18] observed *Washington Post* correspondent Jim Hoagland. The disarray that characterized the Clinton security policy flowed from the "Administration's growing inability to tell the world—and itself—the truth."[19] It was the signature problem of the Clinton years.

Underlying the Clinton security failure was the fact that the administration was made up of people who for 25 years had discounted or minimized the totalitarian threat, opposed America's armed presence abroad, and consistently resisted the deployment of America's military forces to halt Communist expansion. National security advisor Sandy Berger was himself a veteran of

---

[15]Following the U.S. victory against the Taliban, the government of Yemen had second thoughts and began cooperating with Washington.
[16]Page, op. cit.
[17]Mylroie, op cit. p. 147
[18]Ibid.
[19]Ibid.

the Sixties "anti-war" movement which abetted the Communist victories in Vietnam and Cambodia, and created the "Vietnam War syndrome" that made it so difficult afterwards for American presidents to deploy the nation's military forces.

Berger had also been a member of "Peace Now," the leftist movement seeking to pressure the Israeli government to make concessions to Yasser Arafat's PLO terrorists. Clinton's first national security advisor, Anthony Lake, was a protégé of Berger, who had introduced him to Clinton. All three had met as activists in the 1972 McGovern presidential campaign, whose slogan was "Come Home America" and whose primary issue was opposition to the Vietnam War, based on the presumption that the "arrogance of American power" was responsible for the conflict, rather than Communist aggression.[20]

Anthony Lake's attitude towards the totalitarian threat in Southeast Asia was displayed in a March 1975 *Washington Post* article called, "At Stake in Cambodia: Extending Aid Will Only Prolong the Killing."[21] The prediction contained in Lake's title proved to be exactly wrong. Cutting off aid expanded the killing into a genocide. It was not a small mistake for someone who, 17 years later, would be placed in charge of America's national-security apparatus. Lake's article was designed to rally Democratic opposition to a presidential request for emergency aid to the Cambodian regime. The aid was required to contain the threat posed by Communist leader Pol Pot and his insurgent Khmer Rouge forces. At the time, Republicans warned that, if the aid was cut, the regime would fall and a "bloodbath" would ensue. This fear was solidly based on reports that had begun accumulating three years earlier, concerning "the extraordinary brutality with which the Khmer Rouge were governing the civilian population in areas they controlled."[22] But the Democratic-controlled Congress, heeding

[20]David Halberstam, *War in a Time of Peace*, Scribner, 2001, p. 20
[21]March 9, 1975
[22]Peter W. Rodman, *More Precious Than Peace: Fighting and Winning the Cold War in the Third World*, Scribner, 1994, p. 185

Lake's advice, dismissed these warnings as so much "anti-Communist hysteria" and voted to deny the aid.

In his *Post* article, Lake advised fellow Democrats to view the Khmer Rouge not as a totalitarian force—which it was—but as a coalition embracing "many Khmer nationalists, Communist and non-communist," who only desired independence. It would be a mistake, he wrote, to alienate Pol Pot and the Khmer Rouge, lest we "push them further into the arms of their Communist supporters."[23] Lake's left-wing myopia prevailed among the like-minded Democrats, and the following year the new president, Jimmy Carter, rewarded Lake with an appointment as policy planning director of the State Department.

In Cambodia, the termination of U.S. aid led immediately to the collapse of the government, allowing the Khmer Rouge to seize power within months of the congressional vote. The victorious revolutionaries proceeded to implement their plans for a new Communist utopia by systematically eliminating their opposition. In the next three years they killed nearly two million Cambodians, a campaign universally recognized as one of the worst genocides ever recorded.

The Warnings Ignored

For nearly a decade before the World Trade Center's destruction, the Clinton administration was aware that Americans were increasingly vulnerable to attacks that might involve biological or chemical weapons, or even nuclear devices bought or stolen from the broken pieces of the former Soviet Union. This was the insistent message of Republican speeches on the floors of Congress; it was reflected in the warnings of several government commissions and of Clinton's own Secretary of Defense, William Cohen (also a Republican).

In July 1999, for example, Cohen wrote an op-ed piece in *The Washington Post,* predicting a terrorist attack on the American

[23]Ibid.

mainland. "In the past year, dozens of threats to use chemical or biological weapons in the United States have turned out to be hoaxes. Someday, one will be real." But the warnings did not produce the requisite action by the commander-in-chief. Meanwhile, the nation's media looked the other way. The president of the Council on Foreign Relations told *The New Yorker*'s Joe Klein that he "watched carefully to see if anyone followed up on [Cohen's speech]. But none of the television networks and none of the elite press even mentioned it. I was astonished."[24]

The following year, the National Commission on Terrorism, chaired by former Reagan counter-terrorism head Paul Bremer, issued a report with the image of the Twin Towers on its cover. A bipartisan effort led by Jon Kyl and Dianne Feinstein attached the recommendations of the panel to an intelligence authorization bill. But Senator Patrick Leahy, who had distinguished himself in the 1980s by opposing the government's efforts to halt the Communist offensive in Central America, "said he feared a threat to 'civil liberties' in a campaign against terrorism and torpedoed the effort. After the bombing of the USS *Cole,* Kyl and Feinstein tried yet again. This time, Leahy was content with emaciating the proposals instead of defeating them outright. The weakened proposals died as the House realized 'it wasn't worth taking up.'"[25]

After the abortive plot to blow up commercial airliners in the Philippines, Vice President Gore was tasked with improving airline security. A commission was formed, but under his leadership it also "focused on civil liberties" and "profiling"—liberal obsessions that diluted any effort to strengthen security measures in the face of a threat in which all of the proven terrorists were Muslims from the Middle East and Asia. The commission concluded that

---

[24]Joe Klein, "Closework: Why We Couldn't See What Was Right in Front of Us," *The New Yorker,* October 1, 2001, p. 45, http://www.newyorker.com/PRINTABLE/?FACT/011001fa_FACT2

[25]Kevin Cherry, "Clinton Assigns Blame," *National Review Online,* November 8, 2001, http://old.nationalreview.com/comment/comment-cherry110801.shtml

"no profile [of passengers] should contain or be based on ... race, religion, or national origin." According to journalist Kevin Cherry, the FAA also decided in 1999 to seal its passenger screening system from law-enforcement databases, thus preventing the FBI from notifying airlines that suspected terrorists were on board.[26]

In 1993, the FBI identified three charities connected to the Palestinian terrorist organization Hamas that were being used to finance terrorist activities, sending as much as $20 million a year to America's enemies.[27] According to presidential adviser Dick Morris: "At a White House strategy meeting on April 27, 1995—two weeks after the Oklahoma City bombing—the President was urged to create a 'President's List' of extremist/terrorist groups, their members and donors 'to warn the public against well-intentioned donations which might foster terrorism.' On April 1, 1996, he was again advised to 'prohibit fund-raising by terrorists and identify terrorist organizations.'"[28] Hamas was specifically mentioned. Writes Morris: "Inexplicably Clinton ignored these recommendations. Why? FBI agents have stated that they were prevented from opening either criminal or national-security cases because of a fear that it would be seen as 'profiling' Islamic charities. While Clinton was 'politically correct,' Hamas flourished."[29]

In failing to heed the signs that America was at war with a deadly adversary, to overcome the ideological obstacles created by the liberal biases of his party, or to arouse an uninformed public to

---

[26]Ibid.

[27]Barton Gellman, "The Hunt for Bin Laden Part II: Struggles Inside the Government Defined Campaign," *Washington Post,* December 20, 2001, http://www.washingtonpost.com/ac2/wp-dyn/A3616-2001Dec19?language=printer; Dick Morris, "Why Clinton Slept," *NY Post,* January 2, 2002, http://www.angelfire.com/md2/Ldotvets/Bubba_88.html

[28]Morris, "Why Clinton Slept," op. cit.

[29]Ibid. Cf. also Gellman, op. cit., who quotes a member of the Counter-terrorism Strategy Group of the National Security Council: "There was a lack of political will to follow through and allow investigators to proceed on the case [of the Muslim charities that were funding terrorists] ... When I say political, I mean we can't have the public come out and saying we're bashing Muslims."

concern, it was the commander-in-chief who bore primary responsibility.[30] As one former administration official told reporter Joe Klein, "Clinton spent less concentrated attention on national defense than any another President in recent memory."[31] Clinton's political advisor Dick Morris flatly charged: "Clinton's failure to mobilize America to confront foreign terror after the 1993 attack [on the World Trade Center] led directly to the 9/11 disaster." According to Morris, "Clinton was removed, uninvolved, and distant where the war on terror was concerned."[32]

By Clinton's own account, Monica Lewinsky was able to visit him privately more than a dozen times in the Oval Office. But, according to a *USA Today* investigative report, the head of the CIA could not get a single private meeting with the president, despite the Trade Center bombing of February 26, 1993 or the killing of 18 American soldiers in Mogadishu on October 3 of the same year. "James Woolsey, Clinton's first CIA director, says he never met privately with Clinton after their initial interview. When a small plane crashed on the White House grounds in 1994, the joke inside the White House was, 'that must be Woolsey, still trying to get an appointment.'"[33]

Three Missed Opportunities to Get Bin Laden

In 1996 an American Muslim businessman and Clinton supporter named Mansoor Ijaz opened up an unofficial channel between the

---

[30]"Liberals felt that the civil rights of suspected terrorists were more important than cutting off their funds.... Everything was more important than fighting terrorism. Political correctness, civil liberties concerns, fear of offending the administration's supporters, Janet Reno's objections, considerations of cost, worries about racial profiling and, in the second term, surviving impeachment, all came before fighting terrorism." Ibid.

[31]Klein, "Closework," op. cit. p. 47

[32]Dick Morris, *Jewish World Review*, November 14, 2001, http://www.newsandopinion.com/1101/morris111401.asp

[33]Susan Page, "Why Clinton Failed to Stop Bin Laden," *USA Today*, November 13, 2001, http://usatoday30.usatoday.com/news/attack/2001/11/12/clinton-usatcov.htm

government of the Sudan and the Clinton administration. At the same time, "the State Department was describing bin Laden as 'the greatest single financier of terrorist projects in the world' and was accusing the Sudan of harboring terrorists."[34] According to Mansoor, who met with Clinton and Sandy Berger, "President Omar Hassan Ahmed Bashir, who wanted terrorism sanctions against Sudan lifted, offered the arrest and extradition of bin Laden and detailed intelligence data about the global networks constructed by Egypt's Islamic Jihad, Iran's *Hezbollah* and the Palestinian *Hamas.* Among the members of these networks were the two hijackers who piloted commercial airliners into the World Trade Center. The silence of the Clinton administration in responding to these offers was deafening."[35]

President Bashir sent key intelligence officials to Washington in February 1996. Again, according to Mansoor, "the Sudanese offered to arrest bin Laden and extradite him to Saudi Arabia or, barring that, to 'baby-sit' him—monitoring all his activities and associates." But the Saudis didn't want him. Instead, in May 1996 "the Sudanese capitulated to U.S. pressure and asked Bin Laden to leave, despite their feeling that he could be monitored better in Sudan than elsewhere. Bin Laden left for Afghanistan, taking with him Ayman al-Zawahiri, considered by the U.S. to be the chief planner of the September 11 attacks. . . ." One month later, the U.S. military housing complex in Saudi Arabia was blown apart by a 5,000-lb. truck-bomb. Clinton's failure to grasp the opportunity, concludes Mansoor, "represents one of the most serious foreign policy failures in American history."[36]

---

[34]"US Missed Three Chances to Seize bin Laden," *The Sunday Times,* January 6, 2002, http://www.sunday-times.co.uk/article/0,,9004-2001601261,00.html

[35]Ijaz Mansoor, "Clinton Let Bin Laden Slip Away and Metastasize," *Los Angeles Times,* December 5, 2001, http://www.infowars.com/saved%20pages/Prior_Knowledge/Clinton_let_bin_laden.htm

[36]Ibid.

According to a London *Sunday Times* account, based on a Clinton administration source, responsibility for this decision "went to the very top of the White House.[37] Shortly after the September 11 disaster, "Clinton told a dinner companion that the decision to let bin Laden go was probably 'the biggest mistake of my presidency.'" But according to the *Times* report, which was based on interviews with intelligence officials, this was only one of three occasions on which the Clinton administration had the opportunity to seize bin Laden and failed to do so.

When the president's affair with Monica Lewinsky became public in January 1998, and his adamant denials made it a consuming public preoccupation, Clinton's normal inattention to national security matters became subsumed in a general executive paralysis. In Dick Morris's judgment, the United States was effectively "without a president between January 1998 until April 1999," when the impeachment proceedings concluded with the failure of the Senate to convict.[38] It was in August 1998 that the al-Qaeda truck-bombs blew up the embassies in Kenya and Tanzania.

The Failure to Take Security Seriously

Yet this was only half the story. During its eight years, the Clinton administration *was* able to focus enough attention on defense matters to hamstring the intelligence services in the name of civil liberties, to shrink the U.S. military in the name of economy, and to keep the Pentagon from adopting (and funding) a "two-war" strategy; this last because "the Cold War was over" and in the White House's judgment there was no requisite military threat in the post-Communist world that might make it necessary for the United States to be able to fight wars on two fronts.[39] Inattention

---

[37]"US Missed Three Chances to Seize bin Laden," op. cit.

[38]Morris, op. cit.

[39]Tim Weiner, "Two War Strategy Is Obsolete, Panel of Experts Says," *The New York Times*, December 2, 1997. Virtually every penny saved in Vice President Gore's showcase "reinventing government" program came from cuts in the military establishment and America's defenses.

to defense also did not prevent the Clinton administration from pursuing massive social experiments in the military in the name of gender and diversity reform: requiring "consciousness-raising" classes for military personnel, rigging physical standards so women could meet them, and in general undermining the meritocratic benchmarks that are a crucial component of military morale.

While budget cuts forced some military families to go on food stamps, the Pentagon spent enormous sums to re-equip ships and barracks to accommodate co-ed living.[40] All these efforts further reduced the Pentagon's ability to put a fighting force in the field—a glaring national vulnerability dramatized by the war in Kosovo. This diminished the crucial elements of fear and respect for American power in the eyes of adversaries who waited in the wings.[41]

During the Clinton years, the Democrats' insistence that American power was somehow the disturber, rather than the promoter, of international tranquility prompted the White House to turn to multilateral agencies for leadership, particularly the discredited United Nations. While useful in limited peacekeeping operations, the UN was largely a collection of theocratic tyrannies and brutal dictatorships which regularly indicted and condemned the world's most tolerant democracies, specifically the United States, England and Israel, while supporting the very states that provided safe harbors for America's al-Qaeda enemy. Just prior to the World Trade Center attacks, the UN's "Conference on Racism" in Durban, South Africa, engaged in a ritual of America-bashing over "reparations" for slavery and support for Israel, agendas set by the Islamic bloc led by Iran.

During the 1990s, Bill Clinton's most frequent foreign guest was Yasser Arafat, whose allegiance to Iraq and betrayal of America

---

[40]Stephanie Gutman, The Kinder, Gentler Military: How Political Correctness Affects Our Ability to Win Wars, 2001

[41]The war in Afghanistan conducted by the Bush administration relied on U.S. Special Forces, which had not been gender-integrated, and on indigenous allies.

during the Gulf War could not have been more brazen. When Clinton revived the "peace process" in the Arab-Israeli conflict, it failed because of Arafat's failure to renounce the terrorist option. Why renounce terror if there is no price exacted for practicing it?

Clinton and the Military

As recently as 1990, only six Democratic senators had voted to authorize the Gulf War against Iraq. It is true that the Clinton White House was able, during its eight-year tenure, to shed some of the Democrats' normal aversion to the use of American military might. But the Clinton deployments of American forces were often non-military in nature: a "democracy-building" effort in Haiti that failed; flood relief and "peacekeeping" operations that were more appropriately the province of international institutions. Even the conflict Clinton belatedly entered in the Balkans was officially characterized as a new kind of "humanitarian war," as though the old kinds of war for national interest and self-defense were somehow tainted. While the Serbian dictator Milosevic was toppled, "ethnic cleansing," the *casus belli* of the Western intervention, continues, except that the Christian Serbs in Kosovo have now become victims of the previously persecuted Albanian Muslims.

Among Clinton's deployments were also half-hearted strikes using cruise missiles against essentially defenseless countries like the Sudan, or the sporadic bombing of Iraq when Saddam violated the terms of the Gulf peace. The strikes, however, failed in their primary objective, which was to maintain the UN inspections mandated by the Gulf War truce. A negative result of this "Whack-A-Mole" strategy, on the other hand, was the continual antagonizing of Muslim populations throughout the world. The most notorious of these episodes was undoubtedly Clinton's ill-conceived and ineffectual response to the attacks on the African embassies. At the time, Clinton was preoccupied with preparing his defense before a grand jury convened because of his public lies about his White House affair with Monica Lewinsky. Three days after Lewinsky's grand jury appearance, and without consulting the Joint Chiefs of Staff or his national security advisors, Clinton launched cruise missiles into two Islamic countries which he identified as being allied to the terrorists and their leader Osama bin Laden. One of the missiles hit and destroyed a pharmaceutical factory in the Sudan, killing one individual. Since the factory was the sole plant producing medicines for an impoverished African nation, there were almost certainly a number of collateral deaths.

The incident, which inflamed anti-American passions all over the Islamic world, was in conception and execution a perfect reflection of the distorted priorities and reckless attitudes of the Clinton White House. It also reflected the irresponsibility of congressional Democrats, who subordinated the safety concerns of their constituents to providing unified support for the president's misbehavior at home and abroad.

The Partisan Nature of the Security Problem

More than 100 Arabic operatives participated in the September 11 attack on the World Trade Center towers. They did so over a period of several years. They were able to enter the United States with or without passports, and seemingly at will. They received training in flying commercial airliners at American facilities, despite clear indications that some of them might be part of a terrorist campaign. At the same time, Democrats pressed for greater relaxation of immigration policies and resisted scrutiny of foreign nationals on grounds that to do so constituted "racial profiling." To coordinate their terrorist efforts, the al-Qaeda operatives had to communicate with each other electronically on channels that America's high-tech intelligence agencies normally intercept. One reason they were not detected was that the first line of defense against such attacks was effectively crippled by powerful figures in the Democratic Party who considered the CIA, rather than America's enemies, to be the problem.

Security controls that would have prevented adversarial agents from acquiring encryption devices that thwarted American intelligence efforts were casually lifted on orders from the highest levels of government.[42] Alleged abuses by American intelligence operatives became a higher priority than the abuses of the hostile forces they were attempting to contain.[43] Reporter Joe Klein's inquiries led him to conclude that "there seems to be near unanimous agreement among experts: in the ten years since the collapse of the Soviet Union [and the eight years of the Clinton presidency, and the seven since the first Al-Qaeda attack on the World Trade Center] almost every aspect of American national-security—from military operations to intelligence gathering, from border control to political leadership—has been marked by . . . institutional lassitude and bureaucratic arrogance. . . ."[44]

The Democrats' Anti-Intelligence Bill

The Democrats' cavalier attitude towards American security in the years preceding September 11 was dramatized in a bill to cut the intelligence budget sight- unseen, which was introduced every year of the Clinton administration by Senator Bernie Sanders. The fact that Sanders was an extreme leftist proved no problem for the Democrats, still enjoying their long-standing congressional majority, when they appointed him to a seat on the House Intelligence committee. Indeed, why should it be a problem? Shortly before the World Trade Center attack, Senate Democrats made another leftist, California Senator Barbara Boxer—an opponent of the war against Saddam Hussein and a long-time critic of the American military—the chair of the Senate sub-committee on Terrorism.

The Sanders initiative was launched in 1993, after the first al-Qaeda attack on the World Trade Center. In that year, the Democratic-controlled House Intelligence Committee voted to reduce

---

[42]Paul Craig Roberts "Needed: A 'New War' Against The Homegrown Villains" September 15, 2001, http://www.paulcraigroberts.org/2001/09/15/needed-a-new-war-against-the-homegrown-villains/

[43]Thomas Powers, "The Trouble With The CIA," *The New York Review of Books*, January 17, 2002; Gellman, Morris op. cit.

[44]Klein, "Closework," op. cit. p. 45

President Clinton's own authorization request for the intelligence agencies by 6.75 percent. But this was insufficient for Sanders. So he introduced an amendment that required a *minimum* reduction in financial authorization for each individual intelligence agency of at least 10 percent.[45]

Sanders even refused to examine the intelligence budget he proposed to cut: "My job is not to go through the intelligence budget. I have not even looked at it."[46] According to Sanders, the reasons for reducing the intelligence budget were "that the Soviet Union no longer exists," and "that massive unemployment, that low wages, that homelessness, that hungry children, that the collapse of our educational system is perhaps an equally strong danger to this Nation, or may be a stronger danger for our national security."[47] Irresponsible? Incomprehensible? Not to nearly half the Democrats in the House, who voted in favor of the Sanders amendment. Ninety-seven Democrats in all voted for the Sanders cuts, including House Armed Services Committee chair and Berkeley leftist Ron Dellums, along with the entire House Democratic leadership. As terrorist attacks on America intensified year by year during the 1990s, Sanders steadfastly reintroduced his amendment. Every year thereafter, right until the World Trade Center attack, nearly 100 Democrats voted with Sanders to cut the intelligence budget.

According to a study made by political consultant Terry Cooper, "Dick Gephardt (D-MO), the House Democratic leader, voted to cut on five of the seven amendments on which he was recorded. He appears to have 'taken a walk' on two other votes. David Bonior (D-MI), the Democratic Whip and number-two leader, voted for every single one of the ten cutting amendments. Chief Deputy Whips John Lewis (D-GA) and Rosa DeLauro (D-CT)

---

[45]House Amendment 276, to amend HR2330.

[46]Tracy Cooper, research paper on the Sanders-Owens amendment, supplied to the author. Cooper is an independent political consultant. Idem. H5692

[47]Ibid.

voted to cut intelligence funding every time they voted. Nancy Pelosi (D-CA), the Whip-elect, voted to cut intelligence funding three times, even though she was a member of the Intelligence Committee and had the information to know better. Two funding cut amendments got the votes of every single member of the elected House Democratic leadership. In all, members of the House Democratic leadership supported even the Sanders funding cut amendments 56.9 percent of the time."

> Many of the Democrats whose committee positions give them immense say over our national security likewise voted for most or all of the funding cut amendments. Ron Dellums (D-CA), the top Democrat on the Armed Services Committee[48] from 1993 through 1997, cast all eight of his votes on funding cut amendments in favor of less intelligence funding. Three persons who chaired or were ranking Democrats on Armed Services subcommittees for part of the 1993–99 period—Pat Schroeder (D-CO), Neil Abercrombie (D-HI) and Marty Meehan (D-MA)—also voted for every fund-cutting amendment that was offered during their tenures. Dave Obey (D-WI), the senior Democrat on the Appropriations Committee that holds the House's keys to the federal checkbook, voted seven out of eight times to reduce intelligence funding.[49]

In 1994, Republican Porter Goss, a former CIA official and member of the House Intelligence Committee, warned that because of inflation, the cuts now proposed by Sanders-Owens amounted to 16 percent of the 1992 budget and were 20 percent below the 1990 budget. Yet this did not dissuade Dellums, Bonior and roughly 100 Democrats from continuing to lay the budgetary

---

[48]Ibid. "For a while it was renamed the National Security Committee. For the sake of simplicity, though, it's referred to herein as the Armed Services Committee. Similarly, the Defense subcommittee of the House Appropriations Committee, although for a period formally the National Security Subcommittee, is herein consistently called the Defense Subcommittee."

[49]Ibid.

ax to America's first line of anti-terrorist defense. Ranking committee Republican Larry Combest warned that the cuts endangered "critically important and fragile capabilities, such as in the area of human intelligence."[50] In 1998, Osama bin Laden and four radical Islamic groups connected to al-Qaeda issued a *fatwa* condemning every American man, woman and child, civilian and military included. Sanders responded by enlisting Oregon Democrat Peter DeFazio to author an amendment cutting the intelligence authorization again.[51]

The Republicans and National Security Issues

When Republicans took control of the House in 1994, Congressman Floyd Spence, now head of the National Security Committee, expressed his outrage at the Democrats' handiwork in words that were eerily prescient: "We have done to our military and to our intelligence agencies what no foreign power has been able to do. We have been decimating our own defenses.... In this day and time you do not have to be a superpower to raise the horrors of mass destruction warfare on people. It could be a Third World country, a rogue nation, or a terrorist group.... These weapons of mass destruction are chemical, biological, bacteriological.... Anthrax could be released in the air over Washington, DC.... That could happen at any time and people are talking about cutting back on our ability to defend against these things or to prevent them from happening. It is unconscionable to even think about it. It borders on leaving our country defenseless."[52]

Yet the warning signs continued right up to the disaster. Before and after the 1999 *Washington Post* article by Defense Secretary Cohen, "there was a series of more elaborate reports about grand terrorism, by assorted blue-ribbon task forces, which warned of chemical, biological, and nuclear attacks...." A report by former

---

[50]Cooper, Idem. at H5820
[51]Ibid. Idem. at H2957
[52]Ibid.

Senators Hart and Rudman called for a huge "homeland security" campaign that would include—in Joe Klein's summation for *The New Yorker*—"intensive municipal civil defense and crisis response teams, new anti-terrorist detection technology," and a new cabinet-level position of secretary of Homeland Security, which was instituted by the Bush administration shortly after the attack.[53]

Klein—a Democrat and former "anti-war" activist—refused to draw the obvious conclusion from these events and place the responsibility where it belonged, squarely on the shoulders of the Democrats. Instead he wrote: "There can't be much controversy here. Nearly everyone—elected officials, the media, ideologues of every stripe—ignored these reports."[54] Fortunately there is an extensive public record of the intense and ongoing concern of Republican officials and conservative "ideologues" about the nation's security crisis, and their determined if unsuccessful efforts to expose and remedy it. There is an equally extensive public record documenting the Democrats' resistance to strengthening the nation's defenses and the liberal media's efforts to minimize, dismiss or even ridicule attempts by Republicans to do so. The national press's negative treatment of Representative Dan Burton's and Senator Fred Thompson's committee investigations into the efforts by Communist China to influence the 1996 presidential election is a dramatic instance of this pattern, particularly since the liberal media have otherwise made campaign finance reform one of their highest priorities.[55]

In fact, the Chinese poured hundreds of thousands of dollars into the Clinton-Gore campaigns in 1992 and 1996. The top funder of the 1992 Clinton-Gore campaign was an Arkansas resident and Chinese banker named James Riady, whose relationship with Clinton went back 20 years. Riady is the scion of a multi-billion-

---

[53]Klein, op. cit.
[54]Ibid.
[55]Cf. "The Clinton-Gore Security Scandal" below.

dollar financial empire whose throne-room in Jakarta is adorned with two adjacent portraits of Clinton and Chinese leader, Li Peng, the infamous "butcher of Tiananmen Square." Though based in Indonesia, the Riady empire has billions of dollars invested in China, and is a working economic and political partnership with China's military and intelligence establishments. The Riadys gave $450,000 to Clinton's 1992 presidential campaign and another $600,000 to the Democratic National Committee and Democratic state parties; that was just the tip of the iceberg in their working partnership with Clinton.[56]

The question that Democratic obstructions prevented the Thompson and Burton committees from answering was whether these payments resulted in the transfer of U.S. weapons technologies to Communist China. China is known to have transferred such sensitive military technologies to Iran, Libya, North Korea and Iraq. Beginning in 1993, the Clinton administration systematically lifted security controls at the Department of Commerce that had previously prevented the transfer of sensitive missile, satellite and computer technologies to China and other nuclear proliferators. Clinton appointed John Huang, an agent of the Riady interests and communist China, to a senior position at Commerce with top security clearance. Clinton later sent Huang to the Democratic National Committee to take charge of fund-raising for his 1996 campaign.[57]

In May 1999 a bipartisan House committee, headed by Representative Christopher Cox, released a report which was tersely summarized by *The Wall Street Journal* in these harrowing words: "The espionage inquiry found Beijing has stolen U.S. design data for nearly all elements needed for a major nuclear attack on the U.S., such as advanced warheads, missiles and guidance

---

[56]The details of the Clinton-Riady partnership are to be found in William Triplett III and Edward Timperlake, *Year of the Rat*, Regnery, 1998. The book is based on the Burton and Thompson Committee hearings and interviews with national security officials.

[57]Ibid.

systems."[58] Among the factors contributing to these unprecedented losses, most of which took place during the Clinton years, the report identified lax security by the administration.

Two committees of Congress, headed by Dan Burton and Fred Thompson, attempted to get to the bottom of the matter to see if there was any connection between these problems and the Riady-Huang fund-raising efforts, particularly the illegal contributions by foreign agents of the Chinese military and intelligence establishments. The investigations failed because the Committee Republicans were stonewalled by the Clinton administration, by their Democratic colleagues and by the witnesses called. In all, 105 witnesses either took the Fifth Amendment or fled the country to avoid cooperating with investigators. They did this not only with the tacit acquiescence of the Clinton administration but the active help of Clinton officials.[59]

There are scores of Republican congressmen—leaders of military, intelligence and government oversight committees—who attempted to sound the alarm on this front, and who expressed publicly (and to me, personally) their distress at being unable to reach the broad American electorate with their concerns about these national security issues because of the indifference of the liberal media and the stonewalling of the Democrats.[60]

In the year prior to the World Trade Center attack, I met in the Capitol with more than a dozen Republican members of the House, including members of the Armed Services Committee, to discuss how the security issue could be brought before the American public. Given the president's talent for double-talk and the lock-step support from congressional Democrats for his most reckless agendas, and without the possibility of media support for such

---

[58]*The Wall Street Journal,* January 3, 2000

[59]*Year of the Rat,* op. cit.

[60]These included Senators Fred Thompson, James Inhofe and John Kyl, Representatives Dan Burton, Porter Goss, Curt Weldon, Joel Hefley, Tom Tancredo, Peter Hoesktra, Steve Buyer and Tillie Fowler, and members of the Republican congressional leadership such as Chris Cox, J.C. Watts and Tom DeLay.

an effort, not a single member present thought that raising these issues would go anywhere. Even attempting to raise them, they felt, exposed them to political risks. These risks included attacks by Democrats and liberal journalists who would label them "mean-spirited partisans," "right-wing alarmists," "xenophobes" and, of course, "Clinton-bashers."

Although restricted to much smaller platforms than their liberal counterparts, conservative journalists attempted to break the blackout and make the issues public. Bill Gertz, Edward Timperlake and William C. Triplett III wrote books (*Betrayal* and *Year of the Rat*) based on military and intelligence sources and on data collected by the Thompson and Burton committees, that would have shaken any other administration to its roots but received little attention outside conservative circles. Other conservative journalists, including *The Washington Times'* Rowan Scarborough and various writers for *The Wall Street Journal*'s editorial pages, *National Review,* and *The Weekly Standard,* pursued the story but were also unable to reach a broad enough public to make any impact. The conservative side of the ideological spectrum has no apologies to make for the nation's disarming in the face of its security threats. The Democratic Party and its fraternal institutions, the liberal press and the left-wing academy, do.

The Lobby Against America's Intelligence Services

One of the obvious causes of the many security lapses preceding the World Trade Center attack was the post-Vietnam crusade against U.S. intelligence and defense agencies, dating from the Church Committee reforms in the mid-Seventies and led by "antiwar" Democrats and other partisans of the American left. A summary episode reflecting this mood involved CIA operative Robert Baer, described by national security reporter Thomas Powers as "a 20-year veteran of numerous assignments in Central Asia and the Middle East whose last major job for the agency was an attempt to organize Iraqi opposition to Saddam Hussein in the early 1990s—

shuttling between a desk in Langley and contacts on the ground in Jordan, Turkey, and even northern Iraq."

According to Powers, "That assignment came to an abrupt end in March 1995 when Baer, once seen as a rising star of the Directorate of Operations, suddenly found himself 'the subject of an accusatory process.' An agent of the FBI told him he was under investigation for the crime of plotting the assassination of Saddam Hussein. The investigation was ordered by President Clinton's national security adviser, Anthony Lake, who would be nominated to run the [CIA] two years later....[61] Eventually, the case against Baer was dismissed ... but for Baer the episode was decisive. 'When your own outfit is trying to put you in jail,' he told me, 'it's time to go.' Baer's is one of many resignations [in the Directorate of Operations] in recent years...."[62]

Hostility to the CIA during the Clinton years ran so high that intelligence professionals refer to it as the "'Shia' era in the agency," Powers reported. The term referred to the Islamic sect that stresses the sinfulness of its adherents. "We all had to demonstrate our penance," a former CIA station chief in Jordan told Powers. "Focus groups were organized, we 're-engineered' the relationship of the Directorate of Operations and the Directorate of Intelligence"—which meant introducing "uniform career standards" that would apply indiscriminately to analysts and covert operators in the field. This meant high-risk assignments in target countries resulted in no greater advancement up the bureaucratic ladder than sitting at a computer terminal in Langley. "In the re-engineered CIA," comments Powers, "it was possible for Deborah Morris to be appointed the DO's deputy chief for the Near East."[63] "She worked her way up in Langley," an operative told Powers. "I don't think she's ever been in the Near East. She's never run an

[61]Lake's appointment was successfully resisted by the intelligence community.

[62]Powers, op. cit.

[63]The DO is the department of covert operations.

agent, she doesn't know what the Khyber Pass looks like, but she's supposed to be directing operations [in the field]."[64]

The end of the Cold War in 1991 inspired the reformers to close down all the counterespionage groups in the CIA because their expertise was no longer "needed." Spies were passé. "The new order of the day was to 'manage intelligence relationships.'" After interviewing many operatives who had left the CIA in disgust during this period, Powers concluded that in the Clinton years the agency had become more and more risk- averse as the result of "years of public criticism, attempts to clean house, the writing and rewriting of rules, ... efforts to rein in the Directorate of Operations, ... catch-up hiring of women and minorities [and] public hostility that makes it hard to recruit at leading colleges."[65]

A post 9/11 article by Peter Beinart, editor of the liberal *New Republic,* amplified Powers's observations.[66] Beinart speculated that the CIA's lapses may have occurred because of a fundamental mediocrity that had overtaken the institution. This mediocrity was the direct result of the attacks on the agency (and on America's global purposes) by the political left, and of the culture of hostility towards the American government that had been successfully implanted in America's elite universities—once the prime recruiting grounds for the intelligence services. Beinart began with a description of the recent assassination of Abdul Haq in Afghanistan. Haq was potentially the most important leader of the internal opposition to the ruling Taliban. Yet the CIA had failed to provide him with protection. A key element in this disaster was the fact that the CIA did not have a single operative who could communicate with Haq in his native tongue, Dari. Nor did the CIA have a single operative who spoke Pashto, the language of the Taliban, even though al-Qaeda's base had been Afghanistan for years. The problem of reading intercepted intelligence transcripts

---

[64]Ibid.

[65]Ibid

[66]Peter Beinart, *The New Republic,* October 1, 2001.

in Pashto was "solved" by sending the transcripts to Pakistan to be translated by Pakistani intelligence officials—who were also sponsors of the Taliban. Some CIA officials believe it was Pakistani intelligence officials who warned Osama bin Laden to get out of Khost before U.S. missiles were launched into Afghanistan after the embassy bombings in 1998.[67]

The Abdul Haq assassination exposed the enormous human-intelligence gap that had developed within the agency during the post-Vietnam years. As much as 90 percent of America's intelligence budget was being spent on technology, electronic decryption and eavesdropping systems for the National Security Agency, rather than human intelligence based on agents in the field. Without language skills, much of this information itself remained useless. In September 2001, the House Permanent Select Committee on Intelligence concluded: "At the NSA and CIA, thousands of pieces of data are never analyzed or are analyzed 'after the fact'.... Written materials can sit for months and sometimes years before a linguist with proper security clearance and skills can begin a translation."[68]

According to a 1998 article in *The Atlantic* written by a former CIA official, "Not a single Iran-desk chief during the eight years I worked on Iran could speak or read Persian. Not a single Near East Division chief knew Arabic, Persian or Turkish, and only one could get along even in French."[69] These deficiencies become intelligible only when one understands what happened to Middle Eastern studies in American universities in the post-Vietnam decades.

The University Left Against the Nation's Security

The story of the university left's subversion of the field of Middle Eastern studies is recounted in a recent book by Martin Kramer,

---

[67]Powers, op. cit.

[68]Beinart, op. cit.

[69]Reuel Marc Gerecht. Gerecht wrote under the pen-name Edward Shirley.

editor of *The Middle East Quarterly.*[70] As a reviewer summarized Kramer's argument, "In the late seventies, the radical students of the 1960s began to enter the professoriate. The way was cleared for them to wrest power from the Middle East studies establishment when Edward Said's *Orientalism* (1978) crystallized a new understanding of the field."[71] Said was a member of the ruling council of Yasser Arafat's PLO and quickly became one of the most powerful academics in America, eventually heading the Modern Language Association, whose 40,000 members make it the largest professional association of academics. On November 21, 1993, eight months after the World Trade Center bombing, Said wrote an article for *The New York Times Sunday Magazine* with the revealing title "The Phony Islamic Threat." Said's title summarized the intellectual shift in Middle East studies during the previous decade. The new perspective that came to dominate the field was that perceptions of a terrorist threat from Islamic radicals were expressions of "Euro-centric" and racist attitudes by their Western oppressors.

In his book *Orientalism,* Said argued that all previous scholarship on the Middle East was hopelessly biased because it was written by white Europeans, and thus "racist." According to Said, "All Western knowledge of the East was intrinsically tainted with imperialism." In one stroke Said thus discredited all previous scholarship in the field, paving the way for its replacement by Marxist radicals like himself. With the help of his left-wing academic allies, Said's extremist viewpoint created the climate and

---

[70]Martin Kramer, *Ivory Towers on Sand: The Failure of Middle Eastern Studies in America,* published by the Washington Institute for Near East Policy, 2001

[71]Stanley Kurtz, "The Scandal of Middle East Studies," *The Weekly Standard,* November 19, 2001, http://www.weeklystandard.com/Content/Public/Articles/000/000/000/530zyiiu.asp#; Cf. also Martin Kramer, "Terrorism? What Terrorism?!" *The Wall Street Journal,* November 15, 2001, http://www.martinkramer.org/sandbox/2001/11/terrorism-what-terrorism/

context for a revolution in Middle Eastern studies.[72] This was accelerated by the "multiculturalist" attitudes of the university and racial preference policies in faculty hiring, which involved the widespread recruitment of political leftists from the Islamic theocracies of the Middle East. Before Said, "3.2% of America's Middle East area specialists had been born in the region. By 1992, the figure was nearly half. This demographic transformation consolidated the conversion of Middle Eastern studies into leftist anti-Americanism."[73]

In a statement issued ten days after the 9/11 World Trade Center attack, the Middle East Studies Association—the professional organization representing the field—refused to describe the perpetrators of the attack as "terrorists" and preemptively opposed any U.S. military response.[74] Georgetown professor John Esposito, a former president of the Middle East Studies Association and an academic star in the field, had made his name after the first World Trade Center attack by following Said's example and disparaging concerns about Islamic terrorism as thinly veiled anti-Muslim prejudice. He was rewarded by being made a foreign affairs analyst for the Clinton State Department and assigned to its intelligence department.[75]

The language deficiency at the CIA—to which the political takeover of the academic profession greatly contributed—proved crucial at the operational level. But it was only a reflection of the more profound problem that afflicted the intelligence community because of the universities' leftward turn. In Beinart's words, "Today's CIA is a deeply mediocre institution. Its problems aren't legal or financial; they're intellectual. The agency needs a massive

---

[72]Said's thesis was, in fact, an intellectual's version of Pol Pot's order to execute all Cambodians who wore glasses, because as readers they carried with them the bad ideas of the past. Pol Pot's perspective, in turn, was heavily influenced by Sartrean Marxists on Paris's Left Bank, with whom he studied before embarking on his Cambodian crusade.

[73]Kurtz, op. cit.

[74]Kramer, op. cit.

[75]Kurtz, op. cit.

infusion of brainpower." How massive an infusion was indicated in an article Beinart cited: "According to a 1992 *New York Times* story, applicants for the CIA's 'Undergraduate Student Trainee Program' needed only a combined SAT score of 900 and a grade point average of 2.75." Compare that to the average requirements for entrance into top-ranked schools like Harvard or Princeton, which require SAT scores above 1300 and grade point averages of 4.0. Princeton is one of many elite universities that, because of political pressure from the left, officially refuse to allow the CIA to recruit students on their campuses and have refused to do so for more than a decade.

The only places the CIA can recruit its missing brainpower—"the only institutions able to supply the world-class linguists, biologists, and computer scientists it currently lacks—are America's universities." But the universities have long since become the political base of a left that has not given up its fantasies of social revolution and is deeply antagonistic to America and its purposes. The nub of the nation's security problem lies in the fact that, beginning in the 1960s, the political left aimed a dagger at the heart of America's security system. From a vantage of great power in the universities, the media and the Democratic Party, it was able to press the blade home for three decades prior to the World Trade Center disaster.

The main reason the CIA no longer recruits agents from top-ranked schools is that it can't. "The men and women who teach today's college students view the CIA with suspicion, if not disdain," as Beinart gently puts it. The academic left hates the CIA and regards it as an enemy of all that is humane and decent. To make their case, academic leftists drill the nation's elite youth in a litany of "crimes" alleged to have been carried out by the CIA since the late 1940s: the rigging of the Italian and French elections of 1948 against popular Communist parties (whose aim, unmentioned in this academic literature, was to incorporate Western Europe into Stalin's satellite system); the 1951 overthrow of Iranian leader Mosaddegh (a Soviet asset who would have delivered

Iranian oil reserves to Stalin); the overthrow of the Jacobo Arbenz in Guatemala (whom the left portrays as a democrat but was in fact a Communist fellow-traveler who chose to spend his exile years as a privileged guest in Castro's police state); the "Bay of Pigs" (the CIA's failed effort to overthrow the most oppressive Communist regime in the hemisphere); and the "Phoenix Program" in Vietnam (an attempt to prevent a Communist front set up by the Hanoi dictatorship from overthrowing the Saigon government and establishing a Communist police state in the South).[76]

In the perverse view of the academic left, the CIA is an agency of torture, death and oppression for innocent masses all over the world who otherwise would be "liberated" by progressive totalitarian forces. Utilizing the powerful resources of the academy, the left has created a vast propaganda apparatus to establish what is essentially the view of the CIA held by America's most determined enemies. This anti-American propaganda is disseminated under the imprimatur of America's most prestigious university presses including Harvard, California, Duke and Princeton.

University administrations have caved in to these leftists so consistently as to leave little room for maneuver. "When the president of the Rochester Institute of Technology took a brief leave to work for the CIA in 1991," recalls Beinart, "many students and faculty demanded that he resign. Last year, when the government tried to establish a program under which college students would

---

[76]I am very familiar with this litany of CIA crimes now taught as a progressive catechism on American campuses, because as a leftist in the Sixties I wrote the first version of this black record myself *in The Free World Colossus,* which was published in 1965 as a history of the Cold War and became a kind of political bible for the anti-Vietnam movement. As veteran leftist Paul Berman begrudgingly wrote in the August 1986 issue of *The Village Voice,* I was one of the founders of the New Left "and the author of some of its most well-thumbed pages. Other writers figured larger in the awareness of the general public; but no one in those days figured larger among the leftists themselves." He was referring to *The Free World Colossus.*

receive free language instruction in return for pursuing a career in intelligence, the University of Michigan refused. As assistant professor Carol Bardenstein told *Time,* 'We didn't want our students to be known as spies in training.'" Apparently she would prefer them to be helpless targets-in-waiting. For caving in to these pressures, the president of Michigan, Lee Carroll Bollinger, was rewarded by being appointed president of New York's Columbia University shortly after the September 11 World Trade Center bombing.

As Beinart points out, there can be reasonable concerns about the proper functions of a university and the appropriate relationship of government agencies to private institutions of learning, although the University of Michigan is itself a state-financed school. "But most of the squeamishness about training, and encouraging students to work for the CIA doesn't have anything to do with the mission of the academy; it has to do with ideological hostility to the instruments of American power."[77] This ideology is enforced by political correctness in the university hiring process, a bias that virtually excludes conservative academics from obtaining positions at most schools. At Ivy League schools, for example, a study by the Luntz Companies showed that only 3 percent of professors identify themselves as Republicans, with the overwhelming majority holding views well to the left of the American center.[78]

Congressman Dellums and the Democrats' Fifth-Column Caucus

Given the role of universities in shaping the "liberal" culture, the same powerful anti-American, anti-military, anti-CIA sentiments have prevailed in the left wing of the Democratic Party for the last 30 years. The size of this group can be partially gauged by the 58

---

[77]Beinart, op. cit.

[78]Frank Luntz, "Inside the Mind of an Ivy League Professor," *FrontPage Magazine,* August 30, 2002, http://archive.frontpagemag.com/readArticle.aspx?ArtId=22992

congressional Democrats who describe themselves as members of its "Progressive [socialist] Caucus." But its actual influence is far greater.

No political career symbolizes the Democrats' acceptance of radical ideas better than the 27-year tenure of congressman Ron Dellums, who came to the House in the 1970s as the first Sixties radical to penetrate the political mainstream, and who was able—with the encouragement and cooperation of his colleagues—to establish himself as a power player on both the Armed Services and Intelligence committees overseeing the nation's security policy.

A Berkeley radical with vigorously expressed anti-American views, Dellums was an ardent admirer of Fidel Castro's Marxist dictatorship and a relentless opponent of American military power. On his election to Congress in 1970, Dellums went out of his way to announce his radical commitments and pledged to remain faithful to his anti-American roots. "I am not going to back away from being a radical," he said. "My politics are to bring the walls down [in Washington]."[79]

During his long career, Dellums worked hand-in-glove with Soviet front-groups; proposed scrapping all U.S. "offensive weapons;" used his government position to oppose every U.S. effort to block the spread of Communist rule; and, in the Eighties, even turned over his congressional office to a Cuban intelligence agent named Farid Handal, who was organizing a network of "solidarity committees" on U.S. campuses to support Communist guerrilla movements in Central America.[80] When a Democratic White House under Jimmy Carter attempted, in 1979, to reinstitute the draft and increase America's military preparedness after

---

[79]H.Doc. 108-224 Black Americans in Congress 1870-2007; http://www.gpo.gov/fdsys/pkg/GPO-CDOC-108hdoc224/pdf/GPO-CDOC-108hdoc224-2–8–1.pdf

[80]S. Steven Powell, *Covert Cadre: Inside the Institute for Policy Studies*, Green Hill Publ., 1987, p. 260

the Soviet invasion of Afghanistan, Dellums joined a "Stop the Draft" rally of Berkeley leftists, denounced American "militarism" and condemned Carter's White House as "evil."[81]

Dellums's attitude towards America's intelligence services reflected his consistent support for America's international enemies. Just before the 1980 presidential election, with Soviet invasion forces flooding into Afghanistan, with the American embassy held hostage by the new radical Islamic regime in Iran, and with crowds chanting "Death to America" in the streets of Tehran, Dellums told the same Berkeley rally: "We should totally dismantle every intelligence agency in this country piece by piece, nail by nail, brick by brick."[82]

Despite these views, Dellums was no marginalized backbencher in the Democratic House. With the full approval of the Democratic Party leadership and its House caucus, Dellums was made a member of the Armed Services Committee, on which he served throughout the 1980s and 1990s. In the midst of a hot war with Central American Communists, who were seeking to establish a Soviet military base in the Western hemisphere, Democrats made

---

[81]Peter Collier and David Horowitz, *Destructive Generation,* 1989), Summit, p. 161

[82]Cal Thomas, "Will Liberal Democrats Keep U.S. Secrets Safe?" *Los Angeles Times,* February 14, 1991. Dellums replied in a letter to the *Times,* March 5, 1991, accusing his political enemies of taking the quote "out of context." Wrote Dellums: "Their quote out of context printed and reprinted in various forums of my statement that we should 'dismantle every intelligence agency in this country piece by piece, brick by brick, nail by nail,' fails to include my call in the same sentence that 'if there was a need for us to rebuild such organizations that we rebuild them with civil liberties and civil rights and justice to people in mind." The response was as damning as the quote. First, it defended the statement that we should tear down our intelligence agencies by substituting a serious doubt that they should exist (not much of a retraction) and followed that with a completely disingenuous concern for civil liberties—in other words, rights which are already respected by the CIA and other intelligence agencies and about which Ron Dellums has never shown a scintilla of concern when it comes to Communist police states like Cuba.

Dellums chairman of the House Subcommittee on U.S. Military Installations worldwide, where he enjoyed top security clearance. This was done with the specific imprimatur of the Democratic chair of the Armed Services Committee, Les Aspin.

Nor was Dellums alone. He had like-minded allies in both the legislative and executive branches of the Clinton government. Most notoriously, Clinton appointed an anti-military environmental leftist, Hazel O'Leary, to be secretary of Energy, a department responsible for the nation's nuclear weapons labs. O'Leary promptly surrounded herself with other political leftists (including one self-described "Marxist-feminist") and anti-nuclear activists, appointing them as her assistant secretaries with responsibility for the security of the nuclear labs. In one of her first acts, O'Leary declassified eleven *million* pages of nuclear documents, including reports on 204 U.S. nuclear tests, describing the move as an act to safeguard the environment and a protest against a "bomb-building culture."[83]

Having made America's nuclear secrets available to the whole world, including the al-Qaeda network, O'Leary then took steps to relax security precautions at the nuclear laboratories under her control. She appointed Rose Gottemoeller, a former Clinton National Security Council staffer with extreme anti-nuclear views, to be her director in charge of national-security issues. Gottemoeller had been previously nominated to fill the post—long vacant in the Clinton administration—of assistant secretary of Defense for International Security Policy. The appointment was successfully blocked, however, by congressional Republicans alarmed at her radical disarmament agendas. The Clinton

---

[83]This phrase comes from a *Washington Post* report of December 8,1993: "Energy Dept. Discloses 204 Secret Tests," by R. Jeffrey Smith, pp. A1, A9, http://www.highbeam.com/doc/1P2–978677.html

[84]David Horowitz, *Who's Responsible for America's Security Crisis?* Center for the Study of Popular Culture, Los Angeles, CA, 1999, https://secure.donationreport.com/productlist.html?key=5DGIXYHTRFJI

response to this rejection was to put her in charge of security for the nation's nuclear weapons labs.[84]

In the 1980s, a time when the United States was fighting a fierce battle of the Cold War in Central America, Democrats also appointed George Crockett to head the House subcommittee on Western Hemisphere Affairs. Crockett had strong and direct ties to the Communist Party and to pro-Communist organizations. He had begun his career as a lawyer for the Communist Party in Detroit; he was so loyal to its agendas that he was the only House member to refuse to sign a resolution condemning the Soviet Union for its unprovoked shooting-down of a commercial Korean airliner (KAL 007). Crockett was also the only member to vote against a House resolution condemning the Soviet Union in the matter of U.S. Major Arthur Nicholson, who was shot in East Germany and took 45 minutes to bleed to death while the Communists denied him medical aid.[85]

Crockett's appointment came at a time when the Sandinista dictatorship in Nicaragua was engaged in supplying military aid to Communist guerrillas in Guatemala and El Salvador and was building a major Soviet military base on its territory. Dellums and Crockett were the most prominent and probably the most extreme supporters of the Communists in the Democratic caucus; but they had powerful allies in their efforts to protect the Sandinista junta and the Communist guerrillas, which included House leaders like David Bonior and Senators Patrick Leahy and Chris Dodd. Appointed to head the Senate Judiciary Committee in 2001, Leahy became the leader of Democrats' opposition to Bush administra-

---

[85]*Destructive Generation*, op. cit. p. 168

[86]Michael Crowley, "Personal Time," *The New Republic*, November 19, 2001, http://www.newrepublic.com/article/politics/personal-time. Franklin Foer, "Sin of Commission," *The New Republic*, October 8, 2001, http://www.newrepublic.com/article/politics/sin-commission and Stephen F. Hayes, "Patrick Leahy, Roadblock: More Than Any Other Senator, He Has Stalled Anti-Terror Bills," *The Weekly Standard*, October 15, 2001, http://www.weeklystandard.com/Content/Public/Articles/000/000/000/325yzhar.asp; Jerry Seper, "Leahy Challenges Bush on

tion attempts to insert stronger measures into domestic anti-terrorism legislation after the September 11 attacks.[86]

In 1991, Democratic speaker of the House Tom Foley appointed Ron Dellums and five other left-wingers to the sensitive House Intelligence Committee, with oversight over the CIA and other U.S. intelligence agencies. Two years later, Bill Clinton appointed Les Aspin, the left-wing Democrat behind Dellums's political rise, to be his first Secretary of Defense. As Aspin's protégé, Dellums became the chair of the Armed Services Committee, and thus the most important member of the House in overseeing all U.S. military defenses—controlling their purse-strings, and acting as the chief House advisor on military matters to the president himself.

The vote among members of the Democratic caucus to confirm this determined enemy of American power as chairman of the Armed Services Committee was 198–10. In other words, 198 congressional Democrats, including the caucus's entire leadership, saw nothing wrong in placing America's defenses in the hands of one of its most implacable foes. They saw nothing problematic in Dellums's statement that, as head of the Armed Services Committee, he would (in the words of the *Los Angeles Times*) "favor a faster reduction of the armed forces and billions more for economic conversion," calling for a "tripling" of the billions that he would actively seek to be moved out of the defense sector.[87]

The vote to confirm Dellums's new position and authority took place on January 17, 1993.[88] One month later, on February 26, al-Qaeda terrorists bombed the World Trade Center. On Dellums's retirement in 1998, Bill Clinton's third Secretary of Defense, William Cohen, presented him with the "Distinguished Public

---

Military Tribunals," *The Washington Times*, November 16, 2001, http://www.highbeam.com/doc/1G1-80118460.html

[87]James Bornemeier and William J. Eaton, "Pentagon Critic Gains Top Rank on Military Panel," *Los Angeles Times*, January 28, 1993, http://articles.latimes.com/1993-01-28/news/mn-2371_1_military-issue

[88]Ibid.

[89]*Congressional Record*, February 3, 1998, p. 618

Service" medal, the second-highest honor that the Pentagon can bestow on a civilian.[89]

The Party of Blame America First

How could the Democratic Party have become host to—and promoted—legislators whose commitment to America's security was so defective, and whose loyalties were so questionable? How could a party that had led the fight against Hitler, had organized a Cold War alliance to save Europe from Stalin's aggression, and under John F. Kennedy had led the greatest expansion of America's military power in peacetime—how could this party then reach a point where so many of its leaders seemed to regard America itself as the world's problem, rather than "the brightest beacon"—as President Bush put it the day after the 9/11 attacks—"for freedom and opportunity in the world"?[90]

The transformation of the congressional Democrats into a party of the left can be traced to the turbulent decade of the Vietnam War and the 1972 presidential candidacy of Senator George McGovern, whose campaign slogan, "America Come Home," is self-explanatory. George McGovern had been a World War II hero who completed more than 30 bomber missions. But he emerged from combat traumatized by the killing he had witnessed, and transformed into a kind of premature "peacenik." In 1948, he entered politics as an activist in the Progressive Party presidential campaign of Henry Wallace, who was running as an "anti-war" candidate for the pro-Soviet left. Wallace had once been FDR's vice-president, but in 1948 he left the Democratic Party to protest Harry Truman's Cold War policy of "defending free peoples" and opposing Stalin's conquest of Eastern Europe.[91] Although Wallace

---

[90]Comments by President Bush from the Oval Office, *The Boston Globe*, September 12, 2001, p. A18, http://www.boston.com/news/packages/underattack/globe_stories/0912/_Today_our_very_freedom_came_under_attack_+.shtml

[91]A slogan of the campaign was "One, two, three, four, we don't want another war/five, six, seven, eight, win with Wallace in '48."

himself was not a Communist, the Progressive Party was a creation of the American Communist Party and under its political control. The Communist Party, in turn, was controlled by the Kremlin, which had instructed its American supporters to break from the Democratic Party and launch the Progressive campaign in order to weaken America's opposition to Soviet expansion.[92]

Like Wallace, George McGovern was not a Communist or even a radical. But like many otherwise patriotic Americans then and since, he was seduced by the appeasement politics of the left and became permanently convinced that the United States was co-responsible with Stalin for the Cold War by arousing Russians fears of a Western invasion. In McGovern's view, the Cold War could have been averted if Truman had been more accommodating to the Soviet dictator and his designs on Eastern Europe.[93] This anti-anti-communist attitude was a permanent aspect of McGovern's foreign-policy agendas throughout his political career, and reflected the views of the wing of the Democratic Party he came to lead.

At the end of the 1960s, the radicals who had bolted the Democratic Party in 1948 to oppose the Cold War began to return under circumstances that made the party particularly vulnerable to their agendas. In 1968, the Democrats' presidential candidate was Hubert Humphrey, a liberal but also a staunch anti-Communist who wanted to stay the course in Vietnam and prevent a Communist victory. At the Democratic convention that nominated Humphrey, the anti-war radicals staged a riot, which led to a pub-

---

[92]On the Soviet creation and control of the American Communist Party, see John Haynes and Harvey Klehr, *The Secret World of American Communism,* Yale University Press, 1996 and *The Soviet World of American Communism,* Yale University Press, 1998, two volumes in the *Yale Annals of Communism* series, based on the Soviet archives. On the Communist Party's control of the Progressive Party, see John Haynes, Red Scare, Red Menace: Communism and Anti-Communism in the Cold War Era, Ivan R. Dee, 1995.

[93]Radosh, *Divided They Fell: The Demise of the Democratic Party 1964–1996,* Free Press, 1996, pp. 158–9

lic-relations disaster that destroyed Humphrey's chances of becoming president.

The anti-Humphrey plan was the brainchild of radical leader Tom Hayden, who had met with the Vietnamese Communists in Czechoslovakia the previous year, and had gone on to Hanoi to collaborate with the Communist enemy.[94] In the late spring of 1968, Hayden proceeded to plan and then organize a riot at the Democratic Party convention in the full glare of the assembled media.[95] The negative fallout from the chaos in the streets of Chicago, and the Democrats' heavy-handed reaction to the "anti-war" rioters, effectively elected the Republican candidate Richard Nixon the following November.

After Nixon's election, the "anti-war" radicals turned their attention to the Democratic Party with the intention of seizing control of its political machinery.[96] Humphrey's defeat fatally weakened the political power of the anti-Communist forces that had supported him. A series of internal rule-changes pressed by the radicals paved the way for the ascension of the anti-Humphrey left. Their agenda was to remake the party into a left-wing organization which, like the Progressive Party of 1948, would not stand in the way of Communist expansion. The party figure around whom they rallied their forces was McGovern, who had been put in charge of the committee to reform the party's rules. The left's

---

[94]These events are described in *Radical Son*, Free Press, 1997, p. 160. Hayden's collaboration was witnessed by writer Sol Stern, who was a member of the delegation.

[95]Ibid., pp. 165–168. I was an editor of the radical publication *Ramparts* at the time, and interviewed several of the participants who met with Hayden and carried out his instructions, including Weatherman Gerry Long and others.

[96]How they accomplished this is described in Ronald Radosh's important book, op. cit Chapter 6: "McGovernism and the Captured Party"; cf. also Peter Collier and David Horowitz, *Destructive Generation*, Summit, 1989) and Steven Hayward, *The Age of Reagan: The Fall of the Old Liberal Order, 1964–1980*, Prima, 2001. On the subsequent cultural transformation of the old liberalism into new Democratic Party leftism (or "modern liberalism"), see Robert Bork, *Slouching Towards Gomorrah: Modern Liberalism and American Decline*, Regan, 1996.

immediate agenda was to end the Democratic Party's support for the anti-Communist war in Vietnam.

During the Sixties, radicals were intent on making a "revolution in the streets." They were led back into electoral politics by figures like Hayden and his wife-to-be Jane Fonda. Through Hayden's auspices, Fonda had traveled to Hanoi to make anti-American war propaganda for Hanoi, inciting American troops to defect and also aiding the Communists in their denials that they were torturing John McCain and other American POWs.[97] On their return, Hayden and Fonda, with the assistance of radical members like Ron Dellums, gave "anti-war" lectures to the House Democratic Caucus. Although street radicals like Hayden had previously condemned the Democrats and deliberately destroyed the party's presidential candidate, their energies were now directed towards infiltrating the party and shaping its agendas. This compromise of political principle was made painless by McGovern's "Come Home" campaign slogan, which implied that America's military power was the source of the Cold War conflict with Communism instead of its solution.

"Anti-war" leftists became Democratic Party regulars and—in the case of Hillary and Bill Clinton and others—party leaders.[98] Among the more famous activists elected to Congress as Democrats in this period were Ron Dellums, Bella Abzug, Elizabeth Holtzman, Robert Drinan, David Bonior, Pat Schroeder and Bobby Rush, a former Black Panther. Hayden failed to win a congressional seat himself but became a Democratic state assemblyman and then a senator in California. The newly elected radicals spearheaded the Democratic vote to cut off all economic aid to the anti-Communist governments of Cambodia and South Vietnam, even

---

[97]Henry Mark Holzer and Erika Holzer, *Aid and Comfort: Jane Fonda in North Vietnam*, McFarland, 1989)

[98]These events are recounted in Radosh, op. cit., Horowitz, *Radical Son*, pp. 303–5; and Peter Collier, *The Fondas: A Hollywood Dynasty*, Putnam's Sons, 1991.

though American military forces had been withdrawn from Indochina after the 1973 truce. Both regimes fell within months of the cutoff, and there followed the mass slaughter of innocents in both countries by the new Communist rulers.

McGovern's presidential bid was rejected by the voting public. The candidate won only one state (Massachusetts) in losing by the biggest electoral landslide in American history.[99] But the internal party reforms the McGovernites were able to put in place established the left as a power in the Democratic Party. From its newfound position of strength, the left was able to force Nixon's resignation over the Watergate incident and profoundly influence the presidency of Jimmy Carter (1977–1981). Notwithstanding that Carter was a southerner, a Navy man and a self-described conservative—all factors that enhanced his electability—his foreign policy reflected the leftward turn of the party. Of his Secretary of State Cyrus Vance, it was said by a liberal stalwart, "he was the closest thing to a pacifist that the U.S. has ever had as a secretary of state, with the possible exception of William Jennings Bryan."[100]

As president, Carter warned of Americans' "inordinate fear of Communism" as though this, and not Soviet expansion, were responsible for the Cold War.[101] At the end of Carter's term in 1980, his foreign-policy performance was assessed by former Secretary of State Henry Kissinger in these words: "The Carter admin-

---

[99]E.g. Michael Barone, *Our Country,* Free Press, 1990, pp. 508–9; Radosh, op., cit p. 180

[100]The comment was made by Morris Abrams, civil rights lawyer and Democratic Party activist. Cited in Steven F. Hayward, *The Age of Reagan: The Fall of the Old Liberal Order, 1964–1980,* Prima, 2001, p. 542. Hayward describes how the Humphrey Democrats of the centrist Coalition for a Democratic Majority, were frozen out of foreign policy appointments. Ibid., p. 543

[101]Cf. Joshua Muravchik, "Why the Democrats Lost," *Commentary,* January 1985, http://www.commentarymagazine.com/article/why-the-democrats-lost/

[102]Cited in Hayward, p. 535

istration has managed the extraordinary feat of having, at one and the same time, the worst relations with our allies, the worst relations with our adversaries, and the most serious upheavals in the developing world since the end of the Second World War."[102]

Among these "serious upheavals" were the Soviet aggression in Afghanistan (the first crossing of an international border by the Red Army since 1945) and the Sandinista coup in Nicaragua—where the Carter administration stood by while a group of pro-Castro Marxists subverted a democratic revolution, joined the Soviet bloc, and began arming Communist insurgencies in Guatemala and El Salvador. A third debacle was the loss of Iran to Islamic fundamentalists in a 1979 revolution led by the Ayatollah Khomeini. This event transformed Iran into the first radical Islamist state and thus launched the forces that eventually came together in the World Trade Center attacks. The Carter White House underwrote the Islamist victory by withdrawing its support from the existing regime, led by the dictatorial but modernizing Shah. Among the Shah's achievements inciting the hatred of the Iranian mullahs was the lifting of the veil and the education of women. Despite the misogynist and reactionary agendas of the Khomeini revolution, the American left cheered the seizure of power by anti-American radicals as a "Third World" liberation.[103]

Their utopian illusion was short-lived. "Khomeini lost no time in installing a fundamentalist Islamic Republic, executing homosexuals, and revoking, among other security laws, the statute granting women the right to divorce and restricting polygamy."[104] American

---

[103]Waller R. Newell, "Postmodern Jihad: What Osama bin Laden learned from the Left," *The Weekly Standard,* November 26, 2001, http://www.weeklystandard.com/Content/Public/Articles/000/000/000/553fragu.asp. Michel Foucault, perhaps the most influential social thinker among American academics, "welcomed 'Islamic government' as a new form 'of political spirituality' that could inspire Western radicals to combat capitalist hegemony." Foucault described Khomeini himself as "a kind of mystic saint." Ibid.

[104]Hayward, op. cit. pp. 559–560

[105]Ibid.

leftists and liberals had pressured Carter to abandon the Shah because of his repressive police agency, the SAVAK. But "Khomeini's regime executed more people in its first year in power than the Shah's SAVAK had allegedly executed in the previous 25 years."[105]

Clinton Sets the Tone

On November 7, 2001—one month to the day after America began its response to the al-Qaeda attack on the World Trade Center—the man most responsible for the security failures that led to the attack gave to college students at Georgetown a speech that ranks as one of the most disgraceful utterances to pass the lips of a former American president.[106] Without any acknowledgment of his own responsibilities as commander-in-chief, Clinton joined America's enemies in attempting to transfer the blame for the atrocities to his own country. "Those of us who come from various European lineages are not blameless," he explained, reflecting sentiments made familiar by American appeasers since the Wallace campaign of 1948.

Although Europeans in America were the creators of a political democracy that had separated church from state and did not identify a category of people as "infidels," let alone wage wars against them, Clinton reached back in time to recall the Christian crusades against Jews and Muslims a thousand years before. "In the first Crusade, when the Christian Soldiers took Jerusalem, they first burned a synagogue with 300 Jews in it," he said—and then mentioned that some Muslims were killed by the Crusaders as well. "I can assure you that that story is still being told today in the Middle East and we are still paying for it." The former president thus lent legitimacy to the propaganda of the terrorist attackers.

---

[106]Remarks as delivered By President William Jefferson Clinton, Georgetown University, November 7, 2001, http://www.salon.com/2001/11/10/speech_9/

Even as past history, this version of events was woefully deficient. It neglected to mention the Muslim invasions that provoked the Crusades. Did Clinton seriously intend to suggest, moreover, that the Islamists who attacked the World Trade Center would be outraged by the story of martyred Jews, rather than wish the Crusaders had perhaps killed three *million* instead of 300? What was the point of the Clinton story? The Crusades took place a thousand years ago. It is the Muslim world that still hasn't learned to separate religion and state, or to live in peace with those who do not share their beliefs. It is the Muslim world that is still conducting "holy wars." What Christian church in modern America, or in any modern European country, sanctions the murder of "infidels"?

As though the attempt to establish a moral equivalence between the terrorist aggressors and their American victims were not obscene enough, Clinton then added the equally absurd example of black slavery. "Here in the United States," he continued his ethnic insult, "we were founded as a nation that practiced slavery...." In point of historical fact, the United States was founded as a nation dedicated to ending slavery, and did so at an enormous cost in human life. Some of these American lives were also sacrificed to end the Atlantic slave trade and the slave systems that persisted in Africa itself, conducted by Muslims and black Africans. Clinton's idea that Osama bin Laden and the fanatical Islamists at war with America would care in the slightest about the plight of black slaves today—let alone more than a century ago—is an expression of the irrational anti-Americanism that has planted its seeds in the Democratic Party. In fact, one of bin Laden's ideological allies, the Muslim government of the Sudan, still practices slavery against black Christians.[107]

One point Clinton failed to make is that the current leaders of America's war against Islamic racism are two African-Americans, Colin Powell and Condoleezza Rice. There is no

[107]David Horowitz, *Uncivil Wars: The Controversy Over Reparations for Slavery*, Encounter, 2001

example comparable among other states, great or small, of minorities entrusted with a nation's security. Clinton's attempt to smear his own country in order to exculpate himself from his national-security failures is an indication of the internal threat to this nation from homegrown radicals whose political locus is the Democratic Party and the liberal culture.

No Excuses

In August 1998, the chair of the National Commission on Terrorism, Paul Bremer, wrote in *The Washington Post:* "The ideology of [terrorist] groups makes them impervious to political or diplomatic pressures.... We cannot seek a political solution with them." He then proposed that Americans defend themselves: "Beef up security around potential targets here and abroad.... Attack the enemy. Keep up the pressure on terrorist groups. Show that we can be as systematic and relentless as they are. Crush bin Laden's operations by pressure and disruption. The U.S. government further should announce a large reward for bin Laden's capture—dead or alive."[108]

Bremer was not alone. Given these warnings, Andrew Sullivan observed: "Whatever excuses the Clintonites can make, they cannot argue that the threat wasn't clear, that the solution wasn't proposed, that a strategy for success hadn't been outlined. Everything necessary to prevent Sept. 11 had been proposed in private and in public, in government reports and on op-ed pages, for eight long years. The Clinton administration simply refused to do anything serious about the threat."[109]

On January 20, 2001, George W. Bush was sworn in as the 43rd president of the United States. Within months of taking office, he

[108]Andrew Sullivan, "While Clinton diddled," *Salon,* January 9, 2002, http://www.salon.com/2002/01/09/clinton_85/

[109]Andrew Sullivan, "The AWOL President: Clinton's Legacy and 9/11," Salon.com, January 11, 2002, http://www.neoliberalismo.com/awol.htm

[110]Ibid.

ordered a new strategy for combating terrorism that would be more than just "swatting at flies," as he described Clinton's policy. The new plan reached the president's desk on September 10, 2001. Sullivan wrote: "It was too late. But it remains a fact that the new administration had devised in eight months a strategy that Bill Clinton had delayed for eight years."[110]

I

Appreciating the Commander-in-Chief

It has been six months since al-Qaeda terrorists, operating from bases in more than a dozen nations, attacked the World Trade Center and killed 3,000 American civilians on their own soil. A month later, America struck back. Less than two months after that, al-Qaeda's host regime in Afghanistan was destroyed. This victory was accomplished with a minimum of casualties; an international coalition against terror had been forged. No small accomplishment for America's commander-in-chief.

But there are some who can't take yes for an answer. In such quarters, the leader responsible for these triumphs is himself under siege. The Democrats' minority leader thinks the war lacks direction and definition. Others on the left are even more critical. *Salon.com*, for example, has an ongoing series called "Bushed!" whose articles regularly accuse the president of not having done anything right since the military victory in Afghanistan, and more generally of not being up to his job.[1]

These attacks come in an environment of danger that makes them difficult to comprehend, even as partisan gripes. There are an estimated 100 al-Qaeda cells operating within the borders of the United States. During the last decade, 100,000 terrorists have been trained in al-Qaeda's terror camps from the West Bank to Afghanistan with one mission—to kill Americans and destroy the

---

March 11, 2002, http://archive.frontpagemag.com/Printable.aspx?ArtId=24455, http://www.salon.com/2002/03/11/six_months/

[1]Salon Staff, "Bushed!," *Salon.com*, April 30, 2001, http://www.salon.com/2001/04/30/bushed_3/

Great Satan. Last week, U.S. forces engaged undefeated al-Qaeda fighters in the biggest battle of the war in Afghanistan since Tora Bora. In Jerusalem a few days earlier, a suicide bomber from one of Yasser Arafat's terrorist units "waded into a crowd of religious families emerging from Sabbath prayers or bar mitzvah celebrations … [and] approached a group of women with baby strollers before detonating the large nail-packed explosive device on his body."[2] Among the Israeli dead was an 18-month-old girl along with four other children.

Six months ago, in the wake of 9/11, President Bush went before the American people. He told the nation that we were at war and that the war would be a long one. In this, as in other matters affecting this conflict, the president has told the truth—no small matter as far as our security is concerned and, in light of the presidency that preceded his, no small grace. Al-Qaeda first bombed the World Trade Center in 1993 using Palestinian, Egyptian and Iraqi terrorists. Bill Clinton did not even visit the site. For eight years he failed to inform the American people of what our intelligence services knew—that our country was under attack by an international army of religious fanatics whose backers included half a dozen nations armed with weapons of mass destruction, biological and chemical. Nor did Clinton put in place the most basic security measures—at airports, for example—that would have prevented the September attack.

Where are the articles and jeremiads about Clinton's incompetence? Where is the recognition that Clinton was not up to the job as commander-in-chief, and that Bush's response to the war against us has been masterly and responsible in contrast?

---

[2]Tracy Wilkinson and Mary Curtius, "Palestinian Attacks Claim 16 Israelis," *Los Angeles Times*, March 3, 2002, http://pqasb.pqarchiver.com/latimes/access/110011659.html?FMT=ABS&FMTS=ABS:FT&type=current&date=Mar+3%2C+2002&author=TRACY+WILKINSON%3BMARY+CURTIUS&pub=Los+Angeles+Times&edition=&startpage=A.1&desc=The+World%3B+Palestinian+Attacks+Claim+16+Israelis

Even with this response, the future may be worse than we think. The administration is attempting to thwart al-Qaeda plans to poison America's water supplies and destroy our nuclear power plants. A recently released report, which has turned out to be a false alarm, indicated that al-Qaeda was plotting to detonate a "dirty" nuclear bomb in New York City, which could kill 100,000 people. The fact that this was a false alarm is not really reassuring. The reason: we know that 80 out of 132 nuclear "suitcase" bombs built by the Russians are missing from their inventories, and may have fallen into terrorist hands.

We are engaged in a holy war with a medieval enemy that uses 21st-century weapons. It is not George Bush who has made this a war of good versus evil, as his critics bemoan, but a ruthless enemy whose soldiers plan to go to heaven over our dead bodies. Every man, woman and child in America has been targeted for death, while hatred of America, of Christians and of Jews is preached not only across the Muslim world outside the United States but inside our borders as well.

The Washington Post recently ran a story about a Muslim textbook, used in a religious high school, which teaches 11th-graders that "the Day of Judgment can't come until Jesus Christ returns to Earth, breaks the cross and converts everyone to Islam, and until Muslims start attacking Jews." In the al-Qalam All-Girls School in Springfield, Va., seventh-graders learn that Osama bin Laden might actually be a frame-up victim. Students attending Islamic day schools in this country are taught that if a person is a non-Muslim it is okay "to hurt or steal from that person."[3] So why not kill them? A reported 80 percent of the mosques in America are funded by Wahhabi Saudis, the radical sect whose fundamentalist teachings spawned al-Qaeda.[4]

---

[3]Kenneth Adelman, "U.S. Islamic Schools Teaching Homegrown Hate," *FoxNews.com*, February 27, 2002, http://www.foxnews.com/story/0,2933,46610,00.html

[4]Steven Emerson, *American Jihad: The Terrorists Living Among Us*, Free Press, 2002

As we face this enemy, our borders are still porous and our airport security systems a feeble joke. It was recently disclosed, for example, that nine pilots of U.S. commercial jets are themselves illegal immigrants. Equally recently, CBS reporters passed security at airports across the country with fake IDs; the Secretary of Transportation insists on random computer checks instead of scrutiny by time-tested human profiling, in order to avoid the appearance of "discrimination." Better 100,000 dead than one passenger inappropriately profiled! Domestic surveillance—our only real defense—has been hamstrung for decades by laws which prevent the FBI from looking at groups dedicated to destroying the United States, unless they can be shown to have already acted on their deadly agendas and committed criminal acts. The ACLU and other groups are fighting a rearguard battle to preserve these restrictions. As a result of this laxity, as Steven Emerson reports in *American Jihad,* al-Qaeda leaders actually prefer America to other nations when setting up their terrorist cells.

But in the midst of this unprecedented national crisis, which unites all Americans as potential victims, while the administration struggles against time to close the Grand Canyon-size holes in our homeland defenses, the political left is in full-bore attack. Not against al-Qaeda or its domestic allies or the gaps in our security that put us in danger, but against the president and his administration, and in particular his attorney general, who is attempting to reform the system that has already permitted the slaughter of 3,000. *Mr. Ashcroft, why do you want to target Muslims who are here illegally from terrorist countries and subject them to added scrutiny? Have you no decency?*

In other words, it is anti-American business as usual on the political left. Go up to the website of *The Nation,* a magazine which supported every Communist enemy of the United States during the Cold War—from Stalin through Mao to Ho and Fidel—and behold its priorities. Its editors are currently featuring "Enron at Home and Abroad," a *Nation* series attempting to 'Enronize' the Bush administration as a bankruptcy scandal; a story about reparations for a race riot that took place in 1921; articles demonizing Attorney General Ashcroft as a reincarnation of Cotton Mather and Joseph McCarthy; and finally a "Prayer for America" by Democratic congressman Dennis Kucinich, already praised by leftists like Edward Said, which attacks America's commander-in-chief as an imposter and expresses the hope that this nation will not defend itself in the war: "The trappings of a state of siege trap us in a state of fear, ill-equipped to deal with the Patriot Games, the Mind Games, the War Games of an unelected President and his unelected Vice President."[5] Note that Kucinich does not concede we are actually in a state of siege, but suggests rather that the Bush administration has put on the "trappings of a state of siege" with the goal of whipping up a domestic hysteria that will serve its own belligerent agendas. This is exactly what American Communists—and *The Nation*—said about the Truman, Eisenhower and Kennedy administrations and their efforts to defend the West against the Soviet threat during the Cold War.

Speaking for the progressive caucus of the House, Kucinich mocks America's idealistic good with America's practical bad: "Crown thy good, America. Not with weapons of mass destruction. Not with invocations of an axis of evil. Not through breaking international treaties. Not through establishing America as king of a unipolar world." In other words, what is bad in America is the Bush administration's policies—or rather Kucinich's caricature of that program—for defending Americans against al-Qaeda's attacks. Kucinich's attack was echoed by Jimmy Carter, who has spent much of his ex-presidency identifying America, rather than its enemies, as the source of world problems. Carter condemned Bush's post-9/11 reference to the "axis of evil" as itself evil: "I think it will take years before we can repair the damage done by that statement," he told an Emory University conference on the

---

[5]John Nichols, "Kucinich Rocks the Boat," *The Nation*, March 7, 2002, http://www.thenation.com/article/kucinich-rocks-boat

impact of terrorism. A chorus of anti-administration columnists seconded Carter's charge.

What these Bush critics need is a good old-fashioned reality check. Iran, Iraq and North Korea are regimes whose official hatreds of America are not only quite public, but include a religious dimension that makes them far more sinister.[6] All three of these countries are not only developing weapons of mass destruction, but intercontinental missiles to deliver them as well. This is why Bush identified them as an axis of evil: to put them on notice to stop or else. The Bush administration is racing against time to prevent devastating attacks on America that al-Qaeda has already promised. If this takes preventive war against the axis of evil, so be it. If the Israelis had not destroyed Iraq's first nuclear reactor twenty years ago, a nuclear bomb might have already been detonated in a city like New York.

Yet there is a growing drumbeat from the left—including the editorial pages of *The New York Times* —to undermine Bush's public base of support on the war. Have these critics forgotten the lessons of the 1930s, when "anti-war" activists on the left and isolationists on the right refused to take the author of *Mein Kampf* at his word? Why is it so difficult to understand that this nation is engaged in a life-and-death struggle with forces that not only have no compunction about killing millions of Americans but claim to have a religious basis for doing so? While the enemy is busily identifying America as the Great Satan, an entire wing of the American political spectrum is busily assuring their fellow citizens that Iran, Iraq, North Korea and al-Qaeda don't really mean it. These critics adopt a similar attitude towards the Arab-Israel dispute. Yasser Arafat rejects a peace offer that includes 95 percent of his demands and does so by bombing women, children and teenagers. Yet these are regarded as "tactical errors" by Palestinian apologists on the

---

[6]North Korea's hatred properly understood is also religious, albeit the religion of Marxism.

left, rather than as self-evident proofs that there is evil in the Palestinian cause itself—*destroy Israel and the infidel Jews.*

A recent correspondent of mine summarized these views quite aptly: "What grabs anyone who thinks about the events and issues surrounding the war on terrorism, the U.S. and the Israelis is that those who oppose the war think we have a choice. When the rockets of a people who vow your total destruction are being fired into your neighborhood, they say you should do nothing."

Or not so much. *Salon*'s series "Bushed!" expresses its editors' weariness with a commander-in-chief who has just managed the first successful phase of a war to prevent further destructive attacks on their homeland.[7] They don't want a ballistic-missile defense that might forestall a nuclear disaster. They don't want security measures that would include military tribunals, whose purpose is to save a few hundred thousand lives but which might infringe the (nonexistent) civil liberties of America's enemies.

Salon is not *The Nation,* however. David Talbot, *Salon*'s editor, supports America's war even if his colleagues don't. Well, sort of. For he has also indulged in facile bashing of America's leader that he ought to reconsider. Talbot writes in this vein about the president and his Secretary of Defense: "Speaking of Rumsfeld, just what is the secret of this man's appeal? ... Are they [the press] relieved that an administration presided over by a goofy and inexperienced leader—someone who still seems weirdly young at age 55—has a grown-up at home?"[8] If Donald Rumsfeld were actually running George Bush rather than the other way around, others would be pulling the president's strings as well. Why leave out Cheney, the previous press candidate for White House puppet-master-in-chief? And what about Colin Powell, no slouch at bureaucratic infighting himself? If Talbot's assessment were

[7]Salon Staff, "Bushed!," *Salon.com,* April 30, 2001, http://www.salon.com/2001/04/30/bushed_3/

[8]David Talbot, "Bushed!" *Salon,* February 26, 2002, http://www.salon.com/2002/02/26/farflung/

remotely accurate, the White House would resemble the anarchy in Afghanistan, which rightly causes Talbot concern. There would not be a leader running this war; there would be chaos.

For the editor of a magazine who waged a fierce campaign during the Clinton impeachment against personalizing issues of state, Bush-bashing is particularly unseemly. The American people should be grateful for having this particular president in the Oval Office, rather than the man he defeated last year, and Talbot should realize this. In the year and a half since his electoral defeat and in the five months since America was brutally attacked, Al Gore still hasn't figured out what he should do to help lead his country in its time of need.

The American people need George Bush, but George Bush also needs the support of the American people. Only a nation united behind its leader can win a war whose terrain of battle is inside its borders. At this point in the war, despite the defection of the left, 80 percent of the American people understand this and are grateful for a leader who is firm of purpose and resolved to pursue the enemy until he is defeated. The facile Bush critics—particularly those who kept pointing to Clinton's ratings in the polls as a rationale for keeping him in office during the impeachment process—should recognize that on this matter the American people are right.

George Bush is commanding American forces in this war as head of the most ethnically diverse administration in the history of nations. He has shown us a commander who is decisive against our country's enemies in battle, while being generous in extending tolerance to those inside our borders who are from countries that are our enemies. The president has put together both elements of America's strength—its military prowess and its democratic example. Criticism that appreciates the debt already owed to this president is one thing. But criticism that belittles and even demonizes him is no service to our nation and undermines our cause.

2

Free the FBI

While Muslim terrorists penetrate our borders, and inaction by immigration officials daily show that we have no borders and no real ability to keep our enemies out, a surreal battle is taking place within the ranks of the target population itself. The debate is whether Attorney General John Ashcroft and the FBI should have given agents license to keep an eye on suspected terrorists and their ideological supporters, even if they have not yet actually blown up something. The trigger of the debate is the recent decision of the Justice Department to remove restrictions it imposed on itself in 1972, preventing the agency from spying on organizations that have not yet committed a crime. A chorus of so-called civil rights groups has already attacked the decision, calling it an assault on the Constitution, even though it involves no change in the law and no endorsement of illegal behavior.

The 1972 restrictions were adopted by the FBI in the face of a campaign against its practices by the political left. Its focus was the FBI's already discontinued "Cointelpro" program, which was an effort to counter massive civil disobedience and the growing threat from quasi-military radical groups who had gone from demonizing America to planting more than 1,000 bombs, committing acts of military sabotage and killing at least one innocent math professor in Wisconsin in their campaign against the Vietnam War. Of all the

---

June 03, 2002, http://archive.frontpagemag.com/Printable.aspx?ArtId=24461; http://www.salon.com/2002/06/04/cointelpro/

groups targeted by the FBI's Cointelpro program, the one most cited as a victim of official injustice was the Black Panther Party. Plots and alleged acts of political repression against the Panthers became prime justifications for restricting the FBI's actions.

In fact, the Panthers were a heavily armed group prone to violence against their own members and others. In her autobiography published years later, Panther leader Elaine Brown boasted that the Party had more than 1,000 weapons, including rocket launchers and machine guns. But while the Panthers were still a functioning gang, they were perceived as a political party. A fellow-traveling cadre of left-wing lawyers and civil-rights groups, abetted by a willing press, was ready to see the Panthers as victims rather than perpetrators. As a result, the FBI was identified as the villain and neutralized, while the Panthers continued on their radical way. The 1972 restrictions barred the FBI from infiltrating the Panthers and acting to prevent violence before it occurred, making the task of controlling them much more difficult. Aided by the new restrictions, the Panthers were able in the 1970s to murder more than a dozen people, including my friend Betty Van Patter, who was bludgeoned to death in 1974. No one was ever prosecuted for these crimes.

In 1969, a group of SDS New Leftists created the Weather Underground, America's first terrorist cult. The Weathermen were not covert about their anti-American jihad. They issued a public "Declaration of War" against "Amerikkka" and began a campaign of violence that included detonating a bomb in the U.S. Capitol building. In 1970, three of their leaders were blown up while building a nail bomb, which they intended to set off at a dance at Fort Dix. The FBI knew the names of every leader of the Weather Underground and most of its members. But because the fugitives were aided by other leftists, including prominent "civil rights" attorneys, and because the FBI even prior to its self-imposed restrictions was unable to penetrate the leftist networks that protected and supported the terrorist cadre, the government was never able to apprehend them. In the five years before they surfaced themselves, only a handful of Weathermen were ever captured.

And the Weathermen did not have Stinger missiles, anthrax caches or suitcase nuclear devices to make their mayhem really impressive.

All Americans who care for their lives, or for the lives of their families and neighbors—leftists and conservatives alike—should join in praising John Ashcroft for taking those minimal but politically difficult steps to defend their homeland. It would have been better if the FBI had announced that it was specifically targeting mosques where radical Islamic doctrines are preached, instead of churches, synagogues and mosques in general. This blanket approach was obviously adopted to make the agency less vulnerable to attacks from the vocal fellow-travelers of the civil-rights left. The left's strategy is certainly clever: attack as bigoted the idea that *any* Muslims are America's enemies, even the ones who declare that they are, because that's racial profiling. Then, when the government bows to political correctness and announces its sweep will be non-discriminatory and general, proclaim that the FBI is attacking religion.

In fact, 80 percent of America's mosques are funded by the Saudis, who also fund al-Qaeda worldwide.[1] The leader of the first bomb attack on the World Trade Center in 1993, whose aim was to kill 250,000 people, was a blind sheik who operated out of a local mosque. The radical lawyer representing the now-imprisoned blind sheik is under indictment by Ashcroft's Justice Department for helping the prisoner communicate with his terrorist cohorts in the conduct of their violence in the Middle East. The lawyer, Lynne Stewart, is a well-known radical "civil rights lawyer" and former attorney for the Weather Underground terrorists. She is currently also representing three pro-Palestinian teenagers charged with a hate crime: attempting to firebomb an orthodox synagogue

---

[1]Haviv Rettig, "Saudis Have Radicalized 80% of US Mosques," *The Jerusalem Post,* May 12, 2005, http://www.jpost.com/International/Expert-Saudis-have-radicalized-80-percent-of-US-mosques

in New York as a protest against Israel's attempts to defend itself in the Middle East.

The two attorneys defending Stewart have both defended terrorist bombers whose targets were Americans. One of them, Susan Tipograph, was the prime suspect in the escape of a Puerto Rican terrorist from an American prison. Stewart's colleague in defending the teen terrorists, Stanley Cohen, is a lawyer and political advocate for Hamas and a disciple of another Stewart colleague, William Kunstler. Kunstler's Center for Constitutional Rights is a front for left-wing radicals intent on carrying on their own war with America. As an editor for the New Left magazine *Ramparts,* I remember being visited in 1969 by Arthur Kinoy, who with Kunstler was the co-founder of the Center for Constitutional Rights. Kinoy was carrying with him a draft manifesto for a new "Communist Party" (those were the words used to describe it) which he intended to organize with Kunstler. The agendas of the hard left never really change. Support for America's Communist enemies then; support for America's terrorist enemies now.

Following the Ashcroft announcement, I was a guest on Sean Hannity's radio show opposite Francis Boyle, Professor of International Law at Illinois University and self-proclaimed "civil liberties" activist. Professor Boyle went directly on the offensive. The removal by the FBI of its self-imposed restrictions was an assault, he said, on the First and Fourth Amendments, although no one's free speech was in danger and no search and seizure was proposed. Boyle was concerned, he said, for the liberties that made America what it was. Or was he? Francis Boyle is a legal advisor to the terrorist PLO and the terrorist Palestinian Authority, not particularly admirers of the Bill of Rights. His agenda, laid out in the pro-Palestinian Internet magazine *Counterpunch.com,* is "dismantling [the] criminal apartheid regime"[2] in Israel. In fact, Boyle is a

[2]Francis Boyle, "Palestine, Palestinians and International Law," *Counterpunch,* March 31-April 2, 2002, http://www.counterpunch.org/2002/03/31/palestine-palestinians-and-international-law/

supporter of the anti-Israel divestment movement and compares the liberation struggle against Israel to the liberation struggle against South Africa. The proposed destruction of Israel doesn't faze Boyle at all. But then Boyle sees the present Republic of South Africa, which has tragically become the rape, murder and AIDS capital of the world, as "a beacon of hope" for mankind.[3]

While many people in the civil-rights business are genuine liberals, others are people who sympathize with terrorists like the Panthers and the Weathermen, and now Hamas and al-Qaeda. This should be a warning to all Americans who care about their country. It is not only that we have to take the threat to our homeland more seriously. We have to become more sophisticated about the threat we face.

---

[3]Ibid.

3

Know the Enemy (and What He Believes)

The war we have joined is defined by three simple, brutal facts. Our enemy is able to penetrate our borders and strike us in our homes; he can strike us with weapons of mass destruction; and he has made clear that his intention is not to change our policies or to force our withdrawal from some foreign land, but to obliterate us and destroy our civilization. Because of these facts, the imperative of defending ourselves as quickly and effectively as possible is more important in this war than in any we have ever fought. In all wars, the first essential is to know your enemy. Everything you can do to thwart his objectives or to protect your life and the lives of your countrymen depends on this knowledge. If the war is a war of terror, in which stealth warriors target civilians, the importance of this knowledge is greater still.

Who, then, is the enemy that has struck us and threatens our destruction? Officially he has been defined in terms that invoke "terror" and "evil." But these are generic and describe the means by which he has chosen to fight the war; not why he is fighting or how we have become his enemy. They do not tell us *who* he is. The failure to name our enemy is already a source of great weakness in erecting our defenses. Already, in attempting to establish security perimeters at our borders and in our airports and harbors, we have denied ourselves the ability to target the specific groups who have targeted us. The policy that will not identify the enemy

June 25, 2002, http://archive.frontpagemag.com/Printable.aspx?ArtId=24109

by name is a policy that asks us to fight in the dark. Yet every terrorist who slips through our defenses is capable of killing thousands of innocent Americans.

In fact, we already know who our enemy is, no matter how many choose to deny it. Almost a year has passed since the attacks on Wall Street and the Pentagon—the twin symbols of American wealth and power. We have seen the face of the enemy, even if we are still reluctant to name him. We are at war with radical Islam—not all of Islam but with Islamic radicals. And we are—or should be—at war with their allies, the international radical left. Both see us as the embodiment of evil. Both seek our destruction.

The publication of a new al-Qaeda manifesto, translated by the Middle East Media Research Institute (MEMRI) makes the agendas of our Islamic enemies abundantly clear. The statement is called, "Why We Fight America," and was issued by al-Qaeda spokesman Suleiman Abu Gheith. It appeared on an al-Qaeda website hosted by the Center for Islamic Research and Studies. The statement begins by asking why the world is surprised by what happened on 9/11—pretty much the question that Noam Chomsky, Tariq Ali, Edward Said, Barbara Kingsolver, Arundhati Roy and sundry professors at anti-American rallies on college campuses across the country asked within weeks of the horrific attack. And the answer is pretty much the same: "What happened to America [on 9/11] is something natural, an expected event for a country that uses terror, arrogant policy, and suppression against the nations and the peoples, and imposes a single method, thought, and way of life, as if the people of the entire world are clerks in its government offices and employed by its commercial companies and institutions."[1]

Anyone who was surprised by 9/11, the al-Qaeda statement continues, does not understand the root causes of the attack and in

---

[1]Suleiman Abu Gheith, "Why We Fight America," *The Middle East Media Research Institute,* Special Dispatch No. 388, June 12, 2002, http://www.memri.org/report/en/0/0/0/0/0/0/678.htm; (To read the entire transcript): http://www.fecesflingingmonkey.com/0602/memri.htm

particular "the effects of oppression and tyranny on [the victims'] emotions and feelings." Instead, such people must think "that oppression begets surrender, that repression begets silence, that tyranny leaves only humiliation." But, according to al-Qaeda, humiliation, deprivation and oppression inspire righteous rage against the oppressor. And this righteous indignation is what al-Qaeda's war is about. Of course, unlike the Western left, al-Qaeda does not wage its war in the name of an international proletariat and its goal is not a secular socialist utopia. Al-Qaeda's war is about the future world reign of Islam. The al-Qaeda statement asks: How can a Muslim accept humiliation and inferiority, "when he knows that his nation was created to stand at the center of leadership, at the center of hegemony and rule, at the center of ability and sacrifice? ... When he knows that the [divine] rule is that the entire earth must be subject to the religion of Allah—not to the East, not to the West—to no ideology and to no path except the path of Allah? ..."

Credulous apostles of appeasement in the West like Ted Turner and Cherie Blair, wife of British Prime Minister Tony Blair, are so superior in their own minds to the Muslims who hate them that they don't consider the possibility that the Islamic faithful could actually mean what they say. Justifying Arafat's suicide brigades, Blair said: "As long as young people feel they have got no hope but to blow themselves up you are never going to make progress." This is an inanity heard nightly on cable talk shows from the left. It is the propaganda line of Machiavellian spokesmen for the terrorist cause, like PLO spokesman Abdel Rahman and westernized apologists like Hussein Ibish, who equate the terrorists' terror with the victims' responses. But it ignores what the combatants say about themselves and their inspiration, and patronizes them in the process.

The Middle East Media Research Institute has also translated an interview given to the Arab press by the mother of a suicide bomber, who has nothing to say about root causes like poverty or thwarted national desires or "social injustice." What she says is this: "I am a compassionate mother to my children.... Because I love my son, I encouraged him to die a martyr's death for the sake of Allah.... *Jihad* is a religious obligation incumbent upon us, and we must carry it out. I sacrificed Muhammad as part of my obligation. This is an easy thing. There is no disagreement [among scholars] on such matters. The happiness in this world is an incomplete happiness; eternal happiness is life in the world to come, through martyrdom. Allah be praised, my son has attained this happiness.... I prayed from the depths of my heart that Allah would cause the success of his operation. I asked Allah to give me 10 [Israelis] for Muhammad, and Allah granted my request and Muhammad made his dream come true, killing 10 Israeli settlers and soldiers. Our God honored him even more, in that there were many Israelis wounded. When the operation was over, the media broadcast the news. Then Muhammad's brother came to me and informed me of his martyrdom. I began to cry, 'Allah is the greatest,' and prayed and thanked Allah for the success of the operation. I began to utter cries of joy and we declared that we were happy. The young people began to fire into the air out of joy over the success of the operation, as this is what we had hoped for him."[2]

The will to genocide is not specific to the martyrs who blow up little children, but is shared by the community of radical Islam. It comes not from despair but from hope—the hope of heaven, the hope of spreading the realm of Islam and of doing Allah's will. Nothing could be more obvious to anyone paying attention. That is, to anyone paying attention without the screen of liberal arrogance, which denies what it has seen in order to "explain" it. And thereby "understand" it. And thereby surrender to it.

The hope of heaven—or for the global reign of Islam as the path to heaven—is generically the same fanatical inspiration that caused believers in socialism (as a heaven on earth) to kill tens of

---

[2] "An Interview with the Mother of a Suicide Bomber," *The Middle East Media Research Institute,* Special Dispatch No. 391, June 19, 2002, http://www.memri.org/report/en/print683.htm#_edn1

millions of innocent unbelievers during the 20th century. It is the same faith that causes progressive fellow-travelers like Ted Turner, Barbara Kingsolver and Edward Said to support the agendas of America's enemies. And of perverse America-haters, like Gore Vidal and Noam Chomsky, to support any war against their country.

The present war against us may be about humiliation and a sense of inferiority that stems from Islam's centuries of eclipse; but it is not about despair. The new statement from al-Qaeda is not addressed to people who have nothing. Quite the opposite. It is an incitement to people who have something—faith—and who are ready to sacrifice life itself for the glory of Islam: "As long as the Muslim knows and believes ... he will not—even for a single moment—stop trying to achieve [the universal triumph of Islam], even if it costs him his soul ... his time, his property and his son, ..."[3]

This is not a war about land in the Middle East or the structure of a Palestinian state, or a U.S. military presence in the Arabian Peninsula. It is a war about redemption. In this, it exactly parallels the Communist threat from the past. In the eyes of the communists, America stood in the way of heaven—a socialist paradise in which racism, sexism and economic inequality would vanish from the earth. In the eyes of radical Islam, America—the Great Satan—stands in the way of Islam's rule, and thus of human redemption. And for this reason, America must be destroyed.

Thus the al-Qaeda proclamation: "America is the head of heresy in our modern world, and it leads an infidel democratic regime that is based upon separation of religion and state and on ruling the people by the people via legislating laws that contradict

---

[3]Suleiman Abu Gheith, "Why We Fight America," *The Middle East Media Research Institute,* Special Dispatch No. 388, June 12, 2002, http://www.memri.org/report/en/0/0/0/0/0/0/678.htm; (To read the entire transcript): http://www.fecesflingingmonkey.com/0602/memri.htm

the way of Allah and permit what Allah has prohibited. This compels the other countries to act in accordance with the same laws in the same ways ... and punishes any country [that rebels against these laws] by besieging it, and then by boycotting it. By so doing [America] seeks to impose on the world a religion that is not Allah's...."

Americans, wake up! Your enemies hate you for who you are. They hate you because you are democratic and tolerant and unbelieving in Islam's God. They hate you because you are Christians: "America's standing with the Christians of the world against the Muslims has stripped the camouflage from its face."[4] And they hate you because you are Hindus or Buddhists or secularists or Jews.

This war is not a war we are facing. It is a war we are in. Americans have hardly begun to understand this, but the enemy is already keeping score: "We have not reached parity [with America's alleged attacks on Muslims. Therefore], we have the right to kill four million Americans—two million of them children—and to exile twice as many and wound and cripple hundreds of thousands. Furthermore, it is our right to fight them with chemical and biological weapons, so as to afflict them with the fatal maladies that have afflicted Muslims because of the [Americans'] chemical and biological weapons."[5]

Americans have only begun to understand that, if radical Islam is one face of our enemy, the other is the radical left. For two hundred years the radical left has believed in a religion promising a heaven on earth whose end justifies any means. That is why progressives like Lenin and Stalin and Pol Pot killed so many innocent people. That is why radical leftists in America and other European countries have joined in denouncing America's war of

---

[5]Suleiman Abu Gheith, "Why We Fight America," *The Middle East Media Research Institute,* Special Dispatch No. 388, June 12, 2002, http://www.memri.org/report/en/0/0/0/0/0/0/678.htm; (To read the entire transcript): http://www.fecesflingingmonkey.com/0602/memri.htm

self-defense and in abetting the Arab crusade to obliterate Israel, which means exterminating the Jews of the Middle East.

How serious are some American leftists about abetting the war to destroy their own country? Attorney Lynne Stewart is a veteran of the radical left going back to the 1960s, and the lawyer for the "blind sheik" who led the first terrorist attack on the World Trade Center in 1993. She has been a supporter of communist causes and Arab terrorists for her entire professional life and is a hero to progressives at the National Lawyers Guild, the ACLU, *The Nation* and other institutions of the left. In 1995, she was interviewed by *The New York Times* and said this: "I don't believe in anarchistic violence, but in directed violence. That would be violence directed at the institutions which perpetuate capitalism, racism, and sexism, and the people who are the appointed guardians of those institutions, and accompanied by popular support."

The World Trade Center is an institution which perpetuates capitalism and—in the eyes of the left—racism and sexism as well. In the eyes of progressives, America is a land of capitalism, racism and sexism, and the enforcer of capitalism, racism and sexism globally. This is the world that the Islamists call Dar Al-Harb; the world of darkness; the world that is not socialist (for leftist believers) and not Islam (for the Muslim faithful). According to Lynne Stewart and the al-Qaeda spokesman, the people who dwell in Dar Al-Harb and support its profane agendas deserve to die. This is what the present "war on terror" is about. Americans had better understand it sooner rather than later.

4

Sabotaging the Impending War With Iraq

Debating whether the U.S. should go to war is a vital function of any democracy, particularly ours. Abetting dissident military officers by leaking selective classified military data is not. But that is the way *The New York Times* is choosing to wage its campaign to undermine a possible government decision to go to war with Iraq. *The Times'* lead story today quotes unnamed "senior military officers" who claim that the Reagan administration aided the Iraqi regime during the Iran-Iraq war, even though U.S. intelligence knew that Iraq was using poison gas in the war.[1] The claim appears to undercut national security advisor Condoleezza Rice's argument that Iraq's use of poison gas in that war is one of the reasons for a regime-change in that country.

The U.S. came to the aid of Iraq in its conflict with Iran, despite the malevolent nature of the Saddam regime, only when it appeared that Iraq was about to lose the war. It did so in order to prevent the Islamic, terror-supporting government in Iran, a country three and a half times the size of Iraq, from winning the war and dominating the Middle East. Obviously the *Times* story is not a story but an editorial—since crucial factual elements like this

---

August 19, 2002, http://archive.frontpagemag.com/Printable.aspx?ArtId=23189

[1]Patrick E. Tyler, "Officers Say U.S. Aided Iraq In War Despite Use of Gas," *The New York Times*, August 18, 2002, http://www.nytimes.com/2002/08/18/international/middleeast/18CHEM.html

are missing. A responsible editor would have insisted on a more balanced report. Instead, *The Times* decided to abet rogue officers in the Pentagon intent on sabotaging the administration's ability to defend the country against a criminal regime which is involved in terrorist wars against Israel and the United States.

The irresponsibility of *The Times* can be traced to events that happened a generation ago during the war in Vietnam. In particular, its editors should have been prosecuted for abetting the violation of the Espionage Act when they leaked the classified "Pentagon Papers" during the Nixon administration. Instead, they and their political allies succeeded in toppling a president in the midst of not one but two wars (in Vietnam and the Middle East) with deadly consequences for millions of people. Unfortunately, a liberal Supreme Court protected the *Times* editors from the constitutionally mandated consequences of their acts. As a consequence, *The Times* has become a dangerously irresponsible institution with great powers to harm this country. Today's leak is only the latest incident in the *Times'* ongoing abuse of the privilege of a free press. Hopefully, the harm that this has already done to the nation's ability to defend itself in the present war against terror will not be greater still.

5

100,000 Communists March on Washington

In politics, it is important to call things by their right names. Otherwise you are fooling yourself with other people's propaganda. The press is reporting Saturday's "Stop the War" demonstration in Washington as though it were a peace march. Of course it was no such thing. The organizers have no plans to demonstrate in front of the Iraqi embassy, or to call on Saddam Hussein to comply with the 16 Security Council resolutions that have been passed to try to get him to honor the terms of the Gulf War truce he has violated. No, this "anti-war" movement is a regrouping of the communist left—no longer communist in name, but the same left that supported Stalin and Mao, Castro and Ho. Indeed, this communist left, organized by Ramsey Clark and his cohorts, even supports the Serbian war criminal (and communist) Slobodan Milosevic, and of course Saddam Hussein. They are not pacifists and they are not peaceniks. They are anti-American radicals whose dream is a communist revolution in America, but whose immediate agenda is to force America's defeat in the "war on terror" we are now in.

Even the signs saying "Jobs Not War" are not without their Old Left reference-points. This does not mean that the Communist Party USA organized the march—although the Communist Party USA *was* one of its sponsors. The organizing was done by the Workers World Party, a self-styled Marxist revolutionary organization,

---

October 28, 2002, http://archive.frontpagemag.com/readArticle.aspx?ArtId=21486

aligned—I am not making this up—with North Korea's communist regime. The communist slogan in the first May Day parade I participated in, in 1948, was "Peace, Jobs and Democracy." Of course anyone can be for jobs and most of us want to avoid war if possible. But the specific theme of the 1948 May Day parade was stopping America's efforts to prevent Stalin from marching all over Europe. Its slogan, "We don't want another war," meant, "We don't want Harry Truman's Cold War to prevent the communist conquest of Eastern Europe."

The communist left also opposed "American militarism" in the 1930s in an effort to prevent the West from mobilizing to stop Hitler. Their tune changed, of course, when Hitler attacked the Soviet Union in 1941. The "New Left" also opposed the Vietnam War, not because it opposed war but because it wanted the North Vietnamese Communists to win. The real meaning of slogans like "Jobs Not War" is that America is the axis of evil that is plotting war and needs to be disarmed; that the "greatest terrorist state" in the world, in Noam Chomsky's words, is the U.S.A. *We* are the Great Satan, and we deserve to be attacked. This is the real message of the so-called peace movement. It is often covertly and disingenuously expressed. But its message is clear nonetheless. It is a movement of, by and for America's enemies within.

The fact that a movement of America-hating communists, who regard their own country as the enemy and who sympathize with America's terrorist adversaries, should be able to marshal 100,000 activists is a cause for concern. The communist New Left was not able to organize such large demonstrations in support of the communists in Vietnam until the draft was instituted in 1964. There is no draft in this country now. The size of these demonstrations is a reflection of the growth of a treacherous anti-American radicalism that is not organized by a Communist Party *per se,* but is just as dedicated to America's destruction as if it were. The fact that the new technologies of war make it possible for terrorist groups, both foreign and domestic, to inflict enormous damage on industrial democracies like ours, and that our borders are porous and our security capabilities wanting, underscores the daunting dangers posed by this internal threat.

6

A Serious Problem for the Patriotic Left

When conservative talk-show hosts criticize the Democrats' foot-dragging on the war on terror, Democratic Senate majority leader Tom Daschle complains they are promoting hate and endangering his life. When conservatives like myself deplore the sympathies shown by many anti-war activists for America's enemies—sympathies documented by Michelle Goldberg in the pages of *Salon*—columnist Joe Conason accuses me of attempting to incite patriotic mobs against all critics of the war.[1] This is the way leftists attempt to shut down discussion of patriotic loyalties. Here is what Conason wrote: "In many quarters on the right, doubt about war equals hatred of America or worse. This sort of hysteria now pervades the propaganda operations of David Horowitz [whose] *Frontpage* magazine features 'The Fifth Column,' where political adversaries are smeared with treason. Like many right-wingers, he insists that anyone who doesn't enthusiastically support an invasion of Iraq must despise America and love Saddam. Anyone, that is, except for the anti-war skeptics on the right—who somehow escape being branded as traitors."[2]

November 25, 2002, http://archive.frontpagemag.com/Printable.aspx?ArtId=20981

[1]Michelle Goldberg, "Peace Kooks," *Salon*, October 16, 2002 http://www.salon.com/2002/10/16/protest_14; Joe Conason, "Why Conservatives Get a Free Pass for 'Treason'—but Liberals Don't," *Salon*, November 20, 2002, http://www.salon.com/2002/11/20/conservatives_4/

[2]David Horowitz, "The Fifth Column Left Declares War," *FrontPage Magazine*, March 17, 2003, http://archive.frontpagemag.com/readArticle.aspx?ARTID=19245

In fact, I have never equated doubt about the looming war in Iraq with hatred of America. I recently had a *Boston Globe* article by Todd Gitlin, a man with doubts about the war, reposted in *Frontpagemag.com.* In posting it, I changed his title to "A View from the Patriotic Left."[3] The point I was making to my conservative readership was that Gitlin's view was patriotic because it was critical of the hate-America left, even though Gitlin remains a leftist critic of Bush and has been guilty of similar views himself. Documenting America's fifth column is not a plot to suppress leftist critics, let alone all those who do not line up behind the present administration. I do not equate political dissent with treason. Would I for years have written for *Salon,* and spent political capital defending its editors, if I considered them traitors? These charges are absurd and insulting. Conason knows it, and that is what makes his remarks even more distasteful.

"While Horowitz and company focus on easy targets like Noam Chomsky and Ramsey Clark," Conason continues, "their deeper aim is to depict anyone who doesn't line up behind Bush as soft on terror. Aside from scamming a few quick bucks—'Help David Expose the Leftist Plot to Control America's Young Minds!'—that is in fact their only purpose. (Despite its capitalist form, this enterprise strongly resembles communist methods of enforcing the correct line. You can take Horowitz out of the CP, but you can't take the CP out of Horowitz.)"

The vulgar Marxist insinuation that my conservative views are really a scheme to enrich myself is typical, and was the subject of Conason's first attack on me, reacting to my very first *Salon* column. Does anyone wonder why conservatives regard socialism as envy gussied up as a political cause? Although my parents were Communists, after adolescence I never was, either in practice or theory. I was always a new-leftist critic of Communism. My first book, *Student*—published in 1962—was dedicated to Supreme

---

[3]Todd Gitlin, "A View from the Patriotic Left: Gore Vidal and Other America Haters," *FrontPage Magazine,* September 10, 2002, http://archive.frontpagemag.com/readArticle.aspx?ArtId=22742

Court justice and civil libertarian Hugo Black, and explicitly criticized American Communists for their rigid party line and anti-democratic philosophy; it was attacked by a reviewer in the Communist Party's *People's World* for that very reason.

Far from suggesting anything close to the idea that "doubt about war equals hatred of America or worse," I have posted anti-war articles on *Frontpage* by my own columnist, John Zmirak.[4] If Conason wants to claim that I have "smeared [my] adversaries with treason," he should produce the quotes. Whom is he talking about—Jane Fonda? John Walker Lindh? Or Noam Chomsky, who like Fonda traveled to hostile terrain (in this case Pakistan in the middle of the Taliban war) to accuse the United States of crimes against humanity? Visitors to my site and readers of my *Salon* articles know that I have defended specific individuals who are *Dissent* socialists, *Nation* leftists and *Salon* editors. At Horowitz-Watch, a site created by my detractors, I have explicitly dissociated myself from the view that those who criticize the war are *ipso facto* fifth columnists or traitors.[5] "Criticizing American policy is fine," I wrote in my most recent post, "and almost no particular criticism can be labeled 'fifth column.' It's a matter of the individual profile of the critic, and the context of their criticism. I agree that the whole issue is problematic and one needs to be careful in these matters when applying charged labels. But we are also in the middle of a war and it is clear that there is a large constituency in this country that believes America can do no good and that its enemies have 'social justice' on their side." Are these comments controversial?

As it happens, Conason is also 100 percent wrong about my having no enemies to the right. I personally commissioned Myles Kantor to write an article titled "Introduction to the Anti-American Right" and have run articles slamming the anti-war positions of Pat Buchanan's *American Conservative.* I have also contended with

---

[4]http://archive.frontpagemag.com/bioAuthor.aspx?AUTHID=63
[5]http://www.horowitzwatch.blogspot.com/

Justin Raimondo, the right-wing editor of *Antiwar.com,* whose search engine reveals 240 attacks on me, personally.

Conason's column is an attempt to create an atmosphere in which one cannot point to the left's most serious problem: the presence of terrorist sympathizers in its own ranks. To do so would be McCarthyism, right-wing chauvinism, witch-hunting. Yet the problem created by the solidarity of many leftists with America's enemies is not a new one for progressives. During the Cold War, and before the emergence of the New Left, progressives lent their support almost across the board (the *Dissent* camp and the Trotskyists were exceptions) to the Soviet enemy and later to Cuban, Chinese and Vietnamese Communists.

Alienation from one's own country and fifth-column support for its enemies is a problem for the contemporary left, just as it was for the left during the Cold War. Already the national peace demonstrations are in the hands of pro-Saddam, pro-Milosevic, even pro-ayatollah fanatics, as not only Michelle Goldberg but *The Nation*'s David Corn has admirably pointed out. This has already so discredited the left generally that it has probably undone most of the gains it had made with its successful alibi in the wake of the Soviet collapse—that Soviet socialism wasn't "real socialism."

The left's problem in the war on terror is that America has been attacked, that American citizens have been slaughtered in their places of work, and—if the D.C. snipers were (as I believe) a domestic expression of the Islamic *jihad*—in their neighborhoods. Moreover, the left's fifth-column wing has embraced not only anti-Americanism but anti-Semitic, anti-female, religious fanaticism—thus forfeiting every last shred of the left's progressive aura. Sympathy for an enemy 10,000 miles away in Vietnam was one thing. Sympathy for the architects of 9/11 is another. The perils that the patriotic left faces from being connected to an anti-American, terrorist-sympathizing fifth column are measurably increased by the prospect of more 9/11-grade atrocities waiting in the wings. If you think sympathies for the communist devil created problems for radicals during the Cold War, wait until the casualty toll inside America begins to mount. That is why the left needs to have this discussion, which attitudes like Conason's seek to suppress.

Contrary to Conason's claims, it is my view that tactical disagreements over taking on Saddam Hussein at this moment in time don't even qualify for this discussion. It is perfectly legitimate for skeptics to worry about the risks and/or distractions of the war against Iraq, even though it is also my belief that the sooner we do go to war with Saddam, the better. In this hawkish perspective, I happen to be in complete agreement with Al Gore's running-mate, Senator Joseph Lieberman. Conason's article does an immense disservice to the left. By distorting the arguments of critics like myself, he stigmatizes in advance anyone who seeks to raise the problem. By equating critics of the anti-American left with McCarthyites, Conason obscures the problem itself. I may disagree fervently with a David Corn or a Todd Gitlin, or with *Salon*'s editor David Talbot on a host of issues, but I am truly gladdened and encouraged that critics from the left are forthrightly condemning the ugly progressives who side with the enemy.

7

Christopher Hitchens on Anti-Americanism

Anti-Americanism is really all that remains of the program of the political left after the collapse of its socialist dreams. For the whole of the modern era, world history was dominated by the struggle between the revolutionary models of France and the United States. But with the fall of the Berlin Wall in 1989) all this changed. As Christopher Hitchens summarized it in an interview with *The New York Times,* "After the dust settles, the only revolution left standing is the American one. Americanization is the most revolutionary force in the world."[1]

America is revolutionary because it is a society based on institutions and values that are inclusive, tolerant, democratic, anti-authoritarian, libertarian and conservative (skeptical of majorities, based on a deeply held moral individualism). As the president said in the wake of 9/11, the fact that America is a beacon of freedom and opportunity to the world is the reason it is hated by the forces of world reaction—principally Islamic fundamentalism and socialist statism, but also every creed of bigotry, both secular and religious. Americanization is the real threat that al-Qaeda, Saddam Hussein and the American "anti-war" movement have mobilized to oppose. America has been attacked because it is the only

---

December 09, 2002, http://archive.frontpagemag.com/Printable.aspx?ArtId=20774

[1]George Packer, "The Liberal Quandary Over Iraq," *The New York Times,* December 8, 2002, http://www.nytimes.com/2002/12/08/magazine/08LIBERALS.html?pagewanted=all

revolution standing, and an inspiration to those who love freedom everywhere.

The civilizational war we are now engaged in has united what remains of the communist-socialist-left, the remnants of national socialism (particularly the Ba'athists in Syria and Iraq), and radical Islam. This is the unholy alliance that has been forged against us. Even more than during the Cold War, our enemies are entrenched in our own population. Christopher Hitchens suggests that there is a difference between the anti-war movement of the Sixties and the current anti-American movement against the war in Iraq.[2] But there is no such difference. Alexander Cockburn, whose father served Stalin's KGB and who himself supported the Soviet bloc to the bitter end, wrote in response to Hitchens and other critics of the pro-Saddam "anti-war" movement that in supporting Saddam it was no different from the peace movements of the past. In a recent issue of his terrorist support site, Counterpunch.com, Cockburn observed that the anti-war movement of the Sixties was led by Stalinists, Trotskyists and Maoists. Their creed was totalitarian and therefore, as Hitchens would now agree, anti-American. Were self-deluded others drawn to their cause? Certainly. Were some patriotic critics suckered into joining their demonstrations? Probably. But that does not alter the nature of the movements themselves.

What has now changed is not the intention of the leaders of the movement. What has changed is that the enemy is so nakedly the aggressor against *us* (and not, for example, a hapless Third World people like the South Vietnamese). What has changed is not that our declared enemy is more evil than the Soviet enemy, but that he is more *transparently* evil, failing to pay even lip-service to "social justice" and other left-wing values as the communists did. But that is all. The totalitarian agendas of Osama bin Laden and

---

[2]Christopher Hitchens, "Right Concept, Wrong Word", *FrontPage Magazine,* December 9, 2002, http://archive.frontpagemag.com/ReadArticle.aspx?ArtId=20780

Saddam Hussein and Yasser Arafat are no different from those of Stalin and Ho Chi Minh, Fidel Castro and Kim Il Sung.

Hitchens still wants to avoid the obvious in these matters. Instead of confronting the standard progressive activists, he reaches for the standard progressive bogeyman, Pat Robertson: "But what if, just for a moment, one tried to classify something as 'anti-American' for its own sake? My nomination would go to Pat Robertson, who appeared on the television in the immediate aftermath of the September 11 atrocity and declared that the mass murder in New York and Washington and Pennsylvania was a divine punishment for a society that indulged secularism, pornography, and homosexual conduct. Here is a man who quite evidently dislikes his own society and sympathizes, not all that covertly, with those who would use violence and fanaticism to destroy it."[3]

This charge is ridiculous and Hitchens must know it. Robertson apologized publicly and profusely for what he said carelessly and casually in a TV conversation. I agree with Hitchens that Robertson has been guilty of bigotry on more than one occasion. But he has publicly apologized for these lapses as well. This does not excuse his remarks but makes them something short of "anti-Americanism," let alone sympathy for Islamic fanatics out to destroy us. (Where, by the way, are all those leftist apologies for anti-American outbursts during the Vietnam War?) Robertson's writings, despite their eccentricities, are strong defenses of the foundations—political, economic and moral—of America's tolerance and opportunity and inclusiveness. And he has been on the right side of this battle far longer than Hitchens or I.

Nonetheless, Hitchens's intellectual odyssey, which seems to have begun in earnest on 9/11, has brought him to some important conclusions: 1) America is worth defending; 2) American patriotism is progressive; and 3) the triumph of American ideas and institutions is a liberating prospect for most of the world's peoples. In

---

[3]Ibid.

these sentiments, he has brought his own views into harmony with the statement to Congress made by America's president in the wake of 9/11. And Hitchens has seen the irony in the fact that the president's statement also harmonizes with what he (and I) thought we were supporting in the 1960s: "I feel much more like I used to in the '60s"—Hitchens told *The Times,* explaining his support for Deputy Secretary of Defense Paul Wolfowitz's plan to democratize Iraq—"working with revolutionaries."

8

Self-Deception and Appeasement

As we approach the year's end and look towards a future filled with the war, it is sobering (and saddening) to consider how many Americans seem ready to betray their country. The other day I was on a panel with Frank Mankiewicz, former Bobby Kennedy press secretary, former National Public Radio chief, and the man who persuaded George McGovern to run for president in 1972 on a platform of "America Come Home." This was a thinly disguised translation of the left's slogan "Bring the Troops Home," which was consciously designed to help the Communists win the war in Indochina. This is not to say that everybody who endorsed that slogan or the McGovern candidacy also embraced the goal of enabling the Communists to win. But that was the foreseeable practical effect of the policy, and those who endorsed it at the time should have learned their mistake by the result. When the Communists won in Cambodia and Vietnam, they proceeded to slaughter two-and-a-half million Indochinese peasants, creating the bloodbath about which presidents Nixon and Johnson had warned.[1]

Mankiewicz's position on the looming war with Iraq was that it is George Bush's fault. "We are going to have a war," Mankiewicz said, "because our president won't take yes for an answer." Think about that. We have been technically at war with

---

January 2, 2003, http://archive.frontpagemag.com/Printable.aspx?ArtId=20493

[1]http://en.wikipedia.org/wiki/Pol_Pot

Iraq for more than a decade. The war is a result of the Iraq regime's violation of every stipulation of the truce that ended hostilities in the Gulf War. The intervening years have shown that Saddam is a pathological liar who can't be trusted to keep agreements, and a psychopath who tortures and murders the children of his own diplomats to keep them in line. In Iraq, we confront a nation living under unimaginable terror. But the appeasement chorus has forced us into the sick charade of conducting "inspections," even though we know that Saddam has hidden his laboratories and weapons of mass destruction, and that his scientists and officials—even if they have not been corrupted—are too terrified to tell the truth. Yet Frank Mankiewicz is ready to trust Saddam Hussein before he will trust George Bush and the American government. Shame on him.

In this unseemly and dangerous posture he is like Jimmy Carter, according to polls the second most admired American. Carter was recently rewarded with a Nobel Prize by the Norwegian supporters of Middle East terrorism and terrorism generally. The Norwegian Nobel Committee had previously rewarded Guatemalan terrorist Rigoberta Menchú and Palestinian terrorist Yasser Arafat for their "peace" efforts. In fact, Carter's award was for second-hand support of terror—for trusting every international sociopath he has encountered in the last decade, most egregiously the North Korean dictators to whom he gave his personal imprimatur some years ago, allowing Bill Clinton and Al Gore to finance Pyongyang's nuclear-weapons program under the cover of an atoms-for-peace deal.

Appeasers like Mankiewicz and Carter, who have so endangered our future, are but the tip of the iceberg of betrayal. After all, we also have those out-of-control Democratic legislators and overgrown Tinseltown adolescents who actually traveled to Baghdad to give Saddam moral support; we have legions of Middle East studies professors shilling for Hamas and al-Qaeda; and we have college leftists parading their pro-Saddam banners around the quad, having persuaded the city councils in nearly two dozen leftist college towns to pass resolutions refusing to cooperate with the Department of Homeland Security, thus declaring their own war on our War on Terror.

Whence comes this tolerance for evil and sympathy for our enemies? Some of it comes from a radical left that has supported America's totalitarian enemies for generations and has now been enlarged by an unknown cohort of Muslim radicals as well. In his address to the nation after 9/11, President Bush identified the historical continuity in our present foes: "We are not deceived by their pretenses to piety. We have seen their kind before. They are the heirs of all the murderous ideologies of the 20th century. By sacrificing human life to serve their radical visions—by abandoning every value except the will to power—they follow in the path of fascism, and Nazism, and totalitarianism. And they will follow that path all the way, to where it ends: in history's unmarked grave of discarded lies."

But there is also a contingent in this movement of betrayal that has succumbed to the siren-song of the left, and owes its origins to a combination of denial and self-deception. I think that Frank Mankiewicz and the so-called liberals at *The New York Times* fall largely into this category. A democracy like ours lives on dissent. We have succeeded in vanquishing our foes because we are a free society in which principled critics provide a vital ingredient of our success. But saying that we are going to war because our president will not take yes for an answer from a psychopath does not come under the category of principled criticism. It is based on a profound lie about who we are as a nation. It is a betrayal of us.

This passion on the part of liberals like Mankiewicz and Carter comes in part from having absorbed, and then having been addled by, leftist tropes that evil does not exist but is the product of social institutions or of misperceptions based on ignorance and misunderstanding. These leftist tropes give rise to the illusion that governments can fix the messes that individuals create. This leads them, on the one hand, to think that Saddam Hussein can be appeased, and on the other to distrust wealth and success and thus to blame America first. In the minds of these liberals, it seems that *we* are the root cause of all the root causes that inspire madmen to attack us. We even hear now from TV commentator Alan Colmes that the demented dictator Kim Jong Il, who has presided over the starvation of a million of his inhabitants, wouldn't be brandishing a nuclear threat if George Bush had not identified him as part of the "axis of evil." In other words: us bad. This preposterous accusation ignores, among other things, the fact that conservatives warned about the North Korean nuclear threat during the Clinton administration; that they criticized presidential emissary Jimmy Carter for trusting North Korea's dictator and financing his nuclear weapons program under the guise of making him a partner for peace.

An element in these betrayals is the innate human impulse to deny harsh realities, to hope that thinking will make it so. When confronted by evil, appeasement is in fact the most basic human response. The lineup in the 1930s, when Hitler was marching through Europe, was no different from the lineup today. There was no multilateral response to Nazism. There was England. And then there was the United States. If the pacifist betrayers of the West had not been so powerful in the 1930s and Western governments had joined to confront Hitler early, 70 million lives would have been saved. Americans would do well to remember this now.

The heart of the self-deception in America's liberal establishment, however, comes from forgetting the lesson of 9/11 and thinking we are invulnerable. It is this complacency that leaps at the crumbs from dictators' tables and proposes leaving the would-be killers Saddam and Kim Jong Il and Hamas and Hezbollah alone, with the idea that paper agreements will buy peace in our time. They won't.

9

America Under Siege

America's internal enemies turned out in the hundreds of thousands on Saturday in Washington, DC and San Francisco. They were assembled under the auspices of the communist Workers World Party, operating under its front organization A.N.S.W.E.R., to protest America's efforts to defend itself. Once again, the demonstrators pretended to be peace activists, and a willing media establishment encouraged the charade. Neither *The New York Times* nor the *Los Angeles Times*, nor any medium I saw, identified the organizers as communists who have a long record of support for world terror and its leaders, including Kim Jong Il, the Ayatollah Khomeini, Slobodan Milosevic and Saddam Hussein.

As reported by the unfiltered cameras of C-Span, the pretense was pretty thin. One of the featured speakers was a spokesman for the narco-terrorists in Colombia who opened his rant with: "We have to stop America's war against the people of Iraq, and the people of Palestine, Colombia and the world." America is, in fact, supporting the government of Colombia against a brutal communist guerrilla force that has been waging civil war there for half a century. Come to think of it, America's enemies in Palestine are the terrorist organizations Hamas, Palestine Islamic Jihad and the al-Aqsa Martyrs terrorist brigade. And in Iraq, America is opposing a dictator who has slaughtered hundreds of thousands of his own

---

January 20, 2003, http://archive.frontpagemag.com/Printable.aspx?ArtId=20218

people and attempted to swallow the country of Kuwait. The spokesman for the Colombian narco-terrorists was quite candid (and why not, since the American media will present him as a "peace activist" anyway): "As revolutionaries," he said to the crowd, "as progressives, we have to resist American imperialism."

Then came Imam Musa from the mosque Masjid al-Islam. Like most of the cast put together by A.N.S.W.E.R., Imam Musa was also a speaker at the Millions for Reparations March last August—which was more about denouncing America as a racist, imperialist monster than making a case for compensation. (See my report, "Reparations Buffoons on the Washington Mall."[1]) Here is a sample of the rhetoric at that march from Malik Zulu Shabazz (one of the few speakers who was not also at the "peace" event): "The president wants to talk about a terrorist named bin Laden. I don't want to talk about bin Laden. I want to talk about a terrorist called George Washington. I want to talk about a terrorist called Rudy Giuliani. The real terrorists have always been the United Snakes of America."

When he got going, the Imam Musa dotted the i's and crossed any t's that the narco-terrorist spokesman had missed—telling the crowd that the regime-change they wanted was in Washington not Baghdad, and that they really didn't want merely a regime change. "We're calling for a system change," he said. "We won't get any justice as long as that criminal congress is up there. We're calling for revolution. It's revolution time, brothers and sisters. We have to get rid of greedy murderers and imperialists like George Bush in the White House." Imam Musa then led the crowd in the chant the suicide bombers use as they blow up innocent men, women and children—"Allahu Akbar! Allahu Akbar! Allahu Akbar!"

Democratic New York City councilman and former Black Panther Charles Barron was also a speaker at the Millions for

---

[1]David Horowitz, "Reparations Buffoons On the Washington Mall," *FrontPage Magazine*, August 19, 2002, http://archive.frontpagemag.com/readArticle.aspx?ArtId=23179. Included in Volume VI: *Progressive Racism*.

Reparations March, where he announced he needed to assault a white person for his "mental health." At the anti-Iraq war rally he raved: "If you're looking for the axis of evil, then look inside the belly of this beast." He went on to attack America's "monopoly capitalists," who of course were the puppeteers pulling the president's strings. Damu Smith, head of "Black Voices for Peace," returned to Baron's theme and made it specific. "Bush, Cheney and Rumsfeld," he said, "that's the axis of evil." Larry Holmes, "co-founder" of the sponsoring organization which also hosted the Millions for Reparations March, then led the crowd in chants to free two convicted murderers, Mumia Abu Jamal and Jamil Alamin (H. Rap Brown)—also a set-piece at the Millions for Reparations March.

It would be reassuring if one could report that a single speaker or face in the televised crowd dissented from the stew of anti-American, anti-white, anti-Jew hatred or the violent incitements. But not one did. The crowd relished the show and was in total sympathy with its messages.

Another striking fact about this march in support of global terrorism was the presence of prominent Democratic Party officials on the speakers' platform. In San Francisco, the most powerful Democratic legislator in the state, John Burton, screamed, "The president is full of shit" and the president is "fucking with us." In Washington, racial arsonist and Democratic presidential hopeful Al Sharpton was a presence; ex-congresswoman Cynthia McKinney read a speech claiming, "In no other country on the planet do so many people have so little as they do in this country." This from a person who commandeered a taxpayer-funded limousine to take her from her townhouse, one block away, to her congressional offices every morning.

More disturbing by far was the presence of two of the most powerful Democrats in Congress: the potential head of the Ways and Means Committee, Charles Rangel, and the potential head of the Judiciary Committee, John Conyers, the author of the "reparations for slavery" bill and an icon for the organizers of both marches. Rangel's appearance was especially troubling because he has been a nightly face on TV news shows, presenting himself as a patriot and a veteran (he served fifty years ago in Korea) who wanted a military draft so that all America would be involved in the nation's defense. His critics thought he had other agendas, like using conscription to sabotage the war effort. Apparently, they were correct.

Americans who care about their country and its future should think about the following. This anti-American pro-terrorist movement is now larger than the anti-war, pro-communist protest movement was in the Sixties until the very end of the decade. Yet there is no draft now as there was for Vietnam. Before the draft began in the mid-Sixties, the anti-Vietnam movement was tiny. Its demonstrations numbered in the hundreds of participants, not even thousands. The first big manifestation of the anti-American left was the "Stop the Draft March" in Oakland in 1965, which was four years after America's involvement began.

The second thing Americans should think about is the fact that this support movement for America's enemies has a powerful following in the Democratic Party. I am a firm believer in the two-party system. I find it extremely worrying that one party can no longer be trusted with the nation's security. This problem will not be easily fixed. But it won't be fixed at all unless attention is drawn to it, and we cannot do that unless we stop the charade of calling this an anti-war movement and recognize instead that it is an anti-American movement to divide this country in the face of its enemies and give aid and comfort to those who would destroy us.

10

Secessionists Against the War

I'm looking at a full-page advertisement in Sunday's *New York Times* by the celebrated counter-culture author Wendell Berry called "A Citizen's Response to the National Security Strategy of the United States of America."[1] The strategy known as the Bush Doctrine was adopted in September of last year and is available on the White House website. In my view, this is the most important strategy statement made by our government since the Truman Doctrine of 1947. It begins with a recognition that the nation's present war crisis is caused by the fact that we have arrived at a historical crossroads where radical ideologies and modern technologies of mass destruction meet. This requires us to: 1) maintain a military supremacy that cannot be challenged; 2) pre-empt terrorists, fascist and communist alike—Osama bin Laden, Saddam Hussein, Kim Jong Il—who will strike us without warning; and 3) reserve the right to act unilaterally in our self-defense, i.e., be the masters of our fate.

The first thing that struck me about the Berry ad is how wealthy the querulous left has become—the same left which pretends to be the voice of the powerless and the poor. A full page ad in *The New York Times* costs close to $100,000. I have personally seen half a dozen ads since 9/11 that attack corporate America

---

February 9, 2003, http://archive.frontpagemag.com/Printable.aspx?ArtId=19793

[1]Wendell Berry, "A Citizen's Response to the National Security Strategy of the United States of America," *The New York Times*, February 9, 2003, http://www.commondreams.org/views03/0209–11.htm

and the American government, and find ways to sympathize with our nation's enemies. Second-hand Marxism seems to be the only paradigm available to leftist critics of the president and the war. Since *The Times* and the mass media generally have been critical of the war policy and its allegedly "unilateralist" nature, one has to conclude that these deep-pocketed leftists are so unhappy with the media critics of the war, they are willing to squander prodigious amounts of cash to buy a platform for their more radical dissents.

Wendell Berry is wildly unhappy with American democracy and its people because their representatives in two congresses have ratified presidential requests to go to war with Iraq. The first came from Bill Clinton, who requested war powers in 1998 in respect to Iraq; the second was Bush's recent request. Of course Berry does not say this, because like his peers Berry chooses to ignore these ratifications and pretend instead to speak in behalf of the allegedly silent people whose current leader has usurped that power. Radicals who hold this perspective are what I call the secessionists over the war. They want to make their own separate peace with America's enemies, as though the terrorists have not condemned all Americans regardless of race, gender, age or party affiliation.

Berry singles out as its "central and most significant statement" the following passage from the strategy paper: "While the United States will constantly strive to enlist the support of the international community, we will not hesitate to act alone, if necessary, to exercise our right of self-defense by acting preemptively against such terrorists...." A reader of these words who does not harbor intense feelings of hostility towards the United States cannot fail to be impressed by their reasonableness. *While the United States will constantly strive to enlist the support of the international community,* we will defend ourselves against attack, even if it means not waiting for terrorists who have declared their intention to do us harm to actually carry out those intentions. But Berry cannot contain his outrage: "A democratic citizen must deal here first of all with the question, *Who is this 'we'?* It is not the 'we' of the Declaration of Independence, which referred to a small group of signatories bound by the conviction that 'governments [derive] their just power from the consent of the governed.' And it is not the 'we' of the Constitution, which refers to *'the people* [my emphasis—WB] of the United States.' This 'we' of the new strategy can refer only to the President. It is a royal 'we.'" This is because, under the strategy, the president "will need to justify his intention by secret information," and will have to "execute his plan without forewarning." Berry concludes: "The idea of a government acting alone in pre-emptive war is inherently undemocratic, for it does not require or even permit the president to obtain the consent of the governed."

Forget the impracticality of submitting complex geopolitical decisions, based on sensitive intelligence reports, to the general public. The president *already has the consent* of the governed through two votes of Congress. Berry doesn't seem to understand the most basic fact about our constitutional democracy—that it is a representative democracy. It doesn't require Wendell Berry's direct consent or a referendum of the population before the president acts in the nation's defense. Indeed, the Constitution gave the war-making powers to the Senate, in those days an unelected body. Could the founders have known something about democratic passions that Berry doesn't? Perhaps Berry regards Sean Penn's walk-on role as a weapons inspector in Iraq as the *vox populi* in action.

I will not bore readers with Berry's descent into communist bathos, with his argument—familiar from the bilious screeds of Noam Chomsky and Edward Said—that there is really no difference between the terrorists and the United States military. But Berry does not seem to recognize that America has enemies at all. "The National Security Strategy wishes to cause 'terrorism' to be seen 'in the same light as slavery, piracy or genocide'—but not in the same light as war. It accepts and affirms the legitimacy of war." Well, of course. And what is the alternative in this world, except surrender?

Berry takes particularly strong exception to the Bush Doctrine's declaration of independence from the rule of the world's tyrannies, slavocracies and kleptocracies through international instrumentalities like the UN and the World Court. ("We will take the actions necessary to ensure that our efforts to meet our global security commitments and protect Americans are not impaired by the potential for investigations, inquiry, or prosecution by the International Criminal Court [i.e., the court that would prosecute a Pinochet but not a Castro—DH] whose jurisdiction does not extend to Americans and which we do not accept." To which Berry comments: "The rule of law in the world, then, is to be upheld by a nation that has declared itself to be above the law. A childish hypocrisy here assumes the dignity of a nation's foreign policy."[2]

This seems to be the problem defined. Delusional radicals like Berry would like to place the security and freedom of Americans in the hands of international bodies that make a slave-state like Libya the chair of the Human Rights Commission. In the midst of a war in which their country is under siege, they seek to taint it as an outlaw rather than defend it as a nation that seeks to observe the rule of law in a way that its adversaries do not. The rest of us have a charge to keep, and a debt to pay, to those who died for our freedom in wars before this one. We must reaffirm our birthright and acknowledge the great bounties we enjoy as Americans; we must defend our country not only on its military battlefields but here at home on the cultural war front, where a hostile movement of the political left seeks to sap its confidence and destroy its remarkable achievements from within.

---

[2]Wendell Berry, "A Citizen's Response to the National Security Strategy of the United States of America," *Common Dreams,* February 9, 2003, http://www.commondreams.org/views03/0209–11.htm

11

The March to Save Saddam

Millions of activists poured into the streets of cities from Melbourne to New York on Saturday, February 15 to protect Saddam Hussein from an imminent American attempt to disarm and dethrone him and disable his arsenal of chemical, biological and proto-nuclear weapons. They professed concern about Iraqi children (bearing mock bodies to symbolize their alarm) but marched in solidarity with Palestinians and Arabs who kill their own children by strapping bombs to them and telling them to blow up other children—Jewish children—so that they will go to heaven and their families will receive a $25,000 government reward.

In politics, intentions count for nothing; actions are what matter. If the marchers are successful, Saddam will survive to be stronger than ever. All over the Middle East and the Muslim world, fanatical haters of Americans, Christians and Jews will take heart from Saddam's successful defiance, will draw the conclusion that the West is weak, and will be inspired to commit new atrocities against its most defenseless citizens.

All the marches were organized by groups that are well-known supporters of communist totalitarians, and by the fifth-column agents of Islamo-fascism. All the demonstrations promoted Iraqi war propaganda—myths about starving children and about alleged mercenary interests behind American policy. All of them had one

---

February 17, 2003, http://archive.frontpagemag.com/Printable.aspx?ArtId=19705

purpose—to disarm the American forces already in the Middle East and allow Saddam to fight another day. It is true that some of the marchers were well-intentioned or at least not so blind yet that they could look past the evil that is the regime in Iraq. What of it? What could be more irrelevant than splitting critical hairs, when your country is under attack and your actions serve the aggressors?

During the Cold War there were many intelligent souls on the left who joined the "peace" demonstrations in the West organized by Communists and their supporters, but described themselves only as "anti-anti-communists." They meant by this that they knew that communism was bad, but were against the cold warriors who opposed it, and were locked in mortal combat with the Soviet empire. The Gorbachev regime in their eyes was bad, but Ronald Reagan was a "warmonger" and a capitalist, and therefore worse. The anti-anti-communists may have been good at stimulating critical discussion. A democracy can always benefit from dissenters because no political faction has a monopoly on truth. But in practice, the activist opponents of the Cold War encouraged the Communists to hold onto their slave empire and resist the attempts to set their captive nations free. In the end it was Ronald Reagan and the Cold Warriors he led who thwarted the Communists' ambitions, brought down the Soviet empire and liberated more than a billion of its subjects. In the scales of that historic struggle, when it came to mobilizing the military resources that backed the enemy down, the anti-anti-communists ultimately put their weight on the dark side of the scale.

During the Vietnam War—the clearest parallel to present events—the anti-war movement was organized by communists who wanted the other side to win. The non-communists who joined their marches, whatever their intentions, served the same practical end. America was divided at home, and those divisions eventually forced its armies to retreat from the field of battle. As a result, the Communists won and proceeded to slaughter two-and-a-half million peasants between 1975 and 1978.[1] This is the scenario that the people (mostly the same people) who are leading Saturday's protests hope to accomplish: the defeat of the West and the triumph of Islamo-fascism and its friends. Today's "peace" movement—the innocent-intentioned along with the malevolent rest—is a fifth-column army in our midst working for the other side. Already their leaders have warned that if the United States remains determined to oppose the totalitarian evil and stay its intended course, they will act within our borders to "disrupt the flow of normal life" and sabotage the war. This, ultimately, is the most ominous threat Americans face. Abroad we can conquer any foe. The real danger lies at home.

[1]http://en.wikipedia.org/wiki/Pol_Pot

12

The Fifth-Column Left Declares War

Some of us have long warned that the peace movement is not about peace, that it is a fifth column movement to destroy America and give victory to our enemies. Now this fifth column is preparing to move into action to attempt to defeat America in its war against Saddam. On the day after the U.S. military action in Iraq begins, the fifth column is preparing to begin its own war at home. The plan is to cause major disruptions—illegal in nature—in cities across the country to disrupt the flow of normal civic life. These actions will tie up Homeland Security forces and create a golden opportunity for domestic terrorists. The fifth-column left is also planning to invade military bases. Here is a report from *Salon.com*'s Michelle Goldberg:

"[Camp] Vandenberg is about 50 miles north [of] Santa Barbara, Calif. In a few days, activists will start converging on a nearby four-acre plot of land.... They're going to camp there and train to breach the base's security and possibly vandalize some of its equipment. The [leader of the activists] describes the base as 'the electronic nerve center of the global-surveillance-targeting, weapons-guidance, and military-command satellites that will largely direct the war.' The base is 99,000 square acres, with a perimeter running through rugged, wooded terrain. 'If people are committed and determined and in halfway decent physical shape, it is possible to get in, because it's enormous and much of the land

---

March 17, 2003, http://archive.frontpagemag.com/Printable.aspx?ArtId=19245

is still fairly wild,' he says. Within the base, [the action leader] says, are 'major off-limits security zones' that when breached 'set off a series of responses in their own security procedures which require disruption and partial shutdown of regular activities,' which means the base can't operate at full capacity."[1]

Here is the Internet call to arms for New York City, from a group calling itself "No Blood for Oil":

> The No Blood For Oil! Resistance Campaign is calling on all those who oppose the war, to join us in making the first day of concentrated US attack on Iraq an International Day of Civil Resistance! We'll be rallying in New York's Times Square at 5 p.m. that day—or 5 p.m. the next day, if the US assault begins at night—to inaugurate a campaign of civil resistance that will continue as long as U.S. aggression does. THIS MEANS NO BUSINESS AS USUAL! WE JOIN WITH MILLIONS ACROSS THE COUNTRY WHO CALL FOR A 'WORK STOPPAGE' ON THIS DAY! NO WORK, NO SCHOOL, NO BUSINESS AS USUAL! (caps in original)

Similar actions are planned for San Francisco, Los Angeles and the nation's capital, Washington, DC. The DC plan calls for five different actions designed to cause major domestic disruption: "These will be direct action oriented, unpermitted demonstrations to interrupt Business as Usual in the Capital of Capital and to raise the social costs of the US Government to Wage war on Iraq and the world. . . ."[2]

These are the intentions of the so-called peace movement, the actual violence to be spearheaded by the anarchist "Black Bloc," a collection of anarchist "affinity groups" who dress in black with

---

[1]Michelle Goldberg, "The Anti-war Movement Prepares to Escalate," *Salon,* March 14, 2003, http://www.salon.com/news/feature/2003/03/14/war/index_np.html

[2]"Emergency Critical Mass: When War is Called," March 17, 2003, http://lists.mutualaid.org/pipermail/dc-critmass-list/2003-March/000272.html

faces masked to facilitate illegal actions. These are the groups that caused massive disruption and damage during the anti-globalization riots in Seattle, and have wreaked civil havoc in other American cities.

There will also be larger law-breaking demonstrations timed for the day after our soldiers enter Iraq. The stated intent of the large communist-led "peace" organizations (United for Peace and Justice, Not in Our Name and International ANSWER) is to "interrupt the flow of normal life." Since the organizers cannot know the date when military action will begin and thus cannot get permits for their events, these are illegal demonstrations as well, and their goal is sinister. If security forces are tied up, obviously the opportunities for domestic terrorist attacks increase.

Organizers maintain that, even though their actions are designed to tie up Homeland Security forces, they will be "non-violent." Not so the actions of the Black Bloc, who launch their guerrilla operations from the main demonstrations. Here is a sample of their thinking, taken from their literature:

> We contend that property destruction is not a violent activity unless it destroys lives or causes pain in the process. By this definition, private property—especially corporate private property—is itself infinitely more violent than any action taken against it.[3]
> Q: Why do black blocs attack the police?
> A: Because they are in the way. While most anarchists oppose police brutality and seek an end to policing and prisons, our main targets are the rich and powerful. Since the police are the violent face of capitalism, in other words, the guard dogs for the rich, they are on the frontlines when the anarchists come to pursue our class war against the rich.

The military authorities at Vandenberg Air Force Base have already announced that they will use deadly force to repel the

[3]"Anarchist N30 Black Bloc Communiqué," ACME Collective, December 12, 1999, http://www.urban75.com/Action/seattle9.html

saboteurs. Legislators should take forceful measures as well. They could begin by increasing the penalties on existing legislation for this kind of civil disobedience and make them mandatory. This will deter some activists and take others out of commission for the duration of the war. Civil disruption during a Yellow Alert could be made a felony with a mandatory six months in a confined facility and $10,000 fine. If the crime involves violence or is committed during an Orange Alert, the penalties could be increased to one year in jail and a $50,000 fine. If the alert is red, the penalty is two years in jail and a $100,000 fine. Much larger fines should be assessed on the groups that sponsor these actions. Congress should also look to reactivating sedition laws that would meet the threat posed by the deadly seriousness of the radical Fifth Column. These activists are not playing games. They have dedicated their lives to the service of totalitarian enemies of their country. Now the international terrorists have fulfilled their dream: the war has finally come home.

The attempt to sabotage America's war effort is not dissent and should be a wake-up call to all those critics of the efforts by law enforcement to protect us by surveilling anti-American groups. Clearly, both the FBI and our security laws are well behind the curve, since these saboteurs have not been deterred from their deadly ambitions. Criminal subversion and sedition are not protected by the Bill of Rights and the perpetrators should be punished harshly enough to remove them from the battlefield.

13

Scheer vs. Hitchens on the War for Iraq

Last Sunday night, I went to the great debate over Iraq at the Wiltern Theater in Los Angeles. The subject was billed as the Bush administration's war policy on Iraq. Orville Schell, the dean of the School of Journalism at the University of California, which co-sponsored the event, opened the evening with a ritual lament over the alleged absence of a national debate on the issue—until he organized this event. He could have saved his breath.

First, there has been too much debate on the Iraq issue, which should have been decided by 17 UN resolutions and two congressional mandates to liberate this benighted nation from its oppressive and dangerous regime. Second, since the Wiltern debate was organized by institutions dominated by the left—the UC Berkeley School of Journalism and the *Los Angeles Times*—it was nothing like a national debate. On the platform there was not a single conservative or Republican to defend the president and his policy. People who doubt the leftist—not liberal—dominance of the media should reflect on this fact, until it becomes clear to them what has happened to our culture.

To be sure, one of those present was the redoubtable and courageous Christopher Hitchens, who did as good a job defending the American policy as possible given that he still has a lingering foot in the left. But as would become apparent in the course of the

---

March 18, 2003, http://archive.frontpagemag.com/Printable.aspx?ArtId=19223

evening, to hold demagogic charlatans like the *Times'* Robert Scheer to account, Hitchens would have had to rethink his leftist positions on American policy in the Cold War and not just on its policy towards Iraq.

Hitchens began with a yeoman effort to disarm the left-wing audience. If the anti-war left had had its way during the last 13 years, he said, Kuwait would be the 19th Iraqi province, Kosovo would be a part of Greater Serbia with tens of thousands more Albanian Muslims dead, and Afghanistan would still be under the rule of the Taliban. What Hitchens did not say, and what it turned out was important for him to have said, was that if the anti-war left had had its way during the previous 50 years, a billion people would still be living under Soviet communism, and there wouldn't even have been an option to save Kuwait or liberate Afghanistan short of a nuclear war.

This gap in Hitchens's argument allowed the two hardline leftists, Mark Danner and Scheer, to impersonate concerned moralists who would support a sensible American military policy towards Iraq. Containment worked against Stalin, they proclaimed—as though either of them had supported containment against Stalin and his successors. Both of them made another pass at the moral high ground by observing that Rumsfeld and others in the Bush administration had once supported Saddam Hussein and "created" Osama bin Laden by arming the Afghan resistance to the Soviet occupation.

This made Hitchens's faith in American policy towards Iraq appear corrupt and absurd. America's support for Iraq during its war with Iran was not "support for Saddam," as Danner and Scheer maintained. A country more than three times bigger than Iraq, Iran had recently been transformed by the first radical Islamic revolution. Its ayatollahs shared Osama's world vision and were leading crowds a million strong in Teheran chanting "Death to America." Military support for Saddam was a way of preventing a regional victory for these Osamas *avant la lettre,* who would have then controlled the Middle East and 9 percent of the world's oil supply. The policy seemed prudent—particularly since the left and the Democratic Party prevented America from projecting its own power overseas. The same can be said for the anti-American canard that Washington created Osama bin Laden by arming the Afghan resistance, which led to the fall of the Soviet empire and the liberation of a billion slaves of leftist schemes. It was not America that created the Taliban—as Scheer asserted—but the inability of post-Vietnam America to exert influence in that part of the world thanks to the efforts of the "anti-war" left. Unfortunately, Hitchens did not mention any of these facts. He was also too civil to point out that Scheer had made some mistakes of his own. Not only had he opposed America's cold war against the Soviet Union for 30 years; he had actually become a follower of North Korea's own Stalin, Kim Il-Sung. This was Scheer's politics during his years as a member first of the Red Family and then of the Red Sun Rising Commune. If a moral choice is on the table, I'll take Donald Rumsfeld any time.

Even as Scheer was denouncing U.S. "imperialism" during the Cold War, he was busily suggesting that Communists weren't actually so bad, particularly if they were Vietnamese. Scheer wrote a pamphlet in 1965 that was famous enough among radicals to have the moderator of the evening's event refer to it in reverential tones. It was in fact a mendacious tract purveying the Communist propaganda line that the Vietnam War was about an indigenous revolution in the South and not a Communist invasion from the North. After the war was over, the North Vietnamese themselves conceded that they had infiltrated many more regular troops into the South than the Johnson administration claimed, and Scheer's pamphlet denied.[1] Scheer's little tract played a sinister role in

[1]http://en.wikipedia.org/wiki/Vietnam_war. "North Vietnam invaded Laos in 1959, and used 30,000 men to build invasion routes through Laos and Cambodia by 1961. [About 40,000 communist soldiers infiltrated into the south from 1961–63. Ang, Cheng Guan, *The Vietnam War from the Other Side,* Routledge, 2002, pp. 16, 58, 76.] "North Vietnam sent 10,000 troops of the NVA to attack the south in 1964, and this figure increased to 100,000 in 1965." *The Washington Post,* April 23, 1985

convincing young people to oppose their government's effort to save South Vietnam from the fate that befell it. But no one on the platform mentioned the two-and-a-half million Indochinese slaughtered by Scheer's Communist friends when the United States was forced to withdraw because of the pressure of the anti-war protests of the time.

According to Scheer, there is no reason now for the United States not to wait "four months" to give the UN inspections time to work, implying that if the sanctions failed he would then support a U.S. military action—something he has not done in his entire life. No one on the platform discussed the difficulties of keeping 200,000 troops in the desert during the summer heat, or spending a billion dollars a week to do it while Democrats complained about the federal budget, or bivouacking them in an area where they would be a prime target for terrorist attacks while they waited for Saddam to end his cat-and-mouse charade with the UN inspectors. No one on stage discussed the problems of maintaining an overseas military deployment while a fifth-column "peace" movement led by self-identified communists with links to North Korea, Cuba, China and Ramallah organized a domestic opposition with hundreds of thousands of protesters. But that is precisely the situation we face.

I am constantly told that there is a new moderate left which has learned the lessons of the Cold War, has had second thoughts about its long service to the enemy cause, and is prepared to shoulder the responsibilities of American citizenship. I haven't seen much evidence of such a left generally, and there was only a modest manifestation of it on this particular evening. One leftist on the platform did understand that we are engaged in a battle for freedom and was willing to brave a hostile audience to say it. Michael Ignatieff did support the decision to go to war but at the same time couldn't find a single civil word to say about the president who is leading us in this time of national crisis. Two institutions of the national culture sponsoring the event—the *Los*

Angeles Times and Berkeley's School of Journalism—couldn't bring themselves to put a conservative on the platform to confront two unreconstructed anti-American leftists who saw no threat to us from our enemies—"rubbish" is how Mark Danner dismissed the idea—but a threat to others from our "imperialist" selves. *Plus ça change . . .*

14

Black Muslim Traitors

Suppose the traitor who rolled three grenades into the tents of our soldiers in Iraq, killed a captain and wounded 15 others, had been a member of Jerry Falwell's Thomas Road Baptist Church or Robert Schuller's Crystal Cathedral. Do you think his picture might be on the evening news or page one of *The New York Times,* instead of hidden from sight? In fact, the culprit, Hasan Akbar (a.k.a. Mark Fidel Kools) is a black Muslim from South Central Los Angeles and a member of the Masjid Bilal Islamic Center there. What this incident would show us, were the press doing its job, is that there is a connection between the ideas that people devote themselves to and what they actually end up doing. The fact that Akbar's former middle name, which looks adopted as well, is "Fidel" is probably not without significance either.

Last July, the Nation of Islam's spiritual leader, Louis Farrakhan, went to Baghdad where he had this to say: "The Muslim American people are praying to the almighty God to grant victory to Iraq."[1] America needs to wake up to the fact that there is an army of people in this country—some Muslim, some not—who identify with our enemies and pray for their victory. On *Frontpagemag.com* we have described them as a fifth-column left. This

---

March 25, 2003, http://archive.frontpagemag.com/Printable.aspx?ArtId=19101

[1]Thanaa Imam, "Farrakhan in Iraq for 'Solidarity' Visit," UPI, July 6, 2002; http://www.upi.com/Business_News/Security-Industry/2002/07/06/Farrakhan-in-Iraq-for-solidarity-visit/UPI-32511025986484/

has made many progressives angry with us. They claim that we lack proper respect for First Amendment rights and values even though, unlike them, we have never called for the suppression of even hateful speech. They also claim that when we notice dissenters and opponents betraying this country, that observation can have a chilling effect on their treasonous incitements. It certainly can; but it is also the case that real traitors can hide behind free-speech rights, and ideas do have consequences.

In fact, we have never accused all critics of the war of being members of a fifth column or committing treason. We have always been specific in identifying fifth columnists as those opponents of American policy who attack America and its leaders in absolute terms, and who identify with America's enemies like Communist North Korea. Dissenters who are willing to break the law, and tie up Homeland Security forces during a high-terror alert, also declare themselves enemies of America, since they are prepared to endanger their fellow citizens' lives and willfully abet an enemy force.

Examples of absolute hatred are easy to come by. The slogan "Bush is the disease, death is the cure"[2] was on display at many demonstrations against the war. "We Support Our Troops When They Shoot Their Officers"[3]—a banner paraded at an illegal demonstration against the war in San Francisco—is another sign of criminal and treasonous intent. Those who participate in illegal efforts to sabotage homeland defense and who proclaim irrational hatred of America and its leaders are telling us something it is important for us to take note of. They are telling us who they are. They are telling us that they are at war and that we are their enemy. They deserve to be taken seriously, not for their sake but for ours.

---

[2]"Death Threats Against Bush at Protests Ignored for Years," *Zombietime.com,* August 19, 2009, http://www.zombietime.com/zomblog/?p=621#photos

[3]http://www.patriotwatch.com/images/peace_sup.jpg

15

Moment of Truth for the Anti-War Left

Every movement has its moment of truth. For the "anti-war" movement it came at a "teach-in" at Columbia last week, when anthropology professor Nicholas De Genova told 3,000 students and faculty: "Peace is not patriotic. Peace is subversive, because peace anticipates a very different world than the one in which we live—a world where the U.S. would have no place."

De Genova continued: "The only true heroes are those who find ways that help defeat the U.S. military. I personally would like to see a million Mogadishus."[1] This was a reference to the ambush of U.S. forces by an al-Qaeda warlord in Somalia in 1993. The Americans were there on a humanitarian mission to feed starving Somali Muslims. The al-Qaeda warlord was stealing the food and selling it on the black market. In the ambush, 18 American soldiers were killed. Their bodies were then dragged through the streets in an act designed to humiliate their country. In short, for the De Genova leftists, America can do no good, and nothing that is done to America can be worse than it deserves.

The best that could be said of the crowd of Columbia faculty and students is that they did not react to the Mogadishu remark (perhaps they did not know what "Mogadishu" referred to). But

---

March 30, 2003, http://archive.frontpagemag.com/Printable.aspx?ArtId=19000. The war in Iraq began 11 days earlier, on March 19, 2003

[1]Ron Howell, "Radicals Speak Out At Columbia 'Teach-In,'" *Newsday*, March 27, 2003, http://www.nynewsday.com/news/local/manhattan/nyc-propo328,0,6281232.story?coll=nyc-topheadlines-right

they "applauded loudly" when the same professor said: "If we really [believe] that this war is criminal ... then we have to believe in the victory of the Iraqi people and the defeat of the U.S. war machine."[2] Of course, it was not the "Iraqi people" who were fighting us, but their oppressor. Evidently, the American left as represented by faculty and students at one of the nation's elite universities wants America to lose the war with the fascist regime in Baghdad.

The phrase "a million Mogadishus" has a special resonance for those of us who participated in an earlier "anti-war" movement. In 1967, at the height of the conflict in Indochina, the Cuban Communist leader Che Guevara (still an icon among today's radicals) called on revolutionaries all over the world "to create ... two, three, many Vietnams"[3] to defeat the American enemy. It was the Sixties version of a call for *jihad.* At the end of that decade I was the editor of *Ramparts,* the New Left's largest magazine, and edited a book of anti-American essays with the same title: *Two, Three, Many Vietnams.* Tom Hayden, a leader of the New Left then (and later a Democratic state senator and activist against the Iraq war), employed the same slogan to call for armed uprisings inside the United States in a book called *Trial* (1970).

Earlier in the New Left decade, I helped to organize the first protest against the Vietnam War at the University of California, Berkeley. At the time, America had only 300 military advisers in country seeking to prevent the Communist gulag to come. John F. Kennedy was president and had been invited as the commencement speaker. We picketed his appearance with the slogan, "Kennedy's Three R's: Radiation, Reaction and Repression." We didn't want peace in Vietnam. We wanted a revolution in America. Our picket was criticized in the college paper as "disrespectful." Eventually, we got smarter. We calculated that we couldn't attract

---

[2]Ibid.

[3]Ernesto Che Guevara, "Create Two, Three, Many Vietnams," *The Militant,* Vol. 60, No. 36, October 14, 1996, http://www.themilitant.com/1996/6036/6036_33.html

large numbers of people by revealing our deranged fantasies about America, at least not at that more conservative time. We realized that, if we were going to influence the course of the war, we needed the support of a lot of Americans who would never agree with our real agendas. So we changed our slogan to "Bring the Troops Home." That seemed to show care for Americans, while achieving the same goal. If America brought her troops home in the middle of the war, the Communists would win. Which is exactly what happened.

The movement that revealed itself at the Columbia teach-in has the same cynical cleverness at its core. When the Mogadishu remark was made, it was as if the devil had inadvertently exposed his horns, and someone needed to put a hat over them before others got wise. The someone who did that was the demonstration's organizer, Professor Eric Foner, the prestigious head of Columbia's history department. Foner followed De Genova to the speaker's platform. At the time, he let the Mogadishu remark pass while dissociating himself from another De Genova comment to the effect that Americans who described themselves as "patriotic" were "white supremacists." For Foner, this was evidently too self-discrediting.[4]

But by the time a New York *Newsday* reporter called for an interview the next day, Foner had become aware that the Mogadishu remark was also problematic, and indeed had caused some adverse reaction. He told the reporter, "I thought that was completely uncalled for. We do not desire the deaths of American soldiers." Foner did not say (and was not asked) how he thought organizing an anti-American demonstration to protest America's war in Iraq, and expressing the hope that America would lose, would not also serve to encourage the enemy to kill Americans. Eric Foner is no political naïf. He is the scion of a family of well-

---

[4]Ron Howell, "Radicals Speak Out At Columbia 'Teach-In,'" *Newsday,* March 27, 2003, http://www.nynewsday.com/news/local/manhattan/nyc-propo328,0,6281232.story?coll=nyc-topheadlines-right

known American Communists and in the Sixties was a Maoist. After the attacks of 9/11, he wrote an article in the *London Review of Books* saying: "I'm not sure which is more frightening: the horror that engulfed New York City or the apocalyptic rhetoric emanating daily from the White House." After receiving much adverse reaction, he wrote a self-exculpatory piece for *The New York Times* explaining that his uncertainty was actually patriotic.

Foner's cover-up reflects a powerful current in the anti-war movement to derail America's war in Iraq. Until now, the largest organization behind this movement has been "International ANSWER," which is a front for a Marxist-Leninist party with ties to the Communist regime in North Korea. According to a comprehensive report in *The New York Times,* some factions of the left became disturbed that the overtly radical slogans of the International ANSWER protests were "counter-productive."[5] Last fall they met in the offices of People for the American Way to create a new umbrella organization called United for Peace and Justice that would present a more palatable face to the American public. As it happens (but no coincidence), the name of the new organization was similar to that of one of the two main groups behind the national protests of the anti-Vietnam movement: the People's Coalition for Peace and Justice, which was run by the American Communist Party. As it happens, the head of the new organization was a veteran leader of the the Communist-led movement against the War in Vietnam. (The organizer of the other large-scale national demonstrations against that war was the MOBE, which was run by the Trotskyists.)

The group that People for the American Way assembled to create the new Iraq protest organization picked Leslie Cagan to be its head. Cagan is a pro-Castro radical who was still a member of the Communist Party after the fall of the Berlin Wall. Cagan's politics

---

[5]Kate Zernike and Dean E. Murphy, "Anti-war Effort Emphasizes Civility Over Confrontation," *The New York Times,* March 29, 2003, http://www.nytimes.com/2003/03/29/international/worldspecial/29PROT.html

were no less radical and anti-American than International ANSWER's. But she understood the problem of too much candor. "If we're going to be a force that needs to be listened to by our elected officials, by the media," Cagan told the sympathetic *Times* reporter, "our movement needs to reflect the population."[6] In other words, we have to keep our agendas hidden and pretend to be patriotic. Since Cagan's appointment, the *Times* reports that the anti-war left has been hiring Madison Avenue firms to shape its messages. It has been putting up billboards with the slogan "Peace Is Patriotic" to represent its aims.

At the Columbia teach-in, Professor Foner had this to say about patriotism: "I refuse to cede the definition of American patriotism to George W. Bush. I have a different definition of patriotism, which comes from Paul Robeson: The patriot is the person who is never satisfied with his country." It is true that Paul Robeson was never satisfied with his country. He was a leader and icon of the American Communist Party, and he received a Stalin Peace Prize from the mass murderer himself.[7]

The war in America's streets is not about "peace" or "more time for inspections," as it publicly proclaims. It is about which side should lose the war we are now in. The left has made crystal clear its desire that the loser should be us. Even if the left had not made this explicit, a "peace" movement directed at one side makes sense only as an effort to force that side to leave the battle and lose the war. Which is exactly what the Columbia professor said. If this is patriotism, what is treason?

---

[6]Kate Zernike and Dean E. Murphy, "Anti-war Effort Emphasizes Civility Over Confrontation," *The New York Times,* March 29, 2003, http://www.nytimes.com/2003/03/29/international/worldspecial/29PROT.html

[7]Margaret Hunt Gram, "Professors Condemn War in Iraq At Teach-in," *Columbia Spectator,* March 27, 2003; http://www.columbiaspectator.com/vnews/display.v/ART/2003/03/27/3e82ec7193097; http://www.campus-watch.org/article/id/611

16

The War Has Refuted the Opposition

Once again, the left is proved wrong about a war it opposed. In less than two weeks of fighting to liberate Iraq, our troops have brought to light enough facts to destroy every argument the left has made against the war. But don't expect this to put a crimp in its self-righteous arrogance.

I won't even waste time on the fact that Saddam was still lying about obeying the UN resolutions concerning his weapons. The Al Samoud missiles, the stashes of chemical uniforms, the seriousness with which allied commanders are taking the threat of chemical attacks on our troops, are the sickening signs of how incompetent was the Blix operation to disarm Saddam. After the disarmament myth, the left's principal illusion was that Saddam may have been a freelance despot, but he was not a terrorist and certainly not involved with al-Qaeda. The capture and destruction of al-Qaeda's training camp in northern Iraq shows that Iraq was indeed part of an evil axis that included al-Qaeda and Osama bin Laden. Bin Laden's call for a *jihad* in defense of Iraq was actually proof enough. Laurie Mylroie's dissection of Iraq's role in the first World Trade Center bombing and other al-Qaeda attacks was adequate proof before that. The rallying of Palestinian and Syrian terrorists to the Iraqi cause, and the use of Syria and Iran as refuges by the fleeing al-Qaeda soldiers, also establish the obvious. Just as the president said on September 20, 2001, we are in a war with a

---

April 3, 2003, http://archive.frontpagemag.com/Printable.aspx?ArtId=18924

terrorist enemy who has bases in many countries, whose defeat will only be accomplished on a global front and will take years to complete. The ventriloquized speech of the deposed and missing Saddam Hussein through the mouth of the Iraqi information minister, who is calling for an Islamic *jihad* against the allied coalition, is again confirmation of the al-Qaeda-Iraq alliance; particularly since Saddam is not an imam but a fascist *duce* at the head of a secular state.

Why would Osama bin Laden call for a holy war on behalf of an infidel like Saddam Hussein if Saddam weren't his terrorist ally in the *jihad* against America and the West? Why would Saddam impersonate an Islamic paladin, as he recently has, if he hadn't joined the Islamic *jihad* himself? Why would he risk housing an al-Qaeda camp? These are rhetorical questions. No rational person would doubt at this point that the coalition cause is necessary and just.

But the left is anything but rational. Now the left has adopted the Iraq regime's claim that we are the "aggressors" because we weren't attacked. This is quite a hypocrisy. What does the left think Clinton's assault on Bosnia was? Was Milosevic a threat to America's national security? Did he attack us? Yet, aside from Noam Chomsky, there was hardly a leftist complaint about the liberation of Kosovo, which took place without a UN resolution, without a national debate and without authorization from Congress. The hypocrisy is also a lie. There was no aggression committed by America because there was no peace preceding the fighting. Gulf War II is a continuation of Gulf War I, whose truce was violated by Saddam. That is what the 17 UN Security Council resolutions Saddam disregarded were about. The aggression was the Iraq regime's violation of the terms of the truce it had signed. The Iraq War is the resumption of a war that never ended. The left's argument against this renewed war is pathetic. It is fueled by irrational passions—most prominently by the left's hatred of the United States, but secondly by its deranged animus towards George Bush. This is a "peace" movement that should live in infamy.

17

Liberated From Saddam

Baghdad is liberated. In the days to come, it should not be forgotten that if not for one man and one man alone, the people of Iraq would not be celebrating in the streets and pulling down Saddam's statues today. If not for George Bush's decision to go to war, Iraq's jails would still be full and the torture chambers still operating and the weapons mills still turning out the instruments of future destruction. In this war of liberation, America's liberals appeased the monster regime, while radicals offered themselves as human shields to be placed in the way of the liberating forces. My favorite moment this liberation morning came when two Iraqis marched down Baghdad's main street, holding a banner that said: "GO HOME, HUMAN SHIELDS: YOU U.S. WANKERS!"[1] Should we now get ready for apologies from the left? Don't hold your breath. In *The Nation* today, Medea Benjamin, a pro-Castro communist and movement leader, calls for a worldwide effort to send human shields to North Korea, Syria and Iran, the pillars of terrorist power—because they are "threatened" by the United States.[2]

We have come to a historic turning point in the post-Cold War world. We have entered an era that will be defined by a global civil war between the forces of freedom and the powers of Islamo-fascist

April 09, 2003, http://archive.frontpagemag.com/Printable.aspx?ArtId=18786

[1]http://www.brw.net/blog/2003/04/09/troops-in-baghdad/

[2]Medea Benjamin, "Response 3," *The Nation*, April 3, 2003, http://www.thenation.com/article/response-3

and communist totalitarianism. Once again, the progressive left has positioned itself on the dark side of an international civil war. The good news is that America seems to be back. Our military has performed superlatively. Our leadership has stood tall. We should celebrate this and look confidently towards what lies ahead.

PART III

The Anti-War Left in the War

(5/13/2003—11/1/2004)

I

People Against the American Way

You've got to be impressed by the tenacity of leftists. The same people who have been colossally wrong about the war on terror, who clamored for America to sheathe its sword when their country was under attack, who defamed America as an aggressor nation when it was aggressed upon, are again on the attack even though their claims have been refuted by events. They have not taken a moment to reflect on their previous antics, which would have kept the Iraqi oppressors in power and allowed anti-American terrorists to run free in Afghanistan; they have not taken a moment's pause for regrets about blackening America's image or weakening her citizens' resolve in resisting the forces that would bring this nation down. Having attacked their president as a "Nazi" and their country as "the real axis of evil," the left is now complaining about those who have attempted to call them to account.

From Greenwich Village to Hollywood, progressives are sounding the alarm about a "new McCarthyism" and "imminent witch-hunts" because some Americans are revolted by what they said and did. And of course the left is once again—in the same hypocritical breath—presenting itself as a defender of the very American liberties it refused to defend. "A chill wind is blowing in this nation," is how actor and anti-war leftist Tim Robbins characterized the

---

May 13, 2003; http://archive.frontpagemag.com/Printable.aspx?ArtId=18250

situation in his triumphant country on national TV, while complaining about his "persecution" and "silencing."[1]

There is nothing new in these brazen inversions of the facts. Fifty years ago, America was also engaged in a global conflict, and the left's stance was identical. American Communists, organized and funded by Moscow, created the Progressive Party to oppose the Truman Doctrine and the Marshall Plan, America's efforts to defend freedom against the Soviet onslaught. The Progressive Party's mission was to attack America's "Cold War agendas" and to get the United States to disarm unilaterally. Yet when called to account for their disloyalty to country and to democratic values, they presented themselves as victims of a "witch-hunt" and a "Red scare," and champions of the Bill of Rights. And because of the cultural influence of the left and its sympathizers, they were successful. They gave the word "McCarthyism" currency as a name for suppressing progressive ideas, when in practice it has become a scare-word used to suppress attempts to question the left's subversive agendas and commitments. Properly labeled, the early Cold War years would be the era of the "Red threat," when hundreds of thousands of Americans aligned themselves with Joseph Stalin's police state and many became propagandists and spies for the regime in the Kremlin. But thanks to the left's prominent influence in the media and the academy, this treasonous epoch is today known as the era of the "Red *scare,*" as though the actual threat had been mythical.

Leading the current attack on American patriots is the organization People for the American Way, which conducts campaigns of hate and fear aimed principally at Christian conservatives but also at every group that attempts to defend America against the leftist assault. No sooner was the war in Iraq successfully concluded than People for the American Way published a special "report" it called

[1]Tim Robbins, "A Chill Wind is Blowing in This Nation," *Common Dreams,* April 15, 2003, http://www.commondreams.org/views03/0416-01.htm

"Talking Out of Turn: The Right's Campaign Against Dissent."[2] Its indictment begins with this piece of Alice-in-Wonderland logic: "While most people see President Bush's post-9/11 assertion—'Either you are with us, or you are with the terrorists'—as a call for the world community to join America in defeating terrorism, right-wing activists have taken a narrower view. To them, what the President is really saying is 'Either you toe the administration's line, or you're in league with terrorists.' They see Bush's policies toward Iraq as indistinguishable from America's interests.... To them, President Bush is the state and, therefore, dissent is treason." No evidence supports these claims.

The president is an elected leader and the war powers he used were given to him by a vote of the United States Congress in 2002, which included the majorities of both political parties in the Senate. In fact, it was two votes of the United States Congress that authorized the war to change Iraq's regime. The first was four years earlier and also called for "regime change." The "Iraqi Liberation Act," drafted and signed by President Bill Clinton, was passed by overwhelming majorities in both political parties. In other words, opposition to the war against the Saddam regime in Iraq *is* opposition to the policy of the whole American people as represented by its elected government. While this does not make all dissent treason, it certainly does make opposition to America's war in Iraq an opposition to *America*'s war and not to "Bush's war," as progressives and Democrats obstinately claim.

People for the American Way's smear campaign continues in the following vein: "From the beginning, the Right has sought to portray anti-war protesters as radicals. This does not gibe with the facts. A *New York Times* piece on dissenters emphasizes the diversity of the peace movement. While it is true that one group involved in the peace protests, International ANSWER, has socialist ties,

---

[2]People for the American Way, "Talking Out of Turn: The Right's Campaign Against Dissent," April 29, 2003, http://www.sourcewatch.org/index.php?title=Treating_dissent_as_treason

most major anti-war organizations have mainstream connections to groups like the NAACP and the National Council of Churches. These mainstream peace coalitions have gone out of their way to distance themselves from more radical elements and to disavow their tactics." People for the American Way is of course itself a radical organization (although obviously not by its own standards). The *New York Times* story was conveniently written to serve the interests of the left and People for the American Way, which (as *The Times* reported) held a meeting in the People for the American Way offices specifically to discuss the political problem created by the fact that International ANSWER, until then the sponsor of all the national peace demonstrations, was the creation of a Marxist party aligned with North Korea (not merely socialists).[3] A second sponsor of these demonstrations was Not in Our Name—a group organized by leaders of the Revolutionary Communist Party. The meeting in the People for the American Way offices was called to create a new coalition organization, which assumed the name "United for Peace and Justice" and held its first demonstration in New York in March 2003. The organizer and head of the new organization was Leslie Cagan, a pro-Castro Sixties radical who was still a member of the Communist Party after the fall of the Berlin Wall. Cagan put out a call to members of the coalition to "disrupt normal life" once the war started. So much for the "moderates."

As a former anti-war leftist who understands the consequences to which ill-conceived protests lead, I have tried to sound the alarm over the internal threat to the security of this country presented by organizations like International ANSWER, Not in Our Name, United for Peace and Justice and other neo-communist groups.[4] I have done this through articles documenting their activities,

---

[3]Kate Zernike and Dean E. Murphy, "Anti-war Effort Emphasizes Civility Over Confrontation," *The New York Times*, March 29, 2003, http://www.nytimes.com/2003/03/29/international/worldspecial/29PROT.html

published at *Frontpagemag.com,* a site that I edit. People for the American Way is well aware of this and consequently directs some of its slanderous attacks at me: "David Horowitz of the Center for the Study of Popular Culture is perhaps the most rabid advocate of the view that dissent equals treason. Each weekday, Horowitz and his colleagues at *Frontpage* magazine offer new articles on the evils of dissent, liberally sprinkled with such key phrases as 'aid and comfort,' 'clear and present danger,' 'blame America first,' 'hate America Left,' and 'fifth column.' In fact, FrontPage has an entire 'Fifth Column' section containing 380 articles to date."

This is a good illustration of how the left operates without regard for the truth, or for the personal reputations of individuals they are determined to defame. I have never, ever, equated dissent with treason nor given any indication I thought that dissent as such was "evil." Nor does People for the American Way provide any examples that would back up its malicious claim. On the contrary, I specifically and explicitly have asserted the right of critics to dissent from government policies, and I have put actions behind my words. I published, for example, an article on the war by Professor Todd Gitlin—an anti-war dissenter who was even part of the Columbia teach-in at which the infamous wish for a "million Mogadishus" was made.[5] I published Gitlin because, despite his dissent on the war, he denounced the anti-Americanism of the anti-war protests, something that People for the American Way has failed to do. I retitled Gitlin's article, calling it "A View from the Patriotic Left" to emphasize the point. Gitlin returned the favor by demanding I remove the article. Apparently, he didn't want to be tainted by someone as rabid as myself.

The one redeeming aspect of the People for the American Way document is that it provides quotes from the conservatives it

---

[4]David Horowitz, "Neo-Communism," *FrontPage Magazine,* April 22, 2003, http://www.frontpagemag.com/Articles/ReadArticle.asp?ID=7396

[5]Todd Gitlin, "A View from the Patriotic Left: Gore Vidal and Other America Haters," *FrontPage Magazine,* September 10, 2002, http://archive.frontpagemag.com/readArticle.aspx?ArtId=22742

defames which disprove its own accusations. The true test of a radical evidently is to be so far outside the mainstream as to be speaking a different language, so that the plain meanings of English are not what they seem: "A January 21st piece entitled 'The Peace Movement Isn't about Peace,' demonstrates Horowitz's standard *modus operandi*—link dissenters with Communists and dissent with treason. 'When your country is attacked, when the enemy has targeted every American regardless of race, gender or age for death, there can be no peace movement. There can only be a movement that divides Americans and gives aid and comfort to our enemies.... The so-called peace movement today is led by the same radicals who supported America's totalitarian enemies during the Cold War. They marched in support of the Vietcong, the Sandinista Marxists and the Communist guerrillas in El Salvador." And so they did—the organizers and board members of People for the American Way among them.

2

Norman Mailer's Burden

I've been studying America haters (as opposed to America's *critics*) for some time. In the midst of a war, it is especially important to distinguish between genuine dissenters from American policies and those who despise America as such (or what they prefer to call the American "system"—as though the two were separable). The haters wouldn't mind at all the prospect of America's defeat, would think, in fact, that something beneficial would come from it.

America's wars against the oppressive regimes in Afghanistan and Iraq have been especially useful in making this distinction between haters and critics, because in both cases America's adversaries lack redeeming characteristics. There is nothing in either to inspire sympathy for the enemy, nothing to confuse matters. There was no "national liberation" movement in Afghanistan or Iraq, as the left once alleged there was in Vietnam. No illusion that either government was a force for "social justice."

When America goes to war against opponents who are clearly monsters, immoderate criticism of America becomes immediately suspect. Of course there can be honest critics even of these wars—critics whose considerations are tactical and prudential. But there are also critics who are immoderate, who do not regard us as making mistakes but who are convinced, rather, that *we* are the enemy.

July 7, 2003, http://archive.frontpagemag.com/Printable.aspx?ArtId=17358

Here are three rules for identifying the America haters. They are critics for whom:

1. America can do no right.
2. Even the right that America does is wrong.
3. America's wrongs are monstrous.

As it happens, a perfect example of this type of thinking is readily available in the current issue of *The New York Review of Books.* It appears in an article about the Iraq war by novelist Norman Mailer called "The White Man Unburdened."[1] This is enough of a clue already, as it reflects the author's view that America is a racist, imperialist power—and therefore can do no right. Mailer's article asks the question, "Why did we go to war?" and sets up his answer by taking on the evidence from which some might conclude that we have indeed done right. The discoveries of Saddam's mass graves—Mailer observes—appear to show that "we have relieved the world of a monster who killed untold numbers, mega-numbers of victims." But, of course, even the right deeds that a racist and imperialist power appears to do must be wrong.

According to Mailer, a piece of the puzzle is missing: "Nowhere is any emphasis put upon the fact that many of the bodies were of the Shiites of southern Iraq who have been decimated repeatedly in the last twelve years for daring to rebel against Saddam in the immediate aftermath of the Gulf War. Of course, we were the ones who encouraged them to revolt in the first place, and then failed to help them. Why?" Mailer immediately answers his own question. A successful Shiite rebellion "could result in a host of Iraqi imams who might make common cause with the Iranian ayatollahs. Shiites joining with Shiites!" Of course, racists and imperialists will want none of that. Nor does such a prospect cause Mailer himself any concern. Perhaps he forgets that Iran's

---

[1]Norman Mailer, "The White Man Unburdened," *The New York Review of Books,* July 17, 2003, http://www.nybooks.com/articles/archives/2003/jul/17/the-white-man-unburdened/

ayatollahs are the avatars of the Islamo-fascist world movement, and that under their influence the crowds in Teheran not too long ago were chanting "Death to America." Perhaps he is unimpressed by the fact that, in addition to hating America and having imperialistic ambitions, Iran also has long-range missiles and is seeking nuclear warheads, and is the sponsor and host to the largest terrorist army in the world, Hezbollah.

There is another equally obvious answer to Mailer's question, which he does not even consider. The reason we halted our military operation once Kuwait was liberated, and did not proceed to reshape the political landscape of this volatile region, was that there was no regional support for such an adventure; indeed, there was opposition from the Arab states. And from Democrats. Although the first President Bush proceeded in impeccable multilateral fashion—soliciting the Arabs' support—he was barely able to get the congressional authorization he needed to reverse Iraq's conquest of Kuwait. Although he assembled an international coalition of 40 nations, only ten Democratic senators voted to authorize the use of force—even for the limited goal of liberating Kuwait. Three of those senators, Al Gore among them, did so reluctantly and at the last minute. Norman Mailer, and the political left he speaks for, opposed the Gulf War to save Kuwait, and would have opposed the installation of an American approved regime in Baghdad.

These are the reasons why Saddam was left in power and the Shi'as betrayed. Where is Mailer's recognition of his own accountability for *that*? Despite this bad faith, Mailer proceeds with the argument that America is responsible for Saddam Hussein's killing fields: "Today [the Shi'ites] . . . may look upon the graves that we congratulate ourselves for having liberated as sepulchral voices calling out from their tombs—asking us to take a share of the blame. Which of course we will not." In other words, in addition to being mass murderers we're hypocrites, too.

But Mailer is only getting warmed up. In addition to being damned for what we *fail* to do, Americans must be damned for what we are *alleged* to do. Mailer thus damns us for what he claims we did *before* the first Gulf War: "Yes, our guilt for a great part of those bodies remains a large subtext and Saddam was creating mass graves all through the 1970s and 1980s. He killed Communists *en masse* in the 1970s, which didn't bother us a bit." And why should it? This was a power struggle between fascists and Communists who both wanted to see Americans dead. What is Mailer suggesting? That we should have intervened in a Soviet sphere of influence and risked nuclear war to rescue the foot soldiers of the Communist International?

After disposing of his domestic opposition, Saddam invaded Iran, and—according to Mailer—we followed right behind. "Then he slaughtered tens of thousands of Iraqis during the war with Iran—a time when we supported him." Actually there were hundreds of thousands of Iraqis and even more Iranians killed in this war. But we did not "support" Saddam in the sense of approving what he did, as Mailer implies. We only provided aid to Iraq when it looked as if Iran would win and then control the world's oil supplies. The military equipment we supplied to Saddam was to balance the arms Iran was receiving from the Soviet empire, which was in a position to gain major benefits from an Iranian victory. This was classic balance-of-power politics, although one would never know it from Mailer's text. Keeping Iraq independent of Iran seemed merely prudent to Washington at the time. What would Mailer have had us do? If we had allowed Iran to conquer the Middle East, Mailer would have blamed us for the deaths that followed, and for the destructive consequences of an Iraqi defeat. Instead our arms contributed to a military stalemate and a peace, which saved hundreds of thousands of lives that Mailer doesn't consider worth mentioning.

Mailer sums up his distorted account of America's responsibility for all the carnage in Iraq in these words: "A horde of those newly discovered graves go back to that period [before the second Gulf War]. Of course, real killers never look back." *Real killers.* That's us. We can do no right. Even the right that we do is wrong. And the wrongs we do are monstrous.

3

The Party of Sabotage

The Iraq war is now in its fourth month. Before it began, I observed that the neo-communist left was making plans to move from "anti-war" protest to the next stage of resistance and sabotage the war effort itself. When the invasion took place on March 19, the left conducted law-breaking demonstrations in downtown business centers. By tying up first responders and Homeland Security personnel, the chaos in the streets would have facilitated any terrorism that Saddam might have been planning. Fortunately, the forces Bush and Rumsfeld set in motion crushed Saddam's military and toppled his regime. Since the left's war with America is permanent, progressives have now turned their efforts to undermining the occupation of Iraq and the post-war peace, specifically, America's efforts to reshape the Middle East and make it less of a safe harbor for our terrorist foes. Unfortunately for our country, the Democratic Party has begun to follow suit in its own timid way, shedding the mantle of appeasement to become a party dedicated to attacking the remaining war effort.

Since American forces liberated Iraq, not a day has gone by that Democrats have not attempted to undermine the leadership in Washington that brought about the victory on the field of battle. The greatest triumph of American policy since the end of the Cold War has become the unending target of Democratic snipers, including its congressional leaders and virtually all of its presidential

---

July 21, 2003, http://archive.frontpagemag.com/Printable.aspx?ArtId=17135

contenders, who now claim the war they only yesterday supported has cost too much, that the rationale for going to war was deceptive, and that the commander-in-chief is a liar who will sacrifice American youth for no defensible reason. The Democrats are clamoring for congressional investigations to dramatize these charges, which will only serve to tie the administration's hands, distract it from the remaining war tasks and encourage our enemies to resist even further.

No current act of Democratic perfidy has been more disgraceful than John Edward's statement in Iowa—echoed by other Democratic leaders—that the president has lied about the issues of war and peace. Edwards made the charge after conceding that the president's credibility is a crucial element of his ability to function as commander-in-chief, and thus of the nation's security. The statement was disgraceful on many counts. In the first place, it is a lie to say that President Bush lied, specifically in his State of the Union address just prior to the war when he said the British had reported that Iraq was seeking fissionable uranium in Niger. This is now the focus of the Democrat attacks, spearheaded by a national TV campaign launched by the Democratic National Committee. In fact, Bush's 16-word statement about the British intelligence report was true. The report did assert that the Iraqis were seeking fissionable uranium and the British are standing behind their report. But the chorus of Democratic attacks, amplified by a sympathetic media, are steadily sapping the commander-in-chief's credibility and undermining his authority at home and abroad. In a time of war.

Second, the same Democratic Party went to the wall to defend Bill Clinton's lies about war and peace during his administration, shielding him from any inquiry into the missile strikes he ordered in the Sudan, Afghanistan and Iraq. The strikes were unauthorized, and the entire premise of the strike in the Sudan was proven false. What Democrat showed concern about the national security implications of Clinton's credibility during the Lewinsky scandal?

Which one of them cooperated with the congressional investigations into the massive illegal funding of the Clinton campaign by agents of the Chinese military and intelligence services, or into the lax security policies that resulted in China's theft of our nuclear arsenal? None did. America's national security is a low priority on the Democratic Party agenda.

For the record, the United States did not go to war with Iraq because Iraq attempted to make a uranium deal with Niger, or because Iraq did or did not have weapons of mass destruction. It went to war with Iraq to implement UN resolution 1441, an ultimatum to Saddam that was passed by a unanimous vote of the UN Security Council. It went to war for the reasons stated by Democratic Senator Bob Graham, who is now one of the president's chief and most unprincipled attackers. This is what Graham said on Fox News Sunday (6/23/02): "What we're concerned about with Iraq is its intention and capabilities *to develop* weapons of mass destruction, and the merger of that capability with terrorist groups, that is the ultimate nightmare scenario" (emphasis added). Make no mistake: what the Democratic Party is doing now is sabotaging the War on Terror. The securing of Iraq, which borders two terrorist Muslim states in Syria and Iran, is absolutely critical for everything that will follow, including the stabilization of the Middle East and the disarming of Islamic terrorists.

It is a national tragedy that in this hour of national crisis the Democratic Party does not have a leader who will follow the example of Tony Blair, stand up to the saboteurs, and speak out for a bi-partisan front against those who have sworn to destroy us. That Democrats are not rallying around the president in his efforts to carry on the work of peace is an unforgivable betrayal. This is the final destructive legacy of the subversive leadership of Carter, Clinton and Gore. It is they who set the bad example in the first place. And it is they who have never really shed the McGovern delusion: that in the final analysis, America is the root cause of all the root causes that inspire our enemies to attack us.

4

How to Look at the War on Terror

Imagine the date is September 12, 2001. Ask yourself this question: Are you willing to bet that two years will pass and there will not be another terrorist attack on American soil? I will wager there is not one person reading this who would have made that bet two years ago. There is only one reason for the relative security that Americans now enjoy. It is not that the terrorists have given up their violent agendas or their hatred for us. They have not. It is not that America's borders are secure, or that America's internal security systems have been successfully overhauled. There is one reason—and one reason alone—that Americans have been safe for almost two years since the 9/11 attacks. That reason is the aggressive war that President Bush and the American military have waged against international terror and the state powers in Afghanistan and Iraq who support it. The War on Terror has been fought in the streets of Baghdad and Kabul instead of Washington and New York. By taking the battle to the enemy camp, by making the terrorists the hunted instead of the hunters, President Bush and the American military have kept Americans safe.

Now the battlefield of the War on Terror is post-liberation Iraq. The *jihadists* of al-Qaeda and radical Islam and Arab fascism are crawling out of the snakepits of Tikrit and slithering across the borders from terrorist bases in Syria and Iran to attack American troops and anyone helping the American cause. Their goal is self-

---

September 8, 2003, http://archive.frontpagemag.com/Printable.aspx?ArtId=16551

evident: to force the collapse of civil order and to inflict enough casualties on American forces that America will withdraw. Such a withdrawal would be a massive defeat for the forces of order and decency, not only in Iraq but in the world at large. It would be a dramatic victory for the forces of evil.

If Iraq can be secured and become an American ally, then Syrian terrorism and Iranian terrorism and Palestinian terrorism will have no place to hide. American pressure on terrorists everywhere will be dramatically enhanced. If, on the other hand, America withdraws in defeat, then terror will flourish again; not only in Baghdad, Basra and Tikrit, but also in Damascus, Teheran and Ramallah.

The way to think about the War on Terror is to ask yourself who is supporting President Bush and the American military in this life-and-death engagement, and who is not. Help is certainly not coming from the European nations who armed and then appeased Saddam Hussein, who opposed the liberation of Iraq and who now refuse to aid America in securing the peace. Far worse, with exception of fading candidates like Joe Lieberman, it is certainly not coming from the leaders of the Democratic Party who, from the moment Baghdad was liberated, have with ferocious intensity attacked the credibility of America's commander-in-chief, the justification for our mission in Iraq, and the ability of our forces to prevail.

In this mission of sabotage, few political figures have sunk as low as Al Gore. In the wake of the war that went spectacularly well—the swiftest, most casualty-free liberation of a nation on record—Al Gore accused the president of deceit and cynical manipulation of the facts in order to mislead the American public and sacrifice American soldiers for no reason. By linking these accusations to the Florida election recount, he and other Democrats have implied that the war was merely an instrument of a partisan plot to de-legitimize their claim to the White House. Gore's bottom line in his August 7 speech attacking the president's conduct of the War on Terror, was this: "Too many of our soldiers are paying the highest price for the strategic miscalculations, serious misjudgments and historic mistakes that have put them and our nation in harm's way." His attack will be recorded as a milestone in the sad moral decline of one of America's great political parties. In breaking bipartisan ranks in the War on Terror, Gore is seconded by both leaders of the Democratic congressional delegation, by every Democratic presidential nominee with the exceptions of Joe Lieberman and Dick Gephardt, and by the party's politically activist base. It is a dark day for Americans when one of their two major parties cannot be counted on to support the flag when it is committed in battle, and when the battle is America's response to a bloodthirsty aggressor with access to biological, chemical and perhaps even nuclear weapons.

In a Memorial Day speech to American veterans, President Bush had this to say about our adversary: "The terrorists' aim is to spread chaos and fear by killing on an ever widening scale.... They celebrate the murder of women and children. They attacked the civilized world because they bear a deep hatred for the values of the civilized world. They hate freedom and religious tolerance and democracy and equality for women. They hate Christians and Jews and every Muslim who does not share their narrow and violent vision."

The President vowed to stay the course but noted it is only recently that America has done so. "During the last few decades the terrorists grew bolder, believing if they hit America hard, America would retreat and back down." Perhaps the president had in mind al-Qaeda's attack on the World Trade Center in 1993, when President Clinton and Al Gore failed to respond. Perhaps he had in mind al-Qaeda's attack on American troops in Somalia, when President Clinton and Al Gore retreated without response. Perhaps he had in mind the attack on the Khobar Towers, a building housing American soldiers, where President Clinton and Al Gore again failed to respond. Perhaps he had in mind the attack on the USS Cole, when President Clinton and Al Gore were AWOL again.

"Five years ago," the president said, "one of the terrorists [Osama bin Laden] said that an attack could make America run in less than 24 hours. They're learning something different today. The terrorists have not seen America running; they've seen America marching. They've seen the armies of liberation marching into Kabul and to Baghdad." And they know and respect the difference.

Now we are engaged in a war to drive the enemy into the ground. We have taken or killed half of al-Qaeda's leadership; we have destroyed the regime of Saddam Hussein—harbor to terrorists and sponsor of suicide bombers—and captured or killed forty-two of its top fifty-five leaders. The enemy understands the war we are in. It knows that it is fighting for its life in Iraq. In sabotaging the peace in Iraq through its current resistance, its aim is to intimidate America and force our retreat. In his Memorial Day speech, the president addressed this threat: "Retreat in the face of terror would only invite further and bolder attacks. There will be no retreat."

Al Gore and the Democrats need to heed these words and change their course. Unless the Democrats get behind this war, the nation will have no future that is secure.

5

9/11 and the Sixties Generation

While the attacks of September 11, 2001 were a wakeup call for all Americans, they were a particular reckoning for Americans on the political left, and within that group for Americans belonging to the Sixties generation who had launched the "original" anti-war movement over Vietnam. It is members of this generation who led the protests against America's response to 9/11 and the war in Afghanistan and then against the war in Iraq. It is members of this generation who refused to wave the flag on September 12 or any time thereafter, when it was the bracing symbol of a wounded country struggling to defend itself.

Members of this generation went even further, and blamed their own country for the attacks it suffered on September 11. They rejected the call to patriotism and to the defense of their country. "Patriotism threatens free speech with death," spat novelist Barbara Kingsolver. "It is infuriated by thoughtful hesitation, constructive criticism of our leaders and pleas for peace. It despises people of foreign birth who've spent years learning our culture and contributing their talents to our economy.... The American flag stands for intimidation, censorship, violence, bigotry, sexism, homophobia, and shoving the Constitution through a paper shredder."[1] Katha Pollitt, an editor of *The Nation,* was in full accord

---

September 11, 2003, http://archive.frontpagemag.com/Printable.aspx?ArtId=16417

[1]Barbara Kingsolver, "And Our Flag Was Still There," *SFGate.com,* September 25, 2001, http://www.sfgate.com/opinion/openforum/article/And-our-flag-was-still-there-2876076.php

with these sentiments and denied her high-school daughter's request to hang the flag out their apartment window with these words: "Definitely not, I say: The flag stands for jingoism and vengeance and war."[2]

But not everyone in the left was on board for this assault on the homeland. Christopher Hitchens wrote a moving tribute to America in *Vanity Fair* and for the first time in his life came to the conclusion that the country he had lived in for more than 20 years was worth defending, and ultimately adopting. Todd Gitlin, a former president of SDS, the largest student organization of the New Left, and also a sometime contributor to *The Nation,* toured the ruins, searched his conscience, observed his fellow citizens binding their wounds, and concurred with Hitchens:

> I loved these strangers, and others I met in those days, and didn't feel mawkish about it—these new, less aggressive New Yorkers, speaking in hushed voices, or so it seemed, lining up to give blood at the local hospitals on day one, disappointed that no one was collecting it; the cabbies driving in unaccustomed silence ... New Yorkers without their carapaces, stripped down to their unaccustomed cores; no longer islands unto themselves. I took inspiration from the patriotic activists who seem to have brought down Flight 93 over Pennsylvania and probably saved the White House.... It dawned on me that patriotism was the sum of such acts.[3]

And so Gitlin did what for him until that moment would have been unthinkable: he draped a flag from his window. In an article titled "Varieties of Patriotism," Gitlin attempts to explain the defection of his comrades by referring to the shaping experience of their generation in the fires of the Vietnam War.[4] "For a large bloc of Americans, my age and younger, too young to remember World

---

[2]Katha Pollitt, "Put Out No Flags," *The Nation,* September 20, 2001, http://www.thenation.com/article/put-out-no-flags

[3]Todd Gitlin, *The Intellectuals And the Flag,* Columbia University Press, 2005, p. 128

War II—the generation for whom 'the war' meant Vietnam and possibly always would, to the end of our days—the case against patriotism was not an abstraction. There was a powerful experience underlying it: as powerful an eruption of our feelings as the experience of patriotism is supposed to be for patriots. Indeed, it could be said that in the course of our political history we experienced a very odd turn about: The most powerful public emotion in our lives was *rejecting* patriotism."

For activists like Gitlin, who was brought up in a liberal household and at a still impressionable age was sucked into the anti-American radicalism of the Sixties, this testimony may have an air of authenticity. But Vietnam was a long time ago; and apart from such personal circumstances it can have little bearing on the allegiances of a whole generation. *The Nation* and other institutions of the left were anti-American, and had *rejected* patriotism, a long time before Todd Gitlin came of age. They supported Stalin and then Mao and finally the Hanoi Communists, whom they regarded as *Vietnam* "patriots" and bearers of "rice-roots democracy" to a people oppressed by America. Moreover, there was nothing inherent in the Vietnam War that should have made any American turn against his own country. Every year that has passed since the end of the war, and has disclosed the realities of what it was about, attests to this fact.

In probing the mind of the anti-American left, it is instructive to see how, once America was defeated (in no small part through their efforts), the activists turned their backs on the Vietnamese whom they had claimed to love with all the passion they denied their own country. When America left Vietnam, the Vietnamese disappeared entirely from the consciousness of the left. Thousands of innocent Vietnamese were murdered by the communists and hundreds of thousands fled. The communist victors reduced the

---

[4]The article is included in a new book, *The Fight Is for Democracy: Winning the War of Ideas in America and the World,* edited by George Packer. Harper Perennial, 2003

conquered nation to an impoverished gulag. But once the Great Satan was gone, this Vietnam had no place in the conscience of the "anti-war" left.

Since the end of the war, memoir after memoir has appeared from the pens of the victorious Communists; among them Col. Bui Tin, a leader of the Hanoi regime and architect of the Ho Chi Minh Trail, and Truong Nhu Tang, a founder of the National Liberation Front, to name but two. The testimonies of these disillusioned victors confirm what the post-war slaughter had already revealed—that the conflict was not about the liberation of South Vietnam, as the left had maintained. Nor was it about American "oppression" or Vietnamese "nationalists" aspiring to self-determination. It was about the conquest of the South by a ruthless and oppressive communist regime whose ambitions America tried to stop in vain. Far from being an "indefensible war," as Gitlin—still ensnared by false memories and false consciousness—now describes it, the war reflected America's honorable intentions and commitments. Americans can be proud that they tried to save Vietnam from the communist horrors that befell its people after America was forced to leave.

A faithful comrade of Ho Chi Minh, Colonel Bui Tin became disillusioned only when he saw what the Communist victory he had worked so hard to achieve actually meant for his people. In 1995, he wrote: "Nowadays the aspiration of the vast majority of the Vietnamese people, both at home and abroad, is to see an early end to the politically conservative, despotic and authoritarian regime in Hanoi so that we can truly have a democratic government of the people, by the people, for the people."[5] But the aspirations of the Vietnamese people are as invisible to American radicals today as are the testimonies of Iraqis freshly liberated from the prisons and torture-chambers of Saddam Hussein.

---

[5]Bui Tin, *Following Ho Chi Minh: Memoirs of a North Vietnamese Colonel,* C. Hurst & Co., 1994, p. 192

I half believe Gitlin when he says he has accepted and embraced his country, even though he took down his flag "a few weeks after 9/11," and "felt again the old estrangement, the old shame and anger at being attached to a nation" after Bush declared war on the axis of evil. I half believe him even though he opposed the war in Iraq and appeared on a platform at Columbia with a fellow protester who wished America would suffer "a million Mogadishus" and be brought to its knees. I half believe him even though he has written that the very "essence" of American policy in the war on terror is "monumental arrogance"—and that this not only "is the hallmark of Bush's foreign policy, it *is* his foreign policy." Learning the truth—especially when it requires admitting that you were so profoundly and destructively wrong—can be an arduous and painfully slow task.

Todd Gitlin and others like him will have their new patriotism tested over time, as they will their compassion for ordinary people, like the Iraqis, whom America's "runaway bullies" have, in fact, liberated from one of the most oppressive regimes in the modern world—and with no support from "progressives" like them. But there are many more "anti-war" activists on the left who will not have their patriotism tested at all, because it simply does not exist. This is what Richard Rorty called the "spectatorial, disgusted, mocking left" that does not dream of "achieving our country." This left would do well to reflect on what Todd Gitlin has written about the terrible beauty of those days after 9/11: "Patriotism is not only a gift to others, it is a self-declaration: It affirms that who you are extends beyond—far beyond—yourself, or the limited being that you thought was yourself. You are not an isolate. Just as you have a given name and a family name, you also have a national name. One deep truth about September 11 was that a community was attacked, not an assortment of individuals."[6] Just

---

[6]Todd Gitlin, "Varieties of Patriotic Experience" in George Packer, ed., *The Fight is For Democracy: Winning the War of Ideas in America and the World,* Harper Perennial, 2003

so. Those individuals in their identity beyond themselves are what America is about.

The attack on this community is what brought Todd Gitlin and Christopher Hitchens face to face with their feelings for ordinary Americans in the days after 9/11. Gone in these moments was their elitist identification with a mythical international community and their snobbish depreciation of the simple, concrete, authentic loyalties that ordinary, non-intellectual Americans feel for each other and for a country, where—as Gitlin tersely puts it—"diversity is not a feel-good slogan and debate is lifeblood."

I'll buy that, Todd. That's my country too. I'm glad to join hands with you to defend it.

[Unfortunately Gitlin didn't learn from the insights he had in the days after 9/11 and the hopes I had for him proved unfounded.—DH]

6

Stab in the Back

The fact that the president is now on the defensive over the war in Iraq is both puzzling and ominous. The Democratic attack on the credibility of the commander-in-chief has gone on relentlessly for more than ten months, ever since the liberation of Baghdad in April of last year when House Speaker Nancy Pelosi said the war had cost too much. This ferocious attack would be understandable if the war had gone badly or been unjust; if Saddam Hussein had unleashed chemical weapons on the coalition armies, or had ignited an environmental disaster; if the war had resulted in tens of thousands of coalition casualties, or become an endless quagmire, or instigated a wave of terror across the Muslim world—as its opponents had predicted before it began.

But it did not. This was a good war and relatively costless as modern conflicts go. Its result was the liberation of 25 million Iraqis from a monster regime. Its cost was a third of the economic losses resulting from the 9/11 attack. Its relatively painless victory was a tremendous setback for the forces of chaos. The war destroyed a principal base of regional aggression and terror. It prompted a terrorist Libya to give up its chemical and nuclear weapons programs. It encouraged Iran to allow inspections of its nuclear sites. It caused North Korea to consider negotiation and restraint. It induced Pakistan to give up its nuclear-secrets dealer. It made the terrorist regime in Syria more reasonable and pliant. It

February 12, 2004, http://archive.frontpagemag.com/Printable.aspx?ArtId=14195

sent a message across a dangerous world that defiance of UN resolutions and international law, when backed by the word of the United States, can mean certain destruction for outlaw regimes. In all these ways, whatever else one may say about it, George Bush's war has struck a powerful blow for global peace.

The Democrats' current attack on the president's war is an effort—whether Democrats intend it so or not—to reverse these gains. If the president is defeated in the coming election on the issue of war and peace, as Democrats intend, his defeat will send exactly the reverse message to the world of nations. It will tell them that a new American government is prepared to go back to the delusions of pre-9/11, that it will end the war on terror and return to treating terrorists as criminals instead of enemy soldiers. Candidate John Kerry has said this in so many words. It will tell them that the United States will no longer hold governments responsible for the actions of terrorists who operate from their soil, as did Ansar al-Islam, Abu Nidal and Abu Abbas from their bases in Iraq; or for supporting terror, as Saddam Hussein did when he financed suicide bombers in Israel. It will send a signal that tyrants like Saddam Hussein who defy UN ultimatums are likely to be appeased as they were during the Clinton administration, which had the vision to stop Saddam and the Taliban but not the will to use the force at its command to do it. It will declare to the world that the American government is now reluctant to risk even a few American lives to defend international law or stand up for the freedom of those who are oppressed, like the people of Iraq.

The Democrats' personal attack on the president over the war is not only imprudent, it is also unprecedented. Never in our history has a commander-in-chief been attacked on a partisan basis for a war that went well, let alone so well. Never in history has a leader been attacked on a partisan basis for liberating a people or inducing tyrants to give up their weapons of mass destruction. The Democrats' attack on the president is an unprecedented partisan campaign over national security in a time of war. It is a campaign that apparently knows no limits, adopting tactics that are as unscrupulous as they are reckless. Leading Democrats have called the commander-in-chief a "deceiver," a "deserter," a "breaker of promises," a "fraud" who "concocted" the war for personal material gain, a president who risked innocent American lives for a "lie." And all these accusations are made while the war continues, and American troops are in harm's way. All these charges are made while terrorists plot to kill thousands of Americans with biological and chemical and possibly nuclear weapons. The Democrats' campaign is a stab in the back not only for the president but for the nation he serves and which he is sworn to protect.

No one knows what the future will bring. But no one can fail to have noticed that, while the commander-in-chief has carried on an aggressive war against terror in Afghanistan and Iraq, there have been no terrorist attacks on American soil. For two-and- a-half years, while he has waged this war that Democrats are attacking, the American people have been safe. If the American people were now to elect a candidate who has conducted his campaign as an assault on the very war the president has fought to defend us, no one can doubt that our enemies will be encouraged and that our lives will be in greater danger than before. Perhaps there have been elections with higher stakes than the one we are facing this year. But this observer can't remember one.

7

Democrats Hand the Terrorists a Victory at Abu Ghraib

Our Islamic terrorist enemies have won several big victories in recent weeks in Iraq, thanks in no small part to the Democratic wolf pack and its leader John Kerry, who have done their best to turn every American failure into an atrocity that discredits our cause. General Ricardo Sanchez signaled the American retreat on Friday by issuing new guidelines for interrogation in American prisons in Iraq. In the words of *The New York Times,* "the top American commander in Iraq has barred virtually all coercive interrogation practices, like forcing prisoners to crouch for long periods or depriving them of sleep."[1] The purpose of these practices was to get information out of terrorists and jihadists that would save American and Iraqi lives. But no matter, these are less important objectives (or so it seems) than appeasing the outcries of those who didn't want us to fight this war in the first place.

Of course the self-righteous Democrats will take no responsibility for the fact that they have worked relentlessly since the liberation of Baghdad to cripple our efforts in the war. They have attacked the cost of the war, the fact that there is a war, the credibility of the commander-in-chief and so on. Invoking Vietnam, they have in fact

---

May 17, 2004, http://archive.frontpagemag.com/Printable.aspx?ArtId=13005

[1]Eric Schmitt, "Commander Bars Coercive Tactics In Interrogation," *New York Times,* May 15, 2004, http://www.nytimes.com/2004/05/15/world/the-struggle-for-iraq-military-commander-bars-coercive-tactics-in-interrogation.html

divided America's home front on a scale approaching that war, a division that eventually forced our withdrawal. Of course they pretend to do this now (as they did then) out of patriotic zeal. They claim that, because we are Americans, we have to live by a higher standard, which to them means that we have to denounce ourselves in terms appropriate to regimes like Saddam Hussein's. Because of the minor scandal of prisoners being taunted at Abu Ghraib, Senator Kennedy has accused us of having re-opened Saddam's "torture chambers ... under new management," a disgusting lie.[2]

Of course, we have to live by a higher standard than the barbarians we are fighting (not to mention those Middle Eastern tyrannies which are criticizing us). And we obviously do. That's why we don't need 35 congressional investigations, howling media, and a hysterical political opposition to take care of this mess. In fact, we were taking care of it quietly and effectively months before the media savages at *60 Minutes* blew the whistle on Abu Ghraib.

If we lived in a country like Saddam's Iraq or Arafat's West Bank or Assad's Syria, then this outrage would be justified. These were and are monstrous regimes that have no respect for human life. As it happens, we Americans do. We live in a country that *sets the standard* for the rest of the world. The purpose of the left's outcry, then, is not to get the Bush administration to take care of an incident that involved only one prison—actually, one section of one prison and a few lascivious morons. Its purpose is to stigmatize the Bush administration and to damage the American cause in Iraq. And it has succeeded.

Every frontal attack on the Bush administration and the War on Terror encourages our enemies and makes defeating them that much harder. Do Democrats realize this? Of course they do. But they are operating according to a self-exculpating logic that

[2]"Shamefully, we now learn that Saddam's torture chambers reopened under new management - US management." Jeff Jacoby, "Ted Kennedy's Anti-American Slander," *Boston.com,* May 25, 2004, http://www.boston.com/news/globe/editorial_opinion/oped/articles/2004/05/25/ted_kennedys_anti_american_slander?pg=full

absolves them of responsibility for America's defeats. Do you wonder why no Democrat has acknowledged the fact that it is actually "Clinton's army" that has produced the scandal? When our Special Forces, Marines and elite army divisions were conducting the swiftest and most successful military operation in history in the opening weeks of the war, the Democrats with Nancy Pelosi at their head were boasting how this success was achieved by "Clinton's Army," which his policies had shaped. This was to reprove conservatives who had been critics of Clinton's military policies, claiming he had gutted and demoralized the armed forces.

In fact, the Marines who led the invasion were the one service that had resisted Clinton's reforms, while the Abu Ghraib incident could easily be said to be a product of those reforms and the anti-military animus that drove them. The result was a military that was severely downsized, politically corrected, and disrespected. But of course the Democrats are not asking why undertrained reserves were put in charge of a highly sensitive and dangerous prison like Abu Ghraib, whose commander, a female general and product of the Clinton reforms, had never seen duty in the line of fire. Does anyone wonder at the fact that in the center of this sexual mess is a boyfriend-girlfriend team of under-trained reservists, hamburger flippers one week, lords of a prison block the next?

Rumsfeld's decision to field a small fighting force, which obviously contributed to this policy, was the product of 30 years of Democratic attacks on the American military and on America's overseas role as a defender of freedom. Senators Kennedy and Kerry, along with their political colleagues, have conducted a relentless campaign against America and its world role since the early 70s, when both led the attack on America's last ditch effort to save the people of Cambodia and Vietnam from the slaughter the communists had in store for them. Neither man has shown any remorse over the catastrophe his advocacy produced; and neither has altered the views that led to it.

It is a familiar feature of the left never to look back and take responsibility for its acts. Kerry and Kennedy were in full support of President Jimmy Carter when he forced the modernizing, feminist-friendly shah of Iran out of power and gave Islamic terrorists their first big victory in Iran. The Iranian revolution was celebrated by the international left at the time; it directly inspired Osama bin Laden and Islamic radicals from Palestine to Afghanistan to launch their *jihad* against the West. Instead of accepting its own responsibility for creating Osama bin Laden, the left blames America's support of the Afghan resistance to the Soviet invasion. But what else could America have done to help Afghanistan, since a Democratic Congress would not have allowed the sending of American troops?

On Saturday, General Myers tried to rally our forces in Iraq in the face of a divided home front, a world full of critics of our case and of appeasers of the terrorist cause. Myers told them America will win in Iraq because of their unflagging spirit and because of "the basic goodness of America" which inspires them. This is really what our political battles at home are all about. They are about those among us who believe in the basic goodness of America—who therefore don't need to have a national self-flagellation over an incident like Abu Ghraib—and those among us who do not have this belief, and therefore in their hearts want us to lose.

8

Big Lies

As wars go, the conflict in Iraq was (and is) as good as it gets: a three-week military campaign with minimal casualties, 25 million people liberated from one of the most sadistic tyrants of modern times, and the establishment of a military and intelligence base in the heart of the terrorist world. What well-meaning person could oppose this? It was one thing to worry about the war before the fact, as Brent Scowcroft and others did; a military conflict could lead to eruptions in the Muslim world and a conflagration out of control. This was opposition based on honorable intentions, which events have effectively answered.

But the current opposition to the war, now that the Saddam regime has been removed, has no such justification. The war has had enormous beneficial effects with minimal negative consequences. A political monster was taken down. The filling of mass graves with 300,000 corpses was stopped. Plastic shredders for human beings were deactivated. Prisons that held four-to-twelve year olds were closed. A democratic constitution has been drafted. Two-thirds of al-Qaeda's leadership is gone. There hasn't been a terrorist attack in America in more than two-and-a-half years, something no one would have predicted after 9/11. At this point in time, by any objective standard, the Bush war on terror is a triumph.

May 17, 2004, http://archive.frontpagemag.com/Printable.aspx?ArtId=13005

These real-world considerations are why the campaign waged by the Democratic Party and a sympathetic press against the Bush war policy is based not on any analysis of the war itself, but on maliciously concocted claims about the prewar justification for military action. To advance their domestic political agendas, the Democrats hope to convict the administration of "misleading the American public" and wasting American lives through deception and fraud, and thus to defeat Bush at the polls in November. This is the campaign of the big lie, and its success depends on the fact that it is a big lie. Its aim is to shift the terms of the argument to a terrain favorable to critics who have been refuted by events—a terrain entirely irrelevant to the reality of the war itself. To respond to this campaign would require of its targets candor and courage, because the only way to confront it is to impugn the integrity, honesty and goodwill of those who so maliciously prosecute it. Unfortunately, the Bush administration does not seem up to this task of calling its critics to account. This is why it is on the defensive and in serious trouble in its political campaign.

How does this big lie operate? A look at today's top headline in *The New York Times* illustrates it well: "Panel Finds No Qaeda-Iraq Tie."[1] That is the news of the day—similar in its negative spin to the news of the last 32 or 60 days as well. The *Times* headline refers to the report of the 9/11 commission that Mohammed Atta did not meet with Iraqi government officials in Prague prior to 9/11, and that it could find no evidence that Saddam was involved in the 9/11 plot. The *Times* "News Analysis" accompanying the account draws this conclusion: "In questioning the extent of any ties between Iraq and al-Qaeda, the commission weakened the already spotty scorecard on Mr. Bush's justifications for sending the military to topple Saddam Hussein."

Actually, this *Times* reportage is made up of several lies, not

---

[1]Philip Shenon and Christopher Marquis, "Panel Finds No Qaeda-Iraq Tie; Describes a Wider Plot for 9/11," *New York Times*, June 17, 2004, http://www.nytimes.com/2004/06/17/politics/17panel.html?pagewanted=all

just one. First, the panel did not conclude that there was no al-Qaeda-Iraq tie. It concluded that it could not find an al Qaeda-Iraq tie *in respect to the attacks of 9/11*. This is entirely different from the claim that there were no links between al-Qaeda and the Iraqi regime. There are in fact extensive links, which Stephen Hayes and others have detailed.

But that is just the beginning of *The Times'* deception. The bigger lie is that Mohammed Atta's visit to Prague was one of "Mr. Bush's justifications for sending the military to topple Saddam Hussein." Bush made no such claim, certainly not as a justification for the war in Iraq. (*The Times* actually printed Bush's references to Iraq and al-Qaeda links on February 8, 2003; none mentions 9/11.) The justification for sending the military to topple Saddam Hussein was the violation of UN Security Council Resolution 1441 and 16 UN resolutions before that. Resolution 1441 authorized the use of force as of December 7, 2002. Anyone doubting that Saddam defied the UN ultimatum should consult *Disarming Iraq*, the recent memoir written by Chief UN Weapons Inspector Hans Blix. Blix opposed the military option right to the end. But he states very clearly that Saddam failed to meet the requirements of UN Resolution 1441 and showed his contempt for its authority, and that his defiance was a legal justification for the use of force.

The lie about al-Qaeda is just one of a tissue of lies concocted by administration critics about the rationale for the war in Iraq, each of which is designed to distract attention from the legitimacy of the war in Iraq and to express the critics' own unhappiness with the War on Terror itself. *The Times'* "News Analysis" also cites the failure to find WMDs as a further indictment of the administration's rationale for the war. But WMDs were not the rationale for the war. The rationale for the war was Saddam's violation of Security Council Resolution 1441, which called for compliance or "serious consequences."[2] Saddam did not comply. The consequences followed.

---

[2]United Nations Security Council Resolution 1441, November 8, 2002, http://en.wikipedia.org/wiki/United_Nations_Security_Council_Resolution_1441

The rationale for the war was laid out in Bush's September 12, 2002 address to the United Nations General Assembly. He did not refer to an al-Qaeda link. He did not refer to an "imminent threat" (another malicious falsification by critics of the war). What the president said was this: "The conduct of the Iraqi regime is a threat to the authority of the United Nations and a threat to peace. Iraq has answered a decade of UN demands with a decade of defiance. All the world now faces a test, and the United Nations a difficult and defining moment. Are Security Council resolutions to be honored and enforced, or cast aside without consequence? Will the United Nations serve the purpose of its founding, or will it be irrelevant?"

The UN resolutions that Saddam had defied were constituent elements of the truce that Saddam signed at the end of the Gulf War. The truce set the conditions under which the allied forces allowed him to remain in power. Saddam violated the truce. From a legal point of view, the 2003 Iraq war was not a new war but a resumption of the hostilities of 1991, which in fact had been continuing as low-intensity warfare over the no-fly zones maintained by the United States and Britain to prevent Saddam from again dropping poison gas on the Kurds. Many critics of the war argue that, after 17 violated Security Council resolutions, Saddam should have been appeased yet again and given more time to comply. That is a reasonable (if misguided) argument. To claim that the Bush administration misled the American people and waged the war under false pretenses is not.

Critics of the Bush administration have used their fabricated rationales for the war to condemn the president as a liar, a fraud, a deceiver and a traitor. ("He betrayed us," bellowed Gore to a MoveOn.org audience.[3]) These are terms suited to the critics themselves. But the Bush White House has not had the fortitude to

[3]Katharine Q. Seelye, "Gore Says Bush Betrayed the U.S. by Using 9/11 as a Reason for War in Iraq," *New York Times*, February 9, 2004, http://www.nytimes.com/2004/02/09/politics/campaign/09GORE.html

use them (or their political equivalents). The White House had better rethink this reluctance if it intends to retain power in November. In the absence of a strong case by the Bush team, American voters are not going to be able to sort out these lies for themselves

Prior to the inception of hostilities in Iraq in March 2003, the Democratic Party, with honorable exceptions like Senator Lieberman and Minority Leader Gephardt, was a party of appeasers, demanding more time and more offerings to the dictator in Baghdad to avoid a military conflict. From the day Baghdad was liberated in April 2003 and on into the present, the Democratic Party and a willing media have been a chorus of saboteurs—attacking the credibility, integrity and decency of the commander-in-chief; exaggerating, sensationalizing and magnifying every American setback or fault, the orgy of guilt over Abu Ghraib being the most egregious example; tying the hands of American forces in the field and encouraging the enemy to resist. The hard left actually celebrates this resistance. The soft and cowardly left merely encourages it, while pretending not to notice what it is doing. In either case, what we are confronting in this spectacle is an unprecedented event in American political life. In the midst of a good war and a noble enterprise, a major American party is engaged in an effort to stab its own country in the back for short-term political gain; and is willing to do to so by the most underhanded and unscrupulous means.

9

Where Have All the Democrats Gone?

Of all the commentaries on Michael Moore's propaganda film *Fahrenheit 9/11,* the most acute comes from *The New York Times'* conservative columnist David Brooks. In a column facetiously titled "All Hail Moore," Brooks begins with this tongue-in-cheek observation: "In years past, American liberals have had to settle for intellectual and moral leadership from the likes of John Dewey, Reinhold Niebuhr and Martin Luther King, Jr. But now, a grander beacon has appeared on the mountain top, and, from sea to shining sea, tens of thousands have joined in the adulation."[1] Moore's "documentary" is number one at the box office, out-grossing on its opening day, Friday, *White Chicks, Dodgeball, Terminal* and *Shrek 2.*[2]

Underlying this impressive showing is the fact that it has captured the Democratic Party's imagination, not to mention its heart and soul. This is the really significant dimension of Michael Moore's moment. Others have focused on the fact that Moore is a cynical manipulator, an irresponsible *auteur* and a compulsive liar, and beyond that, as Christopher Hitchens has shown in a blistering review in the liberal magazine *Slate,* a world-class phony—attacking the Bush administration's invasion of Iraq for derailing the War on Terror, despite the fact that Moore is on record as

---

June 28, 2004, http://archive.frontpagemag.com/Printable.aspx?ArtId=12432

[1]David Brooks, "All Hail Moore," *New York Times,* June 26, 2004, http://www.nytimes.com/2004/06/26/opinion/26BROO.html

[2]Ibid.

opposing the attack on the Taliban, and thus the War on Terror, as fiercely as he does the war on Saddam.[3]

What is momentous in the Moore phenomenon is that the Democratic Party—or at least its intellectual wing and activist core—has embraced a piece of Marxist agitprop as its most potent election campaign spot. David Brooks provides readers unfamiliar with the Moore creed with some chilling quotes. According to Moore: "The Iraqis who have risen up against the occupation are not 'insurgents' or 'terrorists' or 'the Enemy.' They are the REVOLUTION, the Minutemen, and their numbers will grow—and they will win." In other words, Abu Musab al-Zarqawi, the beheader of Nicholas Berg, is not America's enemy—he is an Islamic reincarnation of Patrick Henry, a harbinger of global freedom, which can only be achieved by the overthrow of the great American oppressor. This obscene formulation is just an excessively vulgar version of the same Marxist fantasy that radicals were peddling in the 1960s about Communist totalitarians like Ho Chi Minh. Not surprisingly, Moore's description of the rationale for the war is vulgar Leninism. In an interview with a Japanese newspaper, cited by Brooks, Moore explained: "The motivation for war is simple. The U.S. government started the war with Iraq in order to make it easy for U.S. corporations to do business in other countries. They intend to use cheap labor in those countries, which will make Americans rich."

What is disturbingly new in this political season is not that there exists a large radical culture that has learned nothing from the fall of Communism, that identifies Americans as agents of evil and George Bush as their Fuehrer-in-Chief. What is new is that they are joined in this electoral campaign by the Democratic Party establishment, along with sensible anti-Communist veterans from the Cold War era like Arthur Schlesinger and Kennedy speech-

[3]Christopher Hitchens, "Unfairenheit 9/11: The lies of Michael Moore," *Slate*, June 21, 2004, http://www.slate.com/articles/news_and_politics/fighting_words/2004/06/unfairenheit_911.html

writer Ted Sorensen who attended Moore's Washington opening along with Senators Tom Harkin, Barbara Boxer, and DNC chairman Terry McAuliffe. How far has this group derangement progressed? *Salon.com,* an Internet journal which, unlike Moore, supported the war on the Taliban, now compares Moore favorably to Solzhenitsyn, Dickens and (of course) Bruce Springsteen.[4]

These eye-popping shifts began developing with disturbing velocity from the moment American troops entered Baghdad, and House minority leader Nancy Pelosi complained that the liberation of 25 million Iraqis was already "too costly." They have proceeded with alarming speed from this high ground to underhanded accusations that the President has betrayed the country, has concocted lies to lead Americans into a war for the benefit of Texas corporations and has wasted the lives of our youth in uniform, while killing and abusing innocent Iraqis for no particular reason—a point Moore pounds home with all the subtlety of a cluster bomb. The impact of these irresponsible and reckless attacks, not only on the tenor of America's political discourse but on the war itself, has been profound.

As a result of the left's propaganda war against the war, the American government is now almost as hamstrung as it was in the post-Vietnam era until 9/11. It could not raise another 100,000 troops, even if they were necessary to pacify Iraq or deal with other challenges without threatening to bring the political house down. It could not threaten, let alone invade, Syria or Iran—even if they were shown to have hidden Saddam's weapons or were engaged in plotting a terrorist attack on the United States. Who would believe the commander-in-chief now? Nor can it rescue black Africans presently being slaughtered by the Muslim Arab government in the Sudan. Michael Moore, his progressive friends, and their campaign of reckless distortion and malicious insinuation have seen to that.

---

[4]Andrew O'Hehir, "'Fahrenheit 9/11': Yea!," *Salon,* June 23, 2004, http://www.salon.com/2004/06/23/fahrenheit_yay/

In this election year, it is unlikely that this popular front between once-sensible liberals and malicious leftists can be broken. The power stakes are too high. But if there is a way to accomplish this, it is to confront those in the Moore audience who are still able to reason with the absurdity of their fundamental premise. This premise is succinctly summarized in an intelligent but ultimately tortured review of Moore's film by David Edelstein that appeared at Slate.com.[5] Edelstein's review shows that he understands the squalid duplicity of Moore, but nonetheless can't extricate himself from the seduction of the idea that the ignoble ends of this film—sabotaging the current war effort—justify the equally disreputable means: "It delighted me. It disgusted me. I celebrate it. I lament it." The crux of his cave-in to bad politics and bad sense is contained in this sentence: "*Fahrenheit 911* must be viewed in the context of the Iraq occupation and the torrent of misleading claims that got us there."

Along with other conservatives in the troubled months gone by, I have many times pointed out that the attacks on the rationale for the war are the real bad faith in the public debate over Iraq. Not one of the misleading claims alleged to have been made by the White House was a formal rationale for the war. The rationale for the war was not WMDs, or an al-Qaeda connection, or an imminent threat. Bush actually said that confronting Saddam was necessary to *prevent* an imminent threat from developing. The rationale for the war was the violation by Saddam of the 1991 truce, the defiance of 16 UN Security Council resolutions to enforce that truth, and a final 17th, unanimously passed Security Council Resolution (1441): an ultimatum to the regime in Iraq to provide proof, by December 7, 2002, that it had destroyed its WMDs "or else." There is not the slightest question that Saddam failed to meet this ultimatum, or indeed that he tried to deceive

---

[5]David Edelstein, "Michael Moore's Fahrenheit 9/11 Is Unfair and Outrageous. You Got a Problem with That?," *Slate*, June 24, 2004, http://www.slate.com/articles/arts/movies/2004/06/proper_propaganda.html

the Security Council by providing it with a false report. Even Hans Blix affirms this in his recent memoir *Disarming Iraq*.

In fact, we know that there were WMDs (and have found some). Moreover, even if there were none, this was not a deception foisted by the Bush administration on others. It was also a contention of the Clinton administration and of the current Democratic Party nominee, John Kerry. The war deadline was imposed by a multilateral coalition of nations acting through the UN Security Council. So this was not unilateral war, as Democrats claim, but a war sanctioned by the international community. It is also true that the UN Security Council failed to vote to enforce its own deadline; but we also know that $10 billion in Oil-for-Food money, stolen by Saddam with the collusion of UN officials, was used to bribe the nations whose votes counted.[6]

We know that there is indeed a link between Saddam and the War on Terror. In addition to ten years of provable links between the Saddam regime and al-Qaeda, and the testimony of the Clinton administration, which identified both parties in its indictment for the bombing of two U.S. embassies in 1998, there is the presence of Abu Musab al-Zarqawi as the commander of the terrorist forces in Iraq.[7] If Zarqawi—an international terrorist linked to al-Qaeda—is heading the resistance in Iraq, then Iraq is the central front of the War on Terror, just as Bush insists. Is there anyone in the sensible opposition who would like to argue that it is a bad idea for the United States to have a military base and a very large CIA station in Iraq, the terror heartland, rather than the regime of Saddam Hussein? If so, make the case. Notwithstanding the

---

[6]Michael Reagan, "Oil for Corruption," *FrontPage Magazine*, April 24, 2003, http://archive.frontpagemag.com/readArticle.aspx?ARTID=18531

[7]Jamie Glazov, "The Al-Qaeda/Saddam Link," *FrontPage Magazine*, January 28, 2004, http://archive.frontpagemag.com/readArticle.aspx?ARTID=14396; Stephen F. Hayes, "Growing Evidence of a Saddam - al-Qaeda Link," *FrontPage Magazine*, July 15, 2003, http://archive.frontpagemag.com/readArticle.aspx?ARTID=17205; Stephen F. Hayes, "Untelling the Truth," *FrontPage Magazine*, June 1, 2004, http://archive.frontpagemag.com/readArticle.aspx?ARTID=12823

emptiness of the left's arguments against these claims, they are irrelevant to the question of whether to support the war and the administration that launched it.

Moreover, the rationale for the war (which is the focus of the entire political debate) is irrelevant if the war is just. Do David Edelstein and all those who are now engaged in this unseemly dance with a Leninist radical like Michael Moore want to argue that the war was *unjust?* Do they want Saddam back in power? Do they think it's a bad thing that America has a military base and a very large intelligence post bordering Syria, Afghanistan and Iran? Do they want us to pull our forces from this front? If so, let them say so, and we'll know whom we're dealing with. Otherwise, they need to stop talking about the "justification" for the war as though it were a substantive issue or something that mattered.

Franklin Roosevelt claimed that Pearl Harbor was a "sneak attack." Yet the United States had broken the Japanese code and therefore should have known the attack was coming. Would it make a difference to anyone if it did? Would that have justified a massive attack on Roosevelt as commander-in-chief comparable to the attack Democrats have mounted on George Bush? Suppose Lincoln had clandestinely sent a special force of Union soldiers to attack Fort Sumter and blame it on the Confederacy. Would that change anyone's view of the Civil War that freed four million slaves? Would David Edelstein have celebrated (while also lamenting) a scurrilous propaganda effort by a pro-slavery fanatic who worked like Michael Moore, defaming Lincoln and attempting to turn the free states against the war? But that is exactly what is happening in America today.

10

Zell Miller: An American War Hero

Michael Kinsley once remarked that a mistake in Washington is when someone tells the truth. What he forgot to mention is that when someone tells the truth, he is made to pay a price for it in political blood; which is why such occasions are so rare. Although there were several stellar speeches given at the Republican convention, including the president's own inspiring finale, it was Zell Miller's stem-winder, about his fellow Democrats' partisanship in a time of war, that made the event for me.

This was the first time in the campaign that any speaker on the Democratic side had summoned the courage to hold his party to account for what they had actually done; for their feckless flight from the field of battle the moment Baghdad was liberated, and for the disgraceful campaign they waged for an entire year to defame, discredit, and ultimately cripple the commander-in-chief of America's forces, who were still fighting terrorist armies in Iraqi streets. This is what made Zell Miller angry; this is what should also anger anyone who cares about the outcome of the war in Iraq, or the security of 300 million Americans, or the American future. This is why Miller got the ovation he did. And this is why he has been so savagely attacked by anti-war "liberals" who can't handle the truth.

Bill Moyers's magazine, *The American Prospect*, which speaks for the Democratic Party left, called Miller's speech a "fascist

---

September 7, 2004, http://archive.frontpagemag.com/Printable.aspx?ArtId=11498

tirade." The normally sober *New Republic* compared Miller adversely to Joe McCarthy and Pat Buchanan. ("Buchanan's speech, after all, was an assault on decency [but] last night Miller declared war on democracy."[1]) Clinton maven Joe Klein declared, "I don't think I've seen anything as angry or as ugly as Miller's speech."[2] I guess Joe hasn't been watching Al Gore, Ted Kennedy or Howard Dean lately, or presidential candidate John Kerry, who called the policy that toppled Saddam, and liberated 25 million Iraqis, "the most inept, reckless, arrogant and ideological foreign policy in modern history." More inept than Jimmy Carter? More ideological than Harry Truman or John F. Kennedy? But then, one of the generic problems of the left is its inability to make even the most modest accounting of its own misdeeds.

I won't spend much time on the wretched accusation by Miller's detractors that he was once a Dixiecrat. This smear comes from a crowd that embraces its *current* racists and defends racial preferences, and bellows *McCarthyism* anytime anyone so much as mentions a previous position or past association reflecting negatively on one of its own. Liberals abhor the "politics of personal destruction," except when they're practicing it themselves.

One unexpected critic in this crowd of low-minded mudslingers is Andrew Sullivan, who should know better. Sullivan dredged up a 40-year-old segregationist quote of Miller's, presenting it as though it were current news.[3] It might well be current news if Miller were still a segregationist in the way, say, that Jane Fonda and John Kerry are still defending their attacks on American soldiers in Vietnam. If Miller had not had second thoughts about his youthful positions on segregation, then dredging up the past might be appropriate. As it happens, he has, and it is not.

---

[1]Jonathan Cohen, "Zellotry," *The New Republic*, September 2, 2004, http://www.tnr.com/doc.mhtml?i=express&s=cohn090204

[2]Jonah Goldberg, "ZellzaPoppin'," *Townhall.com*, September 3, 2004, http://townhall.com/columnists/jonahgoldberg/2004/09/03/zellzapoppin/page/full/

[3]Andrew Sullivan, "The Miller Moment," *Andrewsullivan.com*, September 2, 2004, http://dish.andrewsullivan.com/2004/09/page/9/

Andrew Sullivan has been one of the most interesting commentators on the war in Iraq, defending the president's policies. But lately he has had second thoughts. These seem to have been prompted by his sharp and understandable dissent from the president's policy on gay marriage, a subject that is not only a cause with Sullivan but also a passion. It has prompted him to abandon his support for Bush in the coming election. Reading his most recent commentaries on the Bush presidency, including the outburst against Miller, one is struck by their lack of the very clarity that once distinguished his columns. One cannot help thinking that the emotional nature of the domestic issue has colored his judgments on other policies, including the war. The fact that Sullivan once understood the nature of the war, both at home and abroad, with such acuity makes his critique of Miller one that should be addressed.

Sullivan begins his critique on a false note, adversely comparing Miller's powerful speech to Barack Obama's empty boilerplate at the Democratic convention: "I kept thinking of the contrast with the Democrats' keynote speaker, Barack Obama, a post-racial, smiling, expansive young American, speaking about national unity and uplift." Miller by contrast was mean spirited and "angry." Everybody loves Barack Obama because he is black and a Democrat and yet not a racial charlatan like Sharpton or Jackson. Democrats are thrilled that they finally have a political star who comes across like a Colin Powell or a Condoleezza Rice, so that they can catch up to Republicans on *this* frontier of racial equality and progress. Everyone else is relieved.

With regard to substance, however, Obama's speech was quite empty, full of feel- good sentimentality and politician "uplift." He took no discernible political risks and made no points requiring even a modicum of courage in the way that Colin Powell did at the 2000 Republican convention, when he threw down the gauntlet to his own party on the issues of affirmative action and abortion. Obama said absolutely nothing that would challenge his party's orthodoxies in order to help the constituencies of inner-city poor that he claims as his own: no demurral from the Democrats' destructive racial quota systems, no challenge to the corrupt inner-city public schools his party runs to the detriment of millions of poor black and Hispanic children who are forced to attend them. I have dwelt on this false comparison only to show how easy it is to celebrate a politician whose only achievements are to be not as bad as someone else, and to provide an occasion for people to feel good about themselves by feeling good about him, without having to make any difficult real-world choices. It is just as easy and commonplace for pundits on political matters to smear a man for telling unpleasant truths.

From this false step, Sullivan plunges into the heart of his argument: "Miller's ... assertion was that any dissent from aspects of the War on Terror is equivalent to treason. He accused all war critics of essentially attacking the very troops of the United States. He conflated the ranting of Michael Moore with the leaders of the Democrats." Beware of declarative sentences that slip in weasel words like "essentially." Sullivan's reading of what Miller said is not only off the mark; it is unequivocally false. Here is the quote from Miller's speech that Sullivan uses to prove his point: "Motivated more by partisan politics than by national security, today's Democratic leaders see America as an occupier, not a liberator. And nothing makes this Marine madder than someone calling American troops occupiers rather than liberators."

Sullivan describes this posing of the issue as "gob-smackingly vile." To refute it, he refers to the fact that he himself believes America has liberated Afghanistan and Iraq, yet has used the term "occupation" to describe the American presence. He concludes that Miller's intent is thus "to [claim] that the Democrats were the enemies of the troops, traitors, quislings and wimps ..." But these are all Sullivan's terms, and do not appear anywhere in Miller's speech.

Let us begin by disposing of the canard—repeated *ad nauseam* by Miller's Democrat critics—that the rhetorical contrast between those who regard America as occupying Iraq, and those who regard

America as liberating Iraq, is in fact a false and misleading dichotomy. Of course America is occupying Iraq and would have to occupy any country it intended to liberate. The issue is not the terminology but the substance. If America's mission in Iraq *is* liberating, then it is also noble and deserves to be supported. How is it, then, that the Democratic Party leadership in July 2003, the third month of the U.S. occupation—with American soldiers still dying in the field while terrorists streamed into the country for a holy war against them—launched a relentless campaign to denounce the commander-in-chief of America's forces as a liar, a fraud, a misleader of the American people, a traitor and, worst of all, a reckless, cold-hearted killer of American youth? These were accusations made not just by Michael Moore (and no member the Democratic leadership stepped forward to repudiate Moore) but by Howard Dean, Ted Kennedy, Jimmy Carter, Al Gore and . . . John Kerry. That is the issue. That is the source of the anger. And, like every other Miller critic, Andrew Sullivan doesn't address it.

If you believe that America and her troops *are* a liberating force in Iraq (or if you have a modicum of respect for the truth), you will not proclaim that America has resurrected Saddam's gulag (as Ted Kennedy did), a libel that was trumpeted on Al Jazeera TV to the entire Muslim world. If you want America to win the war in Iraq because you believe that it is a liberating and not an occupying force, then you do not feature a minor prison scandal on the front pages of your national media for a record-breaking number of days. Everyone should be aware that there is a propaganda war that is part of this war, and that should include Democratic politicians whose exploitation of these chinks in America's armor has been as shameless as that of the American media, which is apparently 90 percent Democrat and pro-Kerry.

The most significant fact about the political conflict over Iraq is that Democrats have broken a tradition of bipartisanship in war, which has been the central pillar of American foreign policy going back at least to World War II and Wendell Willkie, a figure with whom Zell Miller began his speech. In 1940, with Hitler marching across Europe and 70 percent of the American people demanding that America stay out of the war, Wendell Willkie, the Republican candidate for president, gave Roosevelt support for an unpopular military draft—*because it was the right thing to do.* Willkie knew it was not the political thing to do. He knew that it might cost him the presidency. But before he died, as Zell Miller recounted, "Willkie told a friend that if he could write his own epitaph and had to choose between 'here lies a president' or 'here lies one who contributed to saving freedom,' he would prefer the latter." Then Miller asked, "Where are such statesmen today? Where is the bipartisanship in this country when we need it most?"

If one were to fault Zell Miller, it would be to point out that there is such a Democrat who put his country above his party. His name is Joe Lieberman. As a former vice-presidential candidate and the conscience of his party during the Clinton impeachment, Joe Lieberman was the Democratic heir-apparent. An acknowledged statesman and much larger figure than any of his Democratic rivals, Joe Lieberman should have won the nomination. But unlike John Kerry, who turned his coat in mid-course, Joe Lieberman refused to back away from his support for the war to liberate Iraq. He sacrificed his bid to be president because he preferred the epitaph, "here lies one who contributed to saving freedom." Today, Joe Lieberman is the invisible man of the Democratic Party, and that is why Zell Miller's charge is so telling and so true: "Now, while young Americans are dying in the sands of Iraq and the mountains of Afghanistan, our nation is being torn apart and made weaker because of the Democrats' manic obsession to bring down our commander-in-chief."

Sullivan's retort is no answer at all: "It is a calumny against Democrats who voted for war in Afghanistan and Iraq and whose sincerity ... should not be in question." This is not about Democrats' sincerity; it is about their judgment. Voting for the war in Iraq in November 2002 is of no help to Americans fighting terrorists in Fallujah and Najaf in 2003 and 2004. The same Democratic leadership that voted for the war has taken half the American people out of the war in the middle of the war. Never before, in the history of American wars abroad, has an opposition led such a scorched-earth campaign against a sitting commander-in-chief. Never in the midst of a war, let alone a good war, let alone a war that we were winning, let alone a war that we have to win.

This is the difference between thinking that your country is the problem—and therefore an occupier—and thinking that your country is a liberator that is capable of making mistakes. There is no way on earth to defend the vicious assaults on the president by Al Gore, Ted Kennedy, Jimmy Carter and John Kerry that go to the heart of his decency and sincerity in conducting this war, and not just to his policies as any honorable criticism would.

Every intelligence agency in the world—including the UN inspectors—reported that Saddam Hussein had weapons of mass destruction. What policy issue is involved in saying—as every Democratic leader has said—that the president "misled" the nation into war? If the president was mistaken, so was every Democrat who supported the war. If the president misled the country, so did John Kerry, who sits on the Senate Intelligence Committee and is privy to all the facts. How can he accuse the president of something he is equally liable for, and not be guilty of bad faith? What does it mean to vote for a war and then to oppose it when the going gets tough—and to oppose it *not* on grounds of what was done in the war but because the reasons for going to war were allegedly wrong? If the war is a liberation (and not merely an occupation) then *that* should be reason enough to support it. The fact that 90 percent of the Democrats at the Boston convention were against the war is ample evidence that they do not consider the war in Iraq a war of liberation, but an imperial occupation.

The 16 words in the president's State of the Union address about Saddam Hussein's efforts to acquire fissionable uranium in Niger, which the Democrats have used to call him a liar, have now been verified by a bipartisan Senate Intelligence Committee investigation. They were true at the time. Yet every national leader of the Democratic Party (Bill Clinton excepted) took the flimsiest excuse, provided by a now-discredited diplomat, to call the president a liar in the middle of a war of noble intentions over this trivial issue. In doing so, they were fully aware that, as John Edwards said: "The most important attribute that any president has is his credibility—his credibility with the American people, with its allies and with the world."[4] If the commander-in-chief's most important asset is his credibility, what justification can Democrats offer for undermining and attempting to destroy this asset while our troops are in harm's way? What, indeed, but rank partisanship and reckless disregard for the security of the American people and the defense of freedom? That is the charge against the Democrats, and it is a charge that will stick.

Far from going over the top in confronting the Democrats' betrayal of the president, of the country he serves, and of the young men and women in harm's way in Iraq who are risking their lives to serve both, Zell Miller was in fact too kind.

---

[4]Adam Nagourney, "Democrats Say Bush's Credibility Has Been Damaged," *The New York Times*, July 14, 2003, http://www.nytimes.com/2003/07/14/politics/campaigns/14DEMS.html

11

One Year After 9/11

Following the 9/11 terrorist attacks, 90 percent of America's citizens supported their nation's response—a warlike response whose first objective was to destroy the Taliban regime in Afghanistan. A year later, more than 90 percent of the members of both political parties—Republicans and Democrats alike—voted to authorize the president to use force if necessary to remove the terror-supporting regime in Iraq. In January 2002, President Bush declared that Iraq was part of an "axis of evil," and that America had to deal with that fact: "If Saddam Hussein does not fully disarm, for the safety of our people and for the peace of the world, we will lead a coalition to disarm him."

Two weeks later, Al Gore gave his full support to the impending confrontation with Iraq: "Since the State of the Union there has been much discussion of whether Iraq, Iran and North Korea truly constitute an 'axis of evil.' As far as I'm concerned, there really is something to be said for occasionally putting diplomacy aside and laying one's cards on the table. There is value in calling evil by its name."[1] This was the first time Gore had spoken on foreign-policy issues since 9/11. He recalled the missed opportunity of the Gulf War when Saddam Hussein had been left in power. "In 1991, I crossed party lines and supported the use of force against Saddam Hussein, but he was allowed to survive his defeat as the

---

September 23, 2004, http://archive.frontpagemag.com/Printable.aspx?ArtId=11266

[1]Elizabeth Wilner, "Combat 'Other' Axes of Evil," *ABC News*, February 12, 2002, http://abcnews.go.com/Politics/story?id=121207&page=1

result of a calculation we all had reason to deeply regret for the ensuing decade. And we still do. So this time, if we resort to force, we must absolutely get it right. It must be an action set up carefully and on the basis of the most realistic concepts. Failure cannot be an option, which means that *we must be prepared to go the limit.*" (emphasis added)

This was the voice of the consensus that led to the war to remove Saddam one year later. Both parties—Democrat and Republican—gave their authorization to the war in a senatorial vote in October 2002. (In the House, more than 100 Democrats voted no.) But only one year after that, and three months after American-led forces had toppled the Saddam regime, the Democratic Party turned its back on the war it had authorized and supported, and proceeded to persuade half the nation to turn their backs on the war as well. Al Gore, Ted Kennedy, John Kerry and other Democratic leaders condemned the war in the most extreme terms, calling it a fraud and a deception. They attacked their own commander-in-chief as a liar who had led the nation into an unnecessary war that sacrificed American lives for nothing more than corporate gain. From the day Baghdad was liberated on April 10, 2003, Democratic leaders and a politically sympathetic media began attacking the president without restraint and did everything possible to undermine the credibility of America's cause.

This episode represents perhaps the most remarkable political about-face in the nation's history. It led to an unprecedented internal opposition to the national purpose in the midst of a shooting war. This was not like the war in Vietnam, which had spawned a similar bout of second thoughts and political opposition. The Vietnam War had gone on for ten years without the prospect of a victory before the Democratic Party turned against it. By contrast, the Iraq victory was swift, and the casualties are still relatively small. Unlike the war it fought in Vietnam, America's war in Iraq is not to defend a dictatorship as the lesser of two evils, but to end one of the most oppressive and evil regimes of the modern age. America has stopped the filling of mass graves, which already contained

300,000 corpses, and shut down the plastic shredders Saddam had used to dispose of his political enemies. It has established a military and intelligence base on the borders of two terrorist states, Syria and Iran. It has diverted the terrorist enemy to a battlefield thousands of miles from Washington and New York, which have consequently not suffered another terrorist attack since September 2001.

Yet despite all this good, a political left in America has managed to turn half the nation against its own commander-in-chief and a war of liberation. The "anti-war" movement was not created overnight but sprang from deep roots in the left-wing movements that preceded and organized it—from the communists who opposed America in the Cold War to the New Leftists who supported America's enemies in Vietnam and Central America and the "social-justice" progressives who condemn America today. These movements entered the Democratic Party during the McGovern campaign of 1972, which promoted the idea that the global problem was not totalitarian communism but American "empire." The same anti-American animus provided the emotional fire of the campaign which has led to the transformation of the Democratic Party into an anti-war party—even when the war is a war to free a people, and when the enemy is a religious, ideology-driven terrorism whose leaders have condemned every American man, woman and child to death.

12

It's Important to Ask the Right Questions

A favorite slogan of the anti-war crowd is, "War is not the answer." Yet everyone, except extreme pacifists, would agree that the answer depends on the question. In some contexts, war *is* the answer. The same may be said for the two questions that dominate the current presidential campaign. Are we safer now than we were on 9/11? Was the war in Iraq a mistake? Supporters of President Bush will answer yes to the first and no to the second; supporters of Senator Kerry will take the opposite view.

As a supporter of the war and of the president, I have noticed a common omission in the arguments of the naysayers, which is their failure to look at the side of the equation that our enemies control. Defending Senator Kerry's contention that this was "the wrong war, in the wrong place, at the wrong time,"[1] William Saletan wrote in a recent issue of *Slate.com:* "How do you ask a man to be the last man to die for a mistake? That's what it all comes down to—this debate, this war, this election."[2] As Saletan shows, if one looks only at the costs of the war and its present status, it's easy to argue that a mistake it is. The war has not been won. A

October 8, 2004, http://archive.frontpagemag.com/Printable.aspx?ArtId=11072

[1]Patricia Wilson, "Kerry on Iraq: 'Wrong War, Wrong Place, Wrong Time'," *Common Dreams,* September 6, 2004, http://www.commondreams.org/headlines04/0906–02.htm

[2]William Saletan, "Is Bush's Biggest Mistake Too Awful to Admit?," *Slate,* October 1, 2004, http://www.slate.com/articles/news_and_politics/ballot_box/2004/10/out_of_the_question.html

thousand Americans and many more Iraqis have died. Iraq is a mess. The price tag for the mess is $ 200 billion. How can it not be a mistake?

This calculation, however, omits two crucial ledger-columns: the cost of having not fought the war at all, and the gains that can be achieved by continuing the war until it is won. If we had not invaded Iraq, Saddam Hussein would still be in power; Abu Musab al-Zarqawi would be in command of an al-Qaeda army in northern Iraq; seventeen UN Security Council resolutions would have been successfully defied; and the largest chemical-weapons factory in the Third World, in Libya, would still be operating, along with an advanced nuclear-weapons plant (both now shut down). And what would the forces of terror—the Zarqawis and Zawahiris—be doing in the face of another toothless appeasement by the world community? That, of course, is the question that Saletan and Kerry, and those who agree with them, cannot answer.

To be fair, they have made a stab at one. In the first presidential debate, Kerry said that the Iraq war was a "diversion" from the War on Terror, though he did not explain how Zarqawi, who is based in Iraq, could be hunted down by a war in Afghanistan. As for Iraq, "We would have had sanctions. We would have had the UN inspectors. Saddam Hussein would have been continually weakening."[3] But the only reason there were UN inspectors in Iraq was that the Bush administration put 200,000 troops on the Iraqi border in preparation for a showdown. The presence of those troops induced Saddam to allow the inspectors in. Does anyone really imagine that we could have kept 200,000 American soldiers in the desert indefinitely, while Saddam Hussein played the same cat-and-mouse game with the inspectors he had been playing since 1991? Or that he would have been weakened by our failure to act on a deadline the Security Council had unanimously endorsed? Can anyone really believe that sanctions were a feasible instrument with which to weaken Saddam Hussein, when he was able to breach them by getting the UN to support a $50 billion "Oil-for-Food" program that undercut the sanctions' impact? Or when he was able to skim 20 percent of that entire program for his personal uses, including the bribing of French, Russian and German politicians to protect his deadly assets?

Was the Iraq war a diversion? Senator Kerry thinks we should have put all our troops into the effort to hunt down Osama bin Laden. But bin Laden hasn't been visible since his escape from the caves of Tora Bora. Three-quarters of his top leadership has been decapitated, and he hasn't been able to mount an attack inside the United States for three years. The most recent al-Qaeda threat is issued in the name of al-Zawahiri, his second-in-command. The most important and destructive terrorist alive today is Abu Musab al-Zarqawi. And he is in Iraq.

Yes, we are safer today because of the wars conducted by the Bush administration than we would have been had our troops stayed home or fought only in Afghanistan. It is true, as the opponents of the president point out, that there is a lot of mayhem in Iraq, and there are a lot of threats in the world. But the mayhem in Iraq is partly caused by internal Iraqi antagonisms and the disarray of the terrorist forces, which is good. The war itself is the only language they understand. The Shi'ite imam, Muqtada al-Sadr, is now seeking to lay down his arms and become a candidate in the upcoming elections. That is the victory we seek. That is the persuasive power of military force—the argument for staying the course, and for keeping this president in office.

---

[3]September 30, 2004 Debate between President Bush and Sen. John Kerry, "Would Bush Lead Another Pre-emptive War?," *CNN.com*, October 1, 2004, http://edition.cnn.com/2004/ALLPOLITICS/10/01/debate.transcript.12/

13

Softening Us Up for the Kill

On Sunday, *The New York Times* featured a political ad counseling defeatism in Iraq—advice that has become commonplace in its pages. It was sponsored by an organization called "Church Folks for a Better America," based in Princeton. The signatories included the same "church folks"—among them William Sloane Coffin, Jr., Robert Drinan, and Robert Edgar of the National Council of Churches—who counseled defeat during the war in Indochina, provided cover for the torturers of American POWs in North Vietnam, and fronted for the Soviet dictatorship's "nuclear freeze" campaign to keep America from matching (and neutralizing) the Soviet missile buildup in Eastern Europe. Robert Edgar was also a leader of the campaign to force Elian Gonzalez back into thc arms of Fidel Castro and his island prison. The church-folks ad is subtitled, "A Call to Recover America's Moral Character," and rehashes the many lies the left is currently using to demoralize Americans' resistance to our terrorist enemies and thus to soften us up for the kill. "Supposedly we went to war to eliminate weapons of mass destruction," the ad proposes. "But there were no weapons of mass destruction."

In the current campaign to undermine the War on Terror, this is the central lie. It is never backed up with statements from the president, declaring the rationale for the war to be weapons of mass destruction—specifically nuclear weapons—because there were no such statements by the president. His concern was

October 26, 2004, http://archive.frontpagemag.com/Printable.aspx?ArtId=10840

Saddam's determination to *acquire* such weapons and the destructive uses that chemical, biological or nuclear weapons could be put to by a madman like Saddam. Here is the rationale for the war—what the president actually said in his State of the Union address on the eve of the invasion:

> Before September 11, many in the world believed that Saddam Hussein could be contained. But chemical agents, lethal viruses and shadowy terrorist networks are not easily contained. Imagine those 19 hijackers with other weapons and other plans—this time armed by Saddam Hussein. It would take one vial, one canister, one crate slipped into this country to bring a day of horror like none we have ever known. We will do everything in our power to make sure that day never comes.... *Some have said we must not act until the threat is imminent. Since when have terrorists and tyrants announced their intentions, politely putting us on notice before they strike? If this threat is permitted to fully and suddenly emerge, all actions, all words, and all recriminations would come too late.* Trusting in the sanity and restraint of Saddam Hussein is not a strategy, and it is not an option.[1] (emphasis added)

This is why we went to war in March 2003. We did not go to war to eliminate weapons of mass destruction, but to prevent Saddam from retaining the ability to develop and produce weapons of mass destruction, as he clearly intended to do—and to provide them to his terrorist allies: Abu Nidal, Abu Abbas, Abu Musab al-Zarqawi, Yasser Arafat and others. The joint congressional resolution, authorizing the use of force in Iraq and passed by majorities in both political parties, Democrats as well as Republicans and by John Kerry and John Edwards in particular, has 23 "whereas" clauses articulating the rationale for the use of force.[2] Only one of

---

[1]George Bush, State of the Union speech, January 28, 2003, *http://www.cnn.com/2003/ALLPOLITICS/01/28/sotu.transcript/*

[2]Authorization For Use Of Military Force Against Iraq Resolution Of 2002—Public Law 107-243—Joint Resolution, October 16, 2002, p. 1497, http://www.gpo.gov/fdsys/pkg/PLAW-107publ243/html/PLAW-107publ243.htm

the 23 focuses on weapons of mass destruction—that is, on actual supposed *stockpiles* of WMDs rather than the programs to develop them.

On the other hand, fully twelve of the clauses refer to Saddam's violation of 16 UN resolutions, which were attempts to enforce the terms of the truce in the 1991 Gulf War. Bush's critics seem to have forgotten them. These are the facts: The United States has been continuously at war with Saddam Hussein since 1990. The conflict in 1990 was caused by Saddam's invasion of Kuwait and was ended by a *cease-fire,* not a peace. The terms of the truce were embodied in UN resolutions 687, 688, and 689, the first three of the sixteen resolutions that Saddam violated.[3] Thirteen subsequent UN resolutions were designed to compel Saddam to adhere to the terms laid out in those three; but they failed to do so, and the UN and the Clinton administration failed to enforce them.

It was Saddam Hussein's violation of these 16 resolutions and then a 17th—Resolution 1441, which was a final ultimatum—that provided the rationale for the war.[4] It was Saddam's determination to *become* an imminent threat. The only significant White House presentation of the case for weapons of mass destruction was the one made by Colin Powell to the UN General Assembly just before the invasion. Powell's presentation focused on laboratories for producing them; and *that* was made *after* the decision to go to war, at British Prime Minister Tony Blair's request. Blair's request came because he was under attack from his Labour left. A recent demonstration in the streets of London by leftists attempting to save the Iraqi dictatorship was, in numbers, the equivalent of four million Americans protesting in Washington. Powell's presenta-

[3]http://en.wikipedia.org/wiki/United_Nations_Security_Council_Resolution_687; http://en.wikipedia.org/wiki/United_Nations_Security_Council_Resolution_688; http://en.wikipedia.org/wiki/United_Nations_Security_Council_Resolution_689

[4]United Nations Security Council Resolution 1441, November 8, 2002, http://en.wikipedia.org/wiki/United_Nations_Security_Council_Resolution_1441

tion to the UN was not the justification for the war. It was a misguided attempt to bring France and Russia on board in enforcing the December 7 deadline, providing political cover for Tony Blair.

The *justification* for the war is contained in the 23 clauses in the congressional authorization and in UN resolution 1441. This resolution called on Saddam to disarm and to provide an accounting for the disposition of all weapons of mass destruction that the UN inspectors had already identified. In his book *Disarming Iraq,* chief UN inspector Hans Blix declares that this resolution was diplomatic language for a war ultimatum and that Saddam failed to meet the terms of the ultimatum. That was why America went to war.

We went to war because we could not maintain 200,000 troops in the desert indefinitely while Saddam played games with the UN inspectors. We went to war because 17 defied UN resolutions had made the word of the UN and the United States meaningless—an extremely dangerous situation if the precedent had been allowed to stand. Here is how Bill Clinton justified the use of force to remove Saddam in 1998, when Saddam expelled the UN inspectors: "If we fail to respond today, Saddam and all those who would follow in his footsteps will be emboldened tomorrow by the knowledge that they can act with impunity, even in the face of a clear message from the United Nations Security Council, and clear evidence of a weapons of mass destruction program."[5] Unfortunately, in 1998 Bill Clinton was preoccupied with an intern named Monica Lewinsky and his government was paralyzed. Consequently, he was unable to respond to this threat except by firing 450 missiles futilely into Iraq, more than the first President Bush had used in the entire Gulf War. No Democrat complained about the cost of these useless strikes, or the aggression they represented.

In the spring of 2003, we went to war against Iraq because to withdraw the 200,000 troops without a war and without Saddam's

---

[5]Text Of Clinton Statement On Iraq to the Joint Chiefs of Staff and Pentagon staff, February 17, 1998, http://www.cnn.com/ALLPOLITICS/1998/02/17/transcripts/clinton.iraq/

acceptance of the UN demands would have been a catastrophic defeat for the forces of international order and peace. It would have meant with absolute certainty that Saddam would reactivate the weapons programs he had launched and spent more than 40 billion dollars to implement before the United States obstructed them. So determined was Saddam to get around the obstacle that those troops placed in his way, he was in the process of negotiating an off-the-shelf purchase of nuclear weapons from North Korea when the coalition forces entered Iraq to remove him.

The leaders of the Democratic Party have betrayed the war they signed onto and in the process have misled the American people about its nature. In doing so, they have gravely damaged our efforts to fight this war, sapped our nation's will to resist, and lent both aid and comfort to our enemies.

William Sloane Coffin, Robert Drinan and the other "folks" in the church of anti-American defeatism were not misled by faulty calculations. They are against this war and all America's wars *because* they are America's wars. But they are ready to exploit the confusions that attend all wars to influence others: "Supposedly we went to war to sever the connections between Saddam Hussein and al-Qaeda. But there were no connections to sever." This claim combines two lies to make one argument. The administration did not justify the war in terms of a connection between Saddam and al-Qaeda. The only reference to al-Qaeda, in the 23 clauses of the congressional authorization justifying the war, is this: "Whereas members of al-Qaeda, an organization bearing responsibility for attacks on the United States, its citizens, and interests, including the attacks that occurred on September 11, 2001, are known to be in Iraq." Which is true. These members of al-Qaeda include the military force known as "Ansar al-Islam," which had a base in northern Iraq, as well as Abu Musab al-Zarqawi, and Abdul Rahman Yasin, one of the perpetrators of the 1993 World Trade Center attack.

The ad continues: "Supposedly we went to war to remove a brutal regime, but we allowed torture cells to exist, including sexual humiliation—and shamelessly photographed the results." This libel is inspired by *The New York Times*-Ted Kennedy school of slanders, morally equating us with Saddam Hussein. We did not "allow torture cells to exist" at Abu Ghraib. As all the world knows, as soon as our military discovered the humiliation games (hardly "torture") that were played by a handful of low-level prison guards, we prosecuted them. Abu Ghraib was a minor incident blown up to major significance by a left-leaning media conducting psychological warfare operations against their own country. Psychological warfare is designed to demoralize the enemy, and that is the apparent intent of running Abu Ghraib stories on the front pages day after day and week after week, inflaming anti-American opinion at home and abroad.

Conducting psychological warfare for the enemy is exactly what William Sloane Coffin, Robert Drinan and John Kerry did during the Vietnam War. Kerry slandered our troops as "war criminals," while Coffin traveled to Hanoi to provide cover for the torturers of our POWs. Both campaigned to force Washington to desert the South Vietnamese and Cambodians, which eventually happened. The result was the slaughter of two and a half million peasants in Indochina. If America cuts and runs this time—as Kerry and the church folks advocate—the bloodbath will not only be in Iraq but will spill into the streets of Washington and New York.

The ad continues: "Supposedly we went to war to establish democracy. But in truth we have still done little to grant 'full sovereignty' to Iraq, and much to keep the country under our control." In fact, the Iraqi people have more sovereignty now than they did under Saddam Hussein or any regime in their country for the last 5,000 years. We have also shown our good intentions in Afghanistan by holding the first real elections there since time immemorial. Anyone not convinced that America is guilty before the fact understands this. There is only one alternative to American authority in Iraq, and that is the authority of Muqtada al-Sadr and

Abu Musab al-Zarqawi. To call for "full sovereignty" now is to invite the rule of the beheaders and the torturers.

The church folks want us out of Iraq—"a clear timetable to end the occupation, not perpetuate it by other means." They suggest that this can be achieved by replacing American forces with "a truly international peacekeeping force to be established by the United Nations." But the failure of the United Nations to enforce its own resolutions is precisely why the United States had to step in and do it for them. In its entire history, the UN has done nothing positive to keep the peace that the United States has not done for it. When the Clinton White House failed step in to prevent the massacres in Rwanda, the UN could not raise the 5,000 troops that would have saved the lives of a million Tutsis. The UN is a moral cesspool. Its Human Rights Commission is run by Libya, and thus Muammar Gaddafi. Ten days before 9/11, its human rights commissioner, Mary Robinson, hosted a hate-fest in South Africa whose agenda was drawn up in Iran and whose targets were the world's most humane and tolerant democracies: the United States, Britain and Israel. The UN secretariat colluded in the theft of $10 billion earmarked to feed Iraqi children. It closed its office in Iraq the first time a bomb blew up in its face. The call for the UN to preside over Iraq's future, instead of the United States, is simply a call to turn over Iraq to the Islamic predators who have already raped its citizens and threatened to destroy us.

By departing from the tradition of bipartisanship in war, by betraying a war policy they authorized, and by conducting a scorched earth campaign against their own commander-in-chief, the Democratic Party has opened the public square to a political menagerie of America-hating radicals. Personified in such figures as Noam Chomsky and Michael Moore, the radicals' agenda is exactly the same as it was during the Cold War and the war in Vietnam: to demoralize our troops, to sap the will of our citizenry, to weaken our ability to stay the course, and to soften us up for the kill.

14

This Is Not about Republicans or Democrats

I have received emails from readers asking why I continue to post Andrew Sullivan's blog on *Frontpagemag.com* because he is supporting the Democrat, John Kerry, in the election. Others demand that I remove his column at once. I have not acceded to their wishes and have no intention of doing so. First, this website is not devoted to Republican politics. It is devoted to the war against terror, against America's fifth-column adversaries and against supporters of our enemies abroad. These adversaries are individuals, like Michael Moore, who consider our terrorist enemies "freedom fighters" and "patriots" and who want them to win. They could include Jimmy Carter, an ex-president who seems never to have met a foreign dictator he didn't like and trust, and who along with Al Gore is responsible for ending the 54-year tradition of bipartisanship in foreign policy by breaking ranks in the middle of a war. His acceptance of a Nobel Peace Prize—an award explicitly designed as a rebuke to an American president at war—reveals a failure of judgment and of basic loyalty to a citizenry under attack. That citizenry should bury Carter's name in everlasting disgrace. He is the self-selected leader of a notorious band of fencesitters in this momentous hour of our destiny, unable to decide whom to fear more: Osama bin Laden or George Bush.

Andrew Sullivan is supporting John Kerry for president (his editorial can be read following this one) because Andrew regards

---

November 1, 2004, http://archive.frontpagemag.com/Printable.aspx?ArtId=10752

Kerry as the "lesser of two risks." The endorsement has elicited a number of emails to this site, renewing the calls for his excommunication. Readers of *FrontPage* who feel this way, and those who don't, need to bear in mind two things. First, this election is not a referendum on whether to retreat or surrender in the War on Terror, as it would have been if the candidate had been Howard Dean or the John Kerry of the primary season. As a result of Kerry's final—and oh-so-cynical—turnaround in the general election, it is about who will fight the war on terror more ferociously and more efficiently. We can live with this choice.

Second, this is a season of poisoned politics and ferocious conflicts. When our country is so divided in wartime, it is important that we keep the faith with those Americans who agree with us on the need for victory but disagree on who is the candidate to achieve that. We should extend this faith to all those Americans who love their country, including Democrats who have been confused in the last year and a half by irresponsible leaders. There are also Republicans who do not understand the centrality of Iraq to the War on Terror. These Republicans mistakenly believe that the war in Iraq is a distraction from the War on Terror, which should be in Afghanistan. They are joined by conservatives who are suspicious of nation-building but have yet to suggest how a conservative policy to leave Saddam in power could have contained the Islamist threat. However we may disagree with them, they are patriots and belong in our camp. There are worthy Democrats who belong there too. Joe Lieberman should have been the Democrats' candidate for President. He has been a model as to what a leader of the opposition should be, but has been effectively neutered by the party's defection from the war it supported and from its frenzy of hatred towards the incumbent George Bush.

Andrew Sullivan—a sometime Democrat and sometime Republican—has been one of the most forthright and insightful defenders of the War on Terror generally and the war in Iraq in particular; and for this the nation is in his debt. He has a firm grasp of the achievements of President Bush in this war, which are even displayed in his column endorsing the Democratic candidate, odd as that may sound and seem. But this is a political season of odd passions and opinions. In criticizing Bush for the Abu Ghraib embarrassment, Andrew has fallen prey to the massive sabotage campaign that has been conducted by the political left. Abu Ghraib was a minor if regrettable incident of the kind that happens in all wars. It was blown out of proportion by leftist media that are more ready to attack George Bush than to confront Saddam Hussein or Abu Musab al-Zarqawi. That is a harsh but inescapable truth.

The sabotage against America's war effort conducted by Howard Dean, Ted Kennedy, Jimmy Carter, Al Gore, Michael Moore, the editors of *The New York Times* and most metropolitan news media is the most disgraceful episode in the history of America's foreign wars. Never before has half the nation been taken out of a war in the midst of a war that we were winning and had to win. How many of the errors attributed to President Bush by Andrew and others are better attributed to the knife they have put in his back? The fact is that no president can be expected to fight a war in these circumstances and not commit serious tactical blunders. His failure to take Fallujah, a crucial error, cannot have been uninfluenced by concern over likely repercussions around civilian casualties from both the domestic left and the international left, which is behind the massive anti-American demonstrations abroad.

Yet the president has blundered in one particular way that cannot be attributed to his internal foes. He has failed to sell the war adequately to the American people, and to answer the charges coming from his left flank. In the presidential television debates, for example, he chided Senator Kerry for saying the war in Iraq was the wrong war in the wrong place at the wrong time. This "confuses" people, the president said. It does more than that, Mr. President. If you are 18 or 19 and risking your young life in Najaf or Fallujah, surrounded by terrorists who want to kill you and get to heaven, and the leader of the Democratic Party says you shouldn't be there in the first place, it does more than confuse you. It demoralizes you. It saps your will to fight. It gets you killed.

John Kerry, Michael Moore, and the war's media detractors are getting Americans killed in Iraq, and also risking a terrorist catastrophe at home because of their pathological hatred of George Bush. The president should be saying so. One reason Kerry should be defeated in this election is to deny these America-haters and America-distrusters a victory. It is important for our country to strike a blow at *them*. But if John Kerry is elected, he will not be an anti-war president. He will have to fight the war in Iraq and disappoint his anti-American allies on the left who want us to lose. No sitting president can back off this fight. We are in a war that we have to win, and we cannot leave before it's over, as we did in Vietnam.

But Kerry will fight the war badly, not just because he does not understand it, and not because he will have to go against the grain of his record of 30 years of anti-military attitudes and appeasement of our Communist enemies. He will fight the war badly because he is a man of extremely bad character, perhaps the worst presidential candidate in this regard on record. As a young man, he went to a war he didn't believe in and returned to betray his comrades in arms; as a candidate he has turned his view of the war 180 degrees and jeopardized the lives of young men and women on the field of battle for political gain. This makes him not only the risky candidate but the reprehensible one.

PART IV

Arguments Over the War

(11/ 26/ 2004—10/ 27/ 2005)

I

Why We Are in Iraq

Just before American and British troops entered Iraq to remove the regime of Saddam Hussein, a videotape of Osama bin Laden was aired on Al Jazeera TV. In that tape, broadcast on February 12, 2003, bin Laden said: "The interests of Muslims and the interests of the socialists coincide in the war against the crusaders."[1] Bin Laden was referring to the fact that, four weeks earlier, millions of leftists had poured into the streets of European capitals and of Washington, San Francisco and New York to protest the removal of Saddam Hussein. Their goal was to prevent the United States and Britain from toppling Saddam and ending one of the cruelest, most repressive regimes in modern times. The protesters chanted "no blood for oil;" they labeled the United States "the world's greatest terrorist state;" they called America's democratic government an "axis of evil;" and they compared America's president to Adolph Hitler.[2]

In America, two groups organized the demonstrations against the war. One was International ANSWER, a Marxist-Leninist sect

---

November 26, 2004, http://archive.frontpagemag.com/ReadArticle.aspx?ArtId=10421

[1]"Bin Laden's Message to Muslims in Iraq: Fight the 'Crusaders,'" *The New York Times,* February 15, 2003, http://www.nytimes.com/2003/02/15/world/threats-and-responses-bin-laden-s-message-to-muslims-in-iraq-fight-the-crusaders.html

[2]"Anti-war Demonstrators Rally Around the World," *CNN.com,* January 19, 2003, http://www.cnn.com/ 2003/US/01/18/sproject.irq.us.protests/. The war, of course, was not about oil. In the end, China, which had opposed the war, reaped the benefits of what became Iraq's oil boom when the United States left.

aligned with the Communist dictatorship in North Korea. The other was United for Peace and Justice, an organization led by Leslie Cagan, a veteran 1960's leftist and member of the Communist Party until after the fall of the Berlin Wall. The Coalition welcomed all factions of the left; it was composed of organizations that ranged from the Communist Party to the National Council of Churches to Muslim supporters of the terrorist *jihad.*

The global protests failed to stop the British and American military effort or save Saddam's regime, which fell six weeks after the initial assault. This victory put an end to the filling of mass graves by the regime; it shut down the torture chambers and closed the prison that Saddam had built for four to twelve-year-olds whose parents had earned his disapproval. But Saddam's forces were not entirely defeated. They regrouped to fight a rearguard guerilla campaign against the American "occupiers." At the same time, the organizers of the anti-war protests continued their efforts, this time in the arena of electoral politics. Their activists marched into the Democratic presidential primary campaigns to support the candidacies of anti-war Democrats Dennis Kucinich and Howard Dean.

The enormous resources in money and manpower that the activists mobilized against the war transformed the campaign of an obscure governor of Vermont into the Democratic frontrunner. Dean condemned America's war in Iraq; he hinted that as president he would make peace at the earliest possible opportunity and withdraw American forces from the Gulf. Electoral politics thus became the left's rearguard attempt to produce the result their prewar protests had failed to achieve: an American defeat in Iraq.

With the resources of the left providing his tailwinds, Howard Dean soared to the top of the presidential pack. In the spring of 2003, just prior to the Iowa caucuses, Dean's nomination appeared so inevitable that he was endorsed by the titular heads of the Democratic Party and by its chief defectors from the war, Jimmy Carter and Al Gore. But other Democrats collectively flinched. Verbal gaffes by the candidate who opined that the world was not safer because of the capture of Saddam, and erupted in a hyper-emotional outburst in Iowa, caused many Democrats to wonder if a nominee so overtly radical could carry the party to victory in the national campaign in November. Within a few weeks, this question was decided as John Kerry and John Edwards responded to the polls by turning 180 degrees and opposing the war. Democrats abandoned Dean and rallied behind them. Kerry's political decision to reverse his views on a matter of war and peace proved to be the most troubling aspect of his candidacy in the eyes of the electorate, and eventually sealed his defeat.

Certain issues beneath the surface of the political conversation carry a charge so great as to shape the conversation itself, issues of "patriotism" and "loyalty," and what constitutes legitimate criticism of government policy in a time of war. To listen to the complaints of the left, one would think that conservative officials were standing ready with pre-drawn indictments for those stepping forward to oppose the war, or uttering any criticisms of government policy in matters pertaining to Iraq. Yet if any side has deployed the charge of treason to silence opposition on the war issue it is the Democrats themselves, who have accused the president of taking the country to war under false pretenses, lying to the American people, and getting Americans killed for no reason except to line the pockets of his Halliburton friends. Al Gore has called the president a traitor; the president has not mentioned Gore's name.

The reality is that that no one takes treason very seriously anymore, and hasn't for a long time. No individual has been charged with treason in the United States in fifty years, not since Tokyo Rose and Axis Sally were tried for broadcasting enemy propaganda to American troops during World War II. Not the Rosenbergs, who stole atomic secrets for the Soviet Union; not Jane Fonda, who in the exact manner of the World War II traitors appeared on enemy radio in the midst of the fighting to denounce American soldiers as war criminals and called on them to defect. Fonda also collaborated with the Communist torturers of American POWs. Yet she was not charged with treason. Nor were spies like Aldrich Ames, or defectors like John Walker Lindh, who joined the Taliban to fight against his own country. So let us not pretend that there is any real threat in the charge of treason capable of chilling the current criticism of America's war effort. If there were, Michael Moore would be in jail instead of on the short list for an Academy Award. When leftists complain that their patriotism is being questioned in an attempt to stifle their criticism, the claim is a smokescreen to prevent others from thinking about the implications of what they have said.

Contrary to impressions conveyed by the left, Republicans have been extraordinarily temperate in confronting those who have assaulted the war and slandered its supporters. In the first presidential debate, for example, President Bush chided his opponent for attacking the war in Iraq as "the wrong war, in the wrong place, at the wrong time."[3] To make that claim "confuses" people, the president said, and is no way to lead a nation engaged in a war. The president's statement was certainly correct as far as it went. But Kerry's statement actually did more than merely confuse people. If you are 19 years old and a Marine in Fallujah being fired on by terrorists and the leader of the Democratic Party—who is within a hair's breadth of being your commander-in-chief—says you shouldn't be there at all, that does more than merely confuse you. It demoralizes you and saps your will to fight. It can get you killed. The reckless Democratic attacks on this war serve to encourage the enemy and demoralize our troops. This is the subject that is suppressed when issues of loyalty and the proper tone of criticism are arbitrarily taken off the table in a time of war.

Treason as a moral rather than a legal issue is not difficult to define. Treason is when your country is at war and you want the other side to win. Are there such people in America, active in the nation's public life? Michael Moore is surely one. On April 12,

---

[3]Bill Kristol, "If John Kerry Were President, . . ." *The Weekly Standard,* September 8, 2004, http://www.weeklystandard.com/Content/Public/Articles/000/000/004/59 2kqbgr.asp

2004, Michael Moore said of our enemies in Iraq, the beheaders of innocents: "They are the REVOLUTION, the Minutemen, and their numbers will grow—and they will win. Get it, Mr. Bush?"[4] There is no doubt whose side of this war Michael Moore is on. Michael Moore wants America to lose; and why shouldn't he, since he sees the United States as a predatory empire illegally in Iraq, and regards "terrorism" as a fiction created by Washington to justify its imperialistic ambitions? Michael Moore's hostility to his own country in time of war is a fact, but what have been the consequences for him? Moore has rooted for the enemy all his life, first in the Cold War and now in the War on Terror, but his treasonous attitudes have made a celebrity of him, not a pariah, and wealthy in the bargain.

A similar observation can be made about the leaders of the anti-war demonstrations, whose careers may not be as well rewarded as Moore's, but who were also freed from any adverse consequences for their behavior. The national mobilizations against the war in Iraq were organized and led by veteran activists who had rooted for the Communist enemy in the Cold War. They did so because, like Moore, they regarded America as an imperialist power and the Soviet Union as an advocate for its oppressed global subjects. In the fall of 2002 and the spring of 2003, similar assumptions guided their efforts to abort America's war in Iraq and save Saddam Hussein.

The anti-war activists are not people for whom peace itself is a significant value. When Saddam was faced with the UN ultimatum to disarm "or else," these opponents of American policy organized no demonstrations at the Iraqi embassy to persuade Saddam to comply. Disarming Saddam was not part of their "anti-war" agenda. In the same revealing way, there were no demonstrations against the genocide the Communists carried out in Indo-

[4]Michael Moore, "Heads Up ... from Michael Moore," *MichaelMoore.com*, April 14, 2004, http://www.michaelmoore.com/words/mikes-letter/heads-up-from-michael-moore

China after America withdrew its forces from Vietnam. In its heart of hearts, the anti-Vietnam movement was not about bringing peace and justice to the Vietnamese and Cambodians; it was about defeating America and helping the Communists to win. The goal of the radicals who organized anti-war demonstrations during the conflicts in Vietnam and Iraq was the same. The issues of the war were only pretexts for their real agenda: America must lose.

This agenda has now been inserted into the political mainstream by a radicalized Democratic Party. During the 2004 presidential election, Michael Moore's *Fahrenheit 9/11* became a campaign spot for the Democrats. Moore presents Saddam's Iraq as a peaceful, even idyllic country cruelly invaded by a callous and deceitful invader. The premier of Moore's anti-American propaganda film was attended by the leaders of the Democratic Party, including senators Clinton, Daschle, Harkin, and Boxer.[5] It is a mark of how far we have slipped morally as a nation when leaders of one of our two great parties are prepared to promote any attack on a sitting president in a time of war. It is a sign that they don't take our enemies seriously.

When progressives are pressed on these issues, they are the first to claim that their dissent is itself patriotism, indeed the only self-respecting patriotism, since for leftists embracing the positive in the American experience is an attitude reserved for right-wing jingoists and yahoos. If America is indeed the greatest terrorist state, as Moore and other leftists contend, then America is actively betraying its own founding principles. If this is the case, loyalty to America would *require* acts of treason. The code of leftists like Michael Moore is: "Loyalty to America is treason to humanity." In their own minds, progressives have no country. They consider themselves "internationalists" and "citizens of the world," while "America is the enemy of humanity," as the national anthem of Michael Moore's Sandinista heroes proclaims.

[5]John Files, "The Like-Minded Line Up for a 9/11 Film," *New York Times*, June 24, 2004, http://www.nytimes.com/ 2004/06/ 24/movies/ 24film.html

Here is how Moore himself defends his disloyalty: "What if there is no 'terrorist threat?' What if Bush and Co. need, desperately need, that 'terrorist threat' more than anything in order to conduct the systematic destruction they have launched against the U.S. Constitution and the good people of this country who believe in the freedoms and liberties it guarantees?"[6] America has no enemies; America is the enemy.

Criticism of government policy is the life-blood of democracy, and that includes war policy. But beginning with the Founders, everyone understands, or used to understand, that there is a necessary trade-off between liberty and security and that, in time of war, sacrifices of the former are regularly made in the interests of the latter. "Loose lips sink ships" was a slogan memorialized on posters during World War II. It was an appeal to Americans to voluntarily restrict their exercise of free speech in order to save their own lives and the lives of their neighbors. It was not regarded as a bid to abolish the Constitution or destroy the First Amendment, which is the way the current left mischaracterizes measures to tighten America's defenses against terror. It was a simple recognition that in war some speech can weaken a democracy's defenses.

In a conflict where the enemy walks among us and can kill thousands of civilians at a stroke, it is important to recognize the difference between criticism made in support of the war effort and criticism designed to undermine it, even if the actual line between them may not always be clear. Before the fighting started in Iraq, some critics voiced a concern that an armed intervention would cause the Arab street to erupt and inflame the Muslim world. This was the concern expressed by former national security advisor Brent Scowcroft.[7] Scowcroft's attack on the president's policy was

---

[6]Michael Moore, "Stupid White Men: Online Chapters," MichaelMoore.com, http://www.michaelmoore.com/stupidwhitemen/onlinechapters/part01

[7]Brent Scowcroft, "Don't Attack Saddam," *The Wall Street Journal*, August 15, 2002, http://online.wsj.com/article/0,,SB1029371773228069195.djm,00.html

harsh, arguing that under no circumstances should America go to war over Iraq. But his comments were obviously offered out of concern for the nation's security. Once the war started, he supported his commander-in-chief. As it turned out, Scowcroft's concerns were proven groundless when Saddam was toppled in one of the swiftest and least costly victories on record, without the consequences that Scowcroft had feared.

A large portion of the criticism against the war, however, has been made on grounds that have nothing to do with American security, and in terms that are far removed from the realities on the battlefield. It is one thing to make dire predictions in advance of a war; quite another to make unsubstantiated claims that attack the moral character of the commander-in-chief and the nation he leads after the war is under way, and while American troops are still under fire. In these circumstances, to say that the president lied to the American people, and sent our troops to die under false pretenses, is more than just criticism. It is sabotage of the war effort, particularly when there is no evidence to substantiate the charge. When political leaders who voted to authorize the war do this, the betrayal is even more indefensible. Yet that is precisely what leaders of the Democratic Party did within two months of the liberation of Baghdad.

Baghdad fell in mid-April 2003. In June, Democratic leaders began assaulting the president as a cynical liar. Their claim was initially based on 16 reasonable words he uttered in a State of the Union address, whose veracity has since been confirmed by a bipartisan Senate Intelligence Committee.[8] As Senator John Edwards, one of the leaders of the attacks, observed, a president's credibility is his most important asset. If that is so, why attack a wartime president for saying British intelligence had reported that

---

[8] "The British government has learned that Saddam Hussein recently sought significant quantities of uranium from Africa," George Bush, State of the Union speech, January 28, 2003, http://www.cnn.com/2003/ALLPOLITICS/01/ 28/sotu.transcript/

Saddam was seeking bomb-making uranium in Niger, when the British had said just that? The vitriolic attacks on the president's integrity while the war was only months old went beyond legitimate criticism; they amounted to an effort to sabotage the American war effort, in hopes that a failed war would lead to a Republican defeat in the November elections.

One aspect of this sabotage was the outcry over the scandal at the Abu Ghraib prison. Such incidents, deplorable in themselves, are common to all wars, but as war crimes go—*as the crimes committed by our enemies in this war go*—the incidents at Abu Ghraib were both minor and isolated, and committed by low-level military personnel. Still, we hold ourselves as a nation to higher standards than our enemies (and most of our friends), and a certain degree of public concern was in order. But when Abu Ghraib is inflated into a major atrocity and appears on the front page of *The New York Times* for more than 60 days (32 of them straight) and is compared by a leading senator to Saddam Hussein's torture chambers, something else is going on.[9] It may have originated as an atrociously irresponsible effort to replace a sitting president. But its clear effect was to wage psychological warfare against one's own country by undermining the moral authority of the commander-in-chief. *The New York Times* and Senator Kennedy expressed more outrage about Abu Ghraib in one day than Imam al-Sistani, the leader of Iraq's Shi'ite population, did throughout the entire episode, about which he said exactly nothing.[10]

During the first year of the Iraq War, the focus of the Democratic attacks was on the rationale for the invasion itself. Democrats claimed that the premise of the war was wrong, and therefore

---

[9]Adam L. Penenberg, "Searching for The New York Times," *Wired.com*, July 14, 2004; "*New York Times* Streak of Page One Stories on Abu Ghraib Ends at 32 Days!," June 2, 2004, http://www.freerepublic.com/focus/f-news/1145998/posts

[10]Jeff Jacoby, "Ted Kennedy's Anti-American Slander," *Boston.com*, May 25, 2004, http://www.boston.com/news/globe/editorial_opinion/oped/articles/ 2004/05/ 25/ted_kennedys_anti_american_slander?pg=full

the war was wrong. But this logic makes no sense. If we were to discover that Abraham Lincoln had contrived to send a secret Union force to attack Fort Sumter and blame it on the Confederacy, would that change our view of whether the Civil War was worth fighting? Yet that seems to be the logic of the opponents of the Iraq War, for whom "missing WMDs" have been construed as a reason for rejecting the war itself. Yet this is a war whose aims and purposes make it very hard to understand how anyone who is a supporter of human rights, or who believes in individual freedom, could be against it. In four years, George Bush has liberated nearly 50 million people in two Islamic countries. He has stopped the filling of mass graves and closed down the torture chambers of an oppressive regime. He has encouraged the Iraqis and the people of Afghanistan to begin a political process that would give them rights they have not enjoyed in 5,000 years. How can one *not* support this war?

The reason critics of the war give for not supporting it is that the president's justification for the invasion was that Saddam possessed WMDs and *that* turned out not to be the case. In addressing this issue, it is important first to remember that the Democrats who are now in full-throated opposition to the war, and who accuse Bush of "dividing the nation," joined him in authorizing it in the first place. Bush requested and secured a resolution for using force in Iraq from both political parties, which is more than his Democratic predecessor did in launching the war in the Balkans. Clinton neither sought nor obtained a congressional resolution to use force.[11] In gauging the sincerity of the Democratic attacks on Bush's war decisions as "unilateral" and "illegal," it is worth remembering that Bill Clinton's failure to seek authorization from Congress didn't seem to bother Democrats at the time.

---

[11]John C. Yoo, Professor of Law, University of California at Berkeley School of Law, "Kosovo, War Powers, and the Multilateral Future," *University of Pennsylvania Law Review*, Vol. 148, No. 5, May 2000; also available at: http://scholarship.law.berkeley.edu/facpubs/156

The "Authorization for the Use of Force" that Bush obtained in October 2002 contains 23 clauses that spell out the rationale for the war.[12] Of the 23, there are only two that even mention *stockpiles* of weapons of mass destruction. If this was the principal argument for the war, the authorization didn't make much of it. What the authorization did stress—in 12 separate clauses—were the 16 UN resolutions that Saddam had ignored or defied. The first three of these, 687, 688 and 689, constituted the terms of the truce in the first Gulf War, whose violation was a legal justification for the war that followed.[13] The other 14 were failed attempts to enforce them. This is why we went to war: to enforce the UN resolutions and uphold international law.

Saddam Hussein had invaded two countries—Iran and then Kuwait—and used chemical weapons against his own people. We went to war with Saddam Hussein in 1991 to force him out of Kuwait, which his invading armies had swallowed. At the end of the war there was no peace treaty, merely a truce that established the conditions by which the allied coalition would allow him to remain in power. They instructed Saddam to disarm and to stop his *programs* to develop weapons of mass destruction. How do we know he had programs for developing weapons of mass destruction? Because he had used chemical weapons against the Kurds. Because his own brother-in-law, who was in charge of his nuclear weapons program, defected and revealed that he did. Because, under the UN resolutions, inspectors were sent into Iraq, located his weapons of mass destruction and destroyed the ones they found. The UN resolutions—backed by the armed power of the United States—partially worked. But only partially, and only for a while. Saddam was forced

[12]"Authorization For Use Of Military Force Against Iraq Resolution Of 2002,"—Public Law 107- 243—Joint Resolution, 107th Congress, October 16, 2002, p. 1497, http://www.gpo.gov/fdsys/pkg/PLAW-107publ243/html/PLAW-107publ 243.htm

[13]http://en.wikipedia.org/wiki/United_Nations_Security_Council_Resolution_687; http://en.wikipedia.org/wiki/United_Nations_Security_Council_Resolution_688; http://en.wikipedia.org/wiki/United_Nations_Security_Council_Resolution_689

to stop the programs the UN inspectors discovered, and was forced to stop repressing the ethnic and religious minorities in Iraq, as the UN resolutions required. But without an occupying army in Iraq, the UN proved unable to hold him to the terms he had agreed to, and he remained an internationally recognized menace. With the help of his allies on the UN Security Council—France, Russia and China—Saddam circumvented the sanctions placed on him, obstructed the inspectors and evaded the terms of the resolutions until finally, in 1998, he expelled the UN inspectors from Iraq altogether.

This broke the truce and resumed the war, though the Clinton administration did not have the ability or will to prosecute it with a ground army. Instead, the president fired 450 missiles into Iraq, more than his predecessor had launched during the entire Gulf War. He also got Congress to authorize an Iraqi Liberation Act, which called for the removal of the Saddam regime by force and was passed by an overwhelming majority in both parties. The act only authorized military help *to Iraqis* trying to overthrow Saddam, since Clinton could not conduct a serious war while he was mired in the Lewinsky scandal. In 1998, at least, Bill Clinton understood, as John Kerry and Tom Daschle and Al Gore also did at the time, that Saddam Hussein had violated the truce and was a threat to the peace. He was an aggressor twice over. He had shown that he was determined to circumvent the UN inspections and the arms control agreements he had signed. Intelligence agencies all over the world believed that Saddam was determined to break the UN sanctions and develop weapons of mass destruction. Why would he expel the UN inspectors if it were not his intention to build weapons of mass destruction and use them? The 2004 Duelfer report found enough evidence to conclude that it was.[14]

Saddam was a self-declared enemy of the United States who expressed his loathing for America in numerous ways—for exam-

---

[14]Comprehensive Report of the Special Advisor to the DCI on Iraq's WMD, with Addendums (Duelfer Report), September 2004, http://www.gpo.gov/fdsys/pkg/GPO-DUELFERREPORT/content-detail.html

ple, by trying to assassinate an American president and by being the only head of state to celebrate the destruction of the World Trade Center on 9/11. Despite leftist claims to the contrary, there were in fact major links between international terrorists, including al-Qaeda, and the Saddam regime. These are documented in Stephen Hayes's *The Connection,* which describes the relations between the government of Iraq, al-Qaeda, and the major world terrorist organizations.[15]

Among other gestures to the *jihad,* the secularist Saddam had the proclamation "*Allahu Akbar*" inserted into the Iraqi flag. He did not adopt this mantra of Islamic martyrs from any religious revelation. He adopted it because Islamic terrorists had made the slogan their war cry and Saddam wanted to join their side.

---

[15]Stephen Hayes, *The Connection: How al-Qaeda's Collaboration with Saddam Hussein Has Endangered America,* Harper, 2004

2

The Path to War

Standing between Saddam and his malevolent ambitions in the fall of 2002 was the uncertain power of the United States. It was uncertain because the first Bush administration had failed to remove Saddam at the end of the Gulf War, and because the Clinton administration was too paralyzed by ideology and circumstances to repair the mistake. After his defeat in the first Gulf War, a still-defiant Saddam had boasted that America could fight a Cold War but couldn't endure ten thousand casualties in a hot one.[1] After America's humiliation in Mogadishu, Osama bin Laden said nearly the same thing: "We have seen in the last decade the decline of the American government and the weakness of the American soldier. He is ready to wage cold wars but unprepared to fight hot wars. This was proven in Beirut when the Marines fled after two explosions, showing they can run in less than twenty-four hours. This was then repeated in Somalia."[2]

November 26, 2004, http://archive.frontpagemag.com/readArticle.aspx?ARTID=10043

[1]David Horowitz, "Why We Are in Iraq, Part II," *FrontPage Magazine,* November 26, 2004, http://archive.frontpagemag.com/readArticle.aspx?ARTID=10043

[2]"Usama bin Ladin: 'American Soldiers Are Paper Tigers,'" *Middle East Quarterly,* December 1998, pp. 73–79, http://www.meforum.org/435/usama-bin-ladin-american-soldiers-are-paper-tigers; *ABC News* Transcript of 1998 Interview with Osama Bin Laden, May 28, 1998, http://abcnews.go.com/ 2020/video/osama-bin-laden-interview-1998–13506629; Osama Bin Laden Interview, May 1998, (*ABC News* Video), http://abcnews.go.com/ 2020/video/osama-bin-laden-interview-1998–13506629

In enemy eyes, America was a paper tiger. This was perhaps the main cause of the miscalculations made by Saddam that led to his fall. But his assessment was correct until 9/11. Before that—ever since the Vietnam truce of 1973—America had shown itself to be a power unwilling and therefore unable to put an army in the field for more than four days. On September 11, 2001, the world changed because the perceptions of an American president changed. George W. Bush understood that the strike against us was a declaration of war. He understood that Islamic terrorists supported by rogue states can get access to terrible weapons and strike at more powerful adversaries with the ability to inflict incalculable damage. America could not wait for such an attack before responding to the threat these regimes represented. The consequences were simply unacceptable. America had to strike *before* the threat became imminent.

Since Saddam had already shown that he would defy all attempts to control him, since he had already demonstrated that he would use weapons of mass destruction, and since he supported the *jihad* against the United States, his regime presented a threat that had to be confronted. John Kerry and other Democratic leaders spoke eloquently to these realities and endorsed the measures taken by the president that led to war. The Bush Doctrine is simply a statement of these realities, along with the will to take the measures necessary to deal with them. It is to engage the war that has been declared against us by terrorists and the regimes that harbor them, including Iran, Syria, and Libya, besides Iraq.

In their attacks on the president, opponents of the war—including the Democratic leaders who once knew better—have said that Iraq was "no threat." But if Iraq was no threat, why was Afghanistan a threat? Afghanistan is a much poorer country than Iraq. It has no great oil reserves; it wasn't about to make a deal with North Korea to buy nuclear weapons "off the shelf," as Saddam was just before American troops crossed his borders. So why was Afghanistan a threat? It was a threat because it provided the terrorists with a base of operations, and from that base they were able to deliver a devastating blow to the United States.

If Afghanistan was a threat, obviously Iraq was an even bigger one, but so was Iran. Some critics of the war want to know why we didn't attack North Korea or Iran. There is a certain hypocrisy to these qualms, since these are the same people who argue that our attack on Iraq was illegitimate. Nonetheless, the question is worth answering. The difference between North Korea and Iraq is that, as bad as North Korea is, it is not part of a formal *jihad* that includes al-Qaeda, Hamas and other Islamic terrorist parties, which Saddam Hussein had joined and, in the case of Hamas, was financing. The difference, finally, between Iran and Iraq is that we were actually at war with Iraq and had been at war since 1991. For ten years, U.S. and British warplanes had participated in daily missions over the "no-fly zones" in northern Iraq in order to prevent Saddam Hussein from dropping poison gas on the Kurds. This was a "low-intensity" war to keep Saddam within the restrictions created by the UN resolutions. The Duelfer Report, issued after Saddam's removal, based on interviews with Iraqi officials and on-site inspections, concluded that Saddam Hussein planned to resume his programs to build weapons of mass destruction once he got past the UN restrictions.[3]

Recall the timeline of the war: after 9/11, Bush declared that Iraq was in defiance of the arms-control and inspection agreements that were designed to keep him under control. Iraq was therefore an international problem. In his State of the Union address on January 20, 2002, the president told Saddam, in effect: You are part of an 'axis of evil' and you are in defiance of the 1991 truce agreements. You need to comply with the terms of the truce you signed, and with the UN resolutions; you need to disarm, open your borders to UN inspectors and give up your ambitions to acquire weapons of mass destruction—*or else.*[4] This ultimatum was delivered 14 months before we actually went to war.

[3]Comprehensive Report of the Special Advisor to the DCI on Iraq's WMD, with Addendums (Duelfer Report), September 2004, http://www.gpo.gov/fdsys/pkg/GPO-DUELFERREPORT/content-detail.html

When Senator Kerry and other critics say the United States "rushed to war," it is difficult to imagine what they are talking about. Shortly after George Bush put Saddam on notice in January 2002, Al Gore gave the first foreign-policy address he had made since the election of 2000. In this speech, Gore praised Bush for identifying Iraq as one of the components of an axis of evil. He noted that Bush had come under criticism for making such a statement, and he made a point of supporting Bush's decision to do so. Saddam's regime was, in fact, evil and a threat to the peace; Gore said America had to do whatever was necessary to deal with the threat he represented, even if we had to do it alone and without our allies' approval.[5] Later, Gore betrayed his own position on Iraq, just as the leadership of the Democratic Party betrayed a war it had signed onto in the hope of gaining a political advantage.

There was no rush to war. In September 2002, nine months after the "axis of evil" speech and six months before the onset of the war, President Bush went to the UN and told its delegates the UN must enforce the resolutions Saddam had defied or become "irrelevant."[6] If the UN Security Council would not meet its obligations, enforce its resolutions and defend the peace, the United States would do it instead. As an earnest of its intent, the United States had begun sending troops to the Gulf. The immediate effect of this was to cause Saddam to readmit the UN inspectors. In the crucial months that followed, the American president said more than once to the Iraqi regime: "You will disarm, or we will disarm you." This was not a rush to war but a deliberate march to a moment of truth in which Saddam's intentions would be tested a

---

[4]Text of President Bush's 2002 State of the Union Address, January 29, 2002, http://www.washingtonpost.com/wp-srv/onpolitics/transcripts/sou012902.htm

[5]Al Gore, "A Commentary on the War Against Terror: Our Larger Tasks," *Council on Foreign Relations*, February 12, 2002, http://www.cfr.org/terrorism/commentary-war-against-terror-our-larger-tasks/p4343

[6]President George W. Bush's Remarks To The United Nations General Assembly, September 12, 2002, http://www.johnstonsarchive.net/terrorism/bushiraqun.html

final time: Disarm, open your borders to unobstructed UN inspections—or else.

In October, following his appearance at the UN, the president went to Congress and got the authorization he needed to use force against Iraq if Saddam persisted in the course of obstruction he had pursued for more than a decade. The vote was 77 to 23 in the Senate, with support from majorities on both sides of the aisle. On November 8, the President won a unanimous 15-to-0 vote in the Security Council for Resolution 1441, an ultimatum that said to Saddam: You will disarm, and you will show that you have disarmed by making a comprehensive report on your weapons of mass destruction, *"or serious consequences"* will follow.[7] The deadline for compliance was set for December 7, 2002.

Chief UN weapons inspector Hans Blix has since written a book on these events, *Disarming Iraq*. Blix is a Swedish leftist who, by his own admission, was against going to war despite Saddam's failure to comply with the UN resolutions.[8] In his book, he acknowledges that UN Resolution 1441 was diplomatic language for an ultimatum of war, and that Saddam had failed to meet its terms.[9] When the December 7 deadline for compliance arrived, the Iraqi regime delivered a 12,000-page report that was essentially a rehash of previous reports and not a serious answer to the

[7]United Nations Security Council Resolution 1441, November 8, 2002, http://en.wikipedia.org/wiki/United_Nations_Security_Council_Resolution_1441

[8]Hans Blix, *Disarming Iraq*, Pantheon, 2004, p. 109

[9]Blix, *Disarming Iraq*, pp. 106: "When the deadline arrived, the Iraq regime provided a report that was generally conceded not to have met the terms of the ultimatum. U.N. chief inspector Hans Blix summarized the Iraqi submission: 'The chemical area of the text was an updated version of a declaration submitted in 1996. The missile part also had largely the same content as a declaration of 1996, with updates added. I reported to the Council that our preliminary examination of the declaration had not provided material or evidence that solved any of the unresolved disarmament issues.' These included the fact that '8,500 liters of anthrax, 2,100 kilograms of bacterial growth media, 1.5 metric tons of VX nerve agent and 6,500 chemical bombs' that the U.N. inspectors had ascertained were at one time in Saddam's possession were unaccounted for.

questions that had been asked. Thousands of weapons were unaccounted for, and the requirements the Security Council had laid down had not been met.

At this point the question was whether yet another ultimatum should be allowed to slip by with no consequences to the defiant regime. If there is never a consequence to violations of international law, then the entire fabric of the law becomes a sham. Neither the word of the United Nations nor of the United States would have any credibility, which would create an extremely dangerous international environment. The only way to deter a threat would be to go to war. Senator Kerry and other critics on the left have suggested that Saddam could have been contained without a war; that the weapons inspections would eventually have worked to disarm the regime. But this is an empty claim. It presumes the United States could maintain 100,000 troops on the Iraqi border indefinitely and focus the main energies of government on keeping one rogue state in check. The only reason the UN inspectors had been readmitted to Iraq after their expulsion was because of Bush's decision to put a massive American military force on the Iraqi border and threaten the regime's survival. Keeping them there after the failure of the ultimatum would have cost $1 billion a week and would have meant maintaining 100,000 troops in the Arab desert where they would be sitting targets for terrorists. Saddam, on the other hand, would have all the time in the world to manipulate "world opinion," delay any result and wear the coalition allies down. The effort to mobilize enough force—diplomatic and military—to produce Saddam's moment of truth on December 7, 2002 had been a year in the making. It should be self-evident that this

(continued) Resolution 1441 had called on Saddam Hussein to document their destruction. Even the French ambassador noted that 'there was no new information in the declaration....' Afterwards Blix wrote of the declaration, 'My gut feelings, which I kept to myself, suggested to me that Iraq still engaged in prohibited activities and retained prohibited items, and that it had the documents to prove it.'"

"alternative" to war was merely a plan for continuing an appeasement that had failed.

In January 2003, one detour remained on the road to war. It was a detour that has since served to obscure the rationale for the war itself. When the UN Security Council deadline passed on December 7, America and Britain were alone among the major powers willing to enforce the resolution they had all authorized. France, which had been Saddam's longtime ally, told Secretary of State Colin Powell that, even though Iraq had now defied the UN resolution, France would veto a decision to go to war "under any circumstances (*quelles que soient les circonstances*)."[10] At the same time, 750,000 anti-war protesters appeared in the streets of London to join the French opposition and say no to war. The size of this demonstration was equivalent to four million protesters in the streets of Washington. Four million American protesters would not even be the full equivalent of the political fact that confronted Tony Blair. The protesters were members of his own party. A proper equivalent would have been four million Republicans marching on Washington to oppose enforcement of the Security Council resolution. To meet this opposition, Blair pleaded with Bush to go back to the Security Council and present whatever intelligence information was required to get a second—albeit entirely superfluous—UN resolution. This was in effect yet another appeasement of Saddam, who had brazenly defied the ultimatum. But because Blair had been a loyal ally, Bush said yes.

In retrospect, he should not have done so. First of all, because it was a futile effort. The French were not going to be convinced. We now know that the French had been bribed with millions of dollars stolen from the UN Oil-for-Food program and the promise of billions of dollars in oil contracts.[11] Second and far more importantly, in making the case, Powell stretched the available evidence and made claims about the existence of actual weapons of mass

---

[10]William Shawcross, *Allies: The US, Britain, Europe and the War in Iraq*, Public Affairs, 2004, p. 148

destruction that proved unsustainable. The reason to go to war was the defiance of the UN ultimatum. But Colin Powell's presentation gave the impression that the reason was Saddam's possession of WMDs, which played into the hands of those who had an interest in turning the debate about the war upside down. It was Colin Powell's presentation that became the basis for the left's unprincipled attack on Bush for "misleading" the nation into war.

The war in Iraq was not about weapons of mass destruction; it was about Saddam Hussein's ten-year defiance of international law and his determination to break the UN's arms control arrangements in order to *acquire* weapons of mass destruction. In his State of the Union speech on January 28, 2003, seven weeks before the fighting began, the president said in so many words that he was not going to wait until Iraq became an imminent threat, until Saddam already had the weapons in place and was about to launch an attack. "Some have said we must not act until the threat is imminent. Since when have terrorists and tyrants announced their intentions, politely putting us on notice before they strike? If this threat is permitted to fully and suddenly emerge, all actions, all words, and all recriminations would come too late. Trusting in the sanity and restraint of Saddam Hussein is not a strategy, and it is not an option."[12] This was the president's message: Saddam will comply with the terms of the UN ultimatum. He will disarm and prove that he has disarmed, or we will disarm him. That in a nutshell is why we are in Iraq.

---

[11]United Nations Oil-For-Food Program: History and Scandals, *DiscoverTheNetworks,* 2005, http://www.discoverthenetworks.org/Articles/oilforfoodhistory.html; United Nations Oil-For-Food Program, *DiscoverTheNetworks,*
http://www.discoverthenetworks.org/printgroupProfile.asp?grpid=6529

[12]George Bush, State of the Union speech, January 28, 2003, http://www.cnn.com/ 2003/ALLPOLITICS/01/ 28/sotu.transcript/

3

Dissenters in a Time of War

The passions provoked by war in a divided nation can be not only unpleasant but dangerous. They can tie our hands, weaken our resolve, and make us vulnerable to those who are determined to destroy us. When lives are at stake—particularly our own—it is easy to abandon common civilities and to think of our opponents as an enemy camp vying for the power to determine our fates. In these circumstances, it is easy to forget the ties that bind us as a nation. In these times, it is easy for the worst passions in each of us to come to the surface, while the worst among us often become leaders of the public debate. Now the presidential election is over and the contest for power decided, and that may provide a window of opportunity in which each of us can work to check these currents and reaffirm our bonds.

The most important thing to be clear about in analyzing these matters is whether the differences are based on good faith disagreements. If they are not, no common front is possible. If they are, then we can agree to disagree and defend our country at the same time. I would not find it possible to embrace people who were supporters of the war for motives that were venal and reasons that were corrupt. The problem for the hardcore left is that it cannot see good in its own country, and therefore cannot support its causes or its wars.

December 10, 2004, http://archive.frontpagemag.com/readArticle.aspx?ARTID=10043

As a supporter of the war, the crucial distinction I make is between those who oppose the war out of love of country and those who don't. Patriotic dissenters criticize the war because they believe the conflict in Iraq reflects flawed decisions, weakens our security and distracts us from the tasks we need to face. Unpatriotic critics are those who oppose the war because they regard America as culpable in its essence, and share a common dream with our enemies of a world that is liberated from American oppression.

This is a view that has been expressed in manifold ways by leftists; for example, at the anti-war "teach-in" held at Columbia University in March 2003, where Professor Nicholas De Genova said he wished for a million American defeats. De Genova told the 3,000 cheering students and faculty who attended the teach-in: "The only true heroes are those who find ways that help defeat the U.S. military.... Peace anticipates a very different world than the one in which we live, a world where the U.S. would have no place."[1] De Genova's views are widely shared on the political left. Professor Robert Jensen of the University of Texas is a prominent "anti-war" activist. As American Marines engaged Sunni terrorists in a fierce battle in Fallujah, Jensen wrote: "The United States has lost the war in Iraq, and that's a good thing.... I welcome the U.S. defeat, for a simple reason: It isn't the defeat of the United States—its people or their ideals—but of that empire. And it's essential the American empire be defeated and dismantled."[2] In

[1]Ron Howell, "Radicals Speak Out At Columbia 'Teach-In,'" *Newsday*, March 27, 2003, http://www.nynewsday.com/news/local/manhattan/nyc-propo328,0,6281232.story?coll=nyc-topheadlines-right

[2]*America, The Tyrant. America Must Fail!*, Kathryn Jean Lopez, *National Review*, December 5, 2004, http://www.nationalreview.com/corner/91500/america-tyrant-america-must-fail-kathryn-jean-lopez; quoting from an editorial entitled "The Upside to Losing Iraq? An Empire Falls," which Robert Jensen wrote for *The Austin American-Statesman* on December 3, 2004, p. A-17; (also published as "A Defeat for an Empire," *Fort Worth Star-Telegram*, December 8, 2004), http://www.commondreams.org/views04/1209- 26.htm

Jensen's mind, the real America whose citizens are dying in Iraq is somehow separate from "its people or their ideals" and should be seen as an evil empire that needs to be destroyed. This was the view of the communist left, which regarded the Cold War as a struggle between the forces of socialism and an American Empire governed by a greedy "ruling class." That made it possible for communists to serve the Soviet enemy while claiming the mantle of "patriotism" for their acts. The same view animates the leaders of the two national "peace" organizations that have coordinated all the major demonstrations against the Iraq War, and are run by Marxist veterans of the previous "anti-imperialist struggle" to defeat the United States.

This is the view of Tom Hayden, who was a leader of the New Left's efforts to support the Communists in Vietnam, and who later became a Democratic state senator in California. In an article called "How to End the Iraq War," Hayden spelled out a concrete plan for Americans who want to defeat their country in war. Ignoring that America is a democracy, and that the vast majority of Americans at the time supported the war, Hayden wrote: "The anti-war movement can force the Bush administration to leave Iraq by denying it the funding, troops, and alliances necessary to its strategy for dominance."[3] This is the voice of a self-declared enemy of the United States, in Hayden's case, a lifelong enemy. Of course this treachery is committed in the name of higher ideals, which Hayden has every right to express. But so do others have a right to judge them for what they are.

There was a refreshing candor to the radicalism of the Sixties, which has been absent in the recent incarnation of the left. Out of disgust with the Stalinist generation that posed as "progressive" and "liberal," the New Left openly proclaimed itself revolutionary and proud of it. It is true that, in order to mobilize large constituencies, leaders of the anti-Vietnam movement claimed their

---

[3]*How to End the Iraq War,* Tom Hayden, *AlterNet,* November 22, 2004, http://www.alternet.org/story/ 20571/how_to_end_the_iraq_war

only agendas were "peace" and "justice;" they organized opposition to the war under the banner "Bring the Troops Home," as though their primary concern was the safe return of American soldiers. But there were also many in their ranks who remained true to the code by flying the flags of the Communist enemy and chanting, "Victory to the Vietcong."[4] Tom Hayden was one of these worthies, even attempting to incite a guerrilla war in American cities in a radical homage to his Communist heroes. In fact, victory for the Communists was the agenda of all New Leftists at the time (bringing the troops home in the middle of a war would accomplish that end), though it is also true that many anti-war liberals were seduced into joining the demonstrations the radicals organized.

It is this coalition of forces on the left, both liberal and radical, that complicates the present task of distinguishing patriots who disagree with the policies in Iraq from anti-American radicals who want to bring down the "empire." The difficulty is increased when the radicals rarely express their goals as candidly as Professor De Genova and Hayden. That is because they are aware that their revolutionary goals constitute an outlaw agenda the vast majority of Americans would reject. It would be far easier to separate this anti-American left from patriotic critics, if the patriotic critics themselves would do some of the separating. It is difficult to locate such a separation when leaders of the Democratic Party are embracing pro-enemy figures like Michael Moore, or when anti-American radicals become Democratic Party legislators, like Hayden. It is difficult when prominent figures in the Democratic Party embrace MoveOn.org radicals, who opposed even the war in Afghanistan, and allow them to be major funders of the Party's campaigns. Further clouding the issue is the existence of an entire Internet industry, funded by liberal donors, whose agenda is to smear supporters of the war as "racists" and "witch-hunters."

---

[4]Sam Marcy, "The American Left," *Columbia University Louis Project*, May 25, 2002, http://www.columbia.edu/~lnp3/mydocs/american_left/marcy.htm

These smear sites include David Brock's MediaMatters, Media-Transparency, PublicEye, NameBase, Disinfopedia, the Southern Poverty Law Center, and the "Rightwing Watch" section of People for the American Way's website. The failure of the patriotic left to dissociate itself from the Tom Haydens and Michael Moores, or from organizations like United for Peace and Justice and MoveOn.org, is often accompanied by venomous attacks on conservatives who do make these distinctions. The technique of lumping opponents for purposes of attack has a name in the left-wing tradition. Trotsky called it attack by "amalgam," as when Stalinists smeared their Bolshevik opponents for allegedly being "in league with Hitler and the Mikado," because all of them were opponents of the Stalin regime.[5]

Stalinists also coined the term "social fascists" to attack democrats and socialists whom they opposed. A post on MediaMatters follows this well-worn pattern, targeting me personally as a critic of the so-called "anti-war" movement. It accuses me of attacking all Democrats as enemies of America. This is the MediaMatters comment: "David Horowitz [says] Democrats, media are 'getting Americans killed in Iraq ... because of their pathological hatred of George Bush.'" In fact, the editorial I wrote, and which MediaMatters even linked, says exactly the opposite, targeting only a radical faction of the Democratic Party. Its headline makes this clear: "This is Not a Magazine About Republicans and Democrats but About a War We Have to Win."[6] In my editorial, which was published the day before the election, I observed that this was "a season of poisoned politics and fierce divisions." I

---

[5] "The Case of Leon Trotsky," Thirteenth Session (Part I), April 17, 1937. Comments read by Leon Trotsky (VI. My "Juridical" Situation), http://www.marxists.org/archive/trotsky/1937/dewey/session13_a.htm

[6] Simon Maloy, "David Horowitz: Democrats, media are 'getting Americans killed in Iraq ... because of their pathological hatred of George [W.] Bush'" *MediaMatters*, November 1, 2004, http://mediamatters.org/research/ 2004/11/01/david-horowitz-democrats-media-are-getting-amer/132221; Cf. Part III, Chapter 14, "This Is Not About Republicans or Democrats" in this volume, above.

attempted to distinguish between patriotic dissenters from the war and those who wanted the United States to lose it. I referred to conservative critics who were suspicious of nation building, and who feared that Iraq was a distraction from the larger War on Terror. Of them I said, "These are patriots and belong in our camp." I have made similar distinctions elsewhere, especially in my book *Unholy Alliance: Radical Islam and the American Left;* but none of this has prevented these critics from accusing me of "McCarthyism."

The other day, I received an email from the writer Sherman Alexie, who is a friend of mine, a leftist, a Democrat and an opponent of the war, but also a man whose eloquent expressions of patriotism I have posted on the website I edit at *Frontpagemag.com.* Sherman is a Spokane Indian, and a talented and lyrical writer. I can't recommend highly enough his novel *Reservation Blues* or his most recent collection of poignant stories, *Ten Little Indians.* The email I received from him was provoked not by anything I had written but by the false representation of my position on the MediaMatters site.

> *Dear David*
> *...Where's your logic? How can you possibly accuse various leftists of dirty tricks and slander when you have accused us anti-war folks and Bush-haters of getting troops killed? There is no larger insult, no greater accusation of evil than that, David. And wildly inaccurate.... David, I guarantee you that I have more friends and family in the military than you do now or have ever had. I know hundreds of current and ex-soldiers. I'm an email pen pal to a dozen friends in Iraq. Republican small town guys who believe in their mission, who love their country and their families, but who count on me to be the anti-war guy even as I send them all of my prayers and support and dirty jokes. It's the whole red state-blue state separation illusion. There are millions of us red state children who became blue state adults and we live and love in both worlds.*
> *Sherman*

I was disappointed that Sherman could think I didn't understand his deep affection for his country, particularly since I had posted his views on my site. I also don't think that being "blue state" is a sign of maturity. But this kind of disagreement is what makes life interesting. In my reply, I pointed out that, in thinking only supporters of the war were making serious charges, he had missed the other side of the conversation. When opponents of the war say the war is not just wrong-headed but based on "lies," that it is a "fraud" concocted for the president's friends in Texas, and that the president and those who support him are getting Americans killed for no reason, that is just as serious an accusation as disloyalty. Moreover, these charges from the left came first and provoked the conservative responses. It is not mere dissent from the war that is "getting Americans killed." It is those extreme attacks on the credibility of the commander-in-chief, and on his moral character in conducting the war.

There will always be dissenters in a democracy. It is the air we breathe. My concern is not with dissenters but with those who have fundamentally broken with America and its purposes and gone over to the enemy camp. It is also about opportunistic leaders of the Democratic Party, like Jimmy Carter, Ted Kennedy and Al Gore, who have broken with the tradition of bipartisanship in foreign affairs and recklessly attacked a wartime president with accusations that are wildly overwrought and misleading.

To call the commander-in-chief a liar and a traitor—as Gore has in so many words, and others have either directly or by implication—is to conduct a classic psychological-warfare campaign advantageous only to the enemy. It is to take aim at the nation's morale when it is engaged in a war with a deadly enemy, to sabotage the war effort and undermine our troops on the field of battle. Political leaders have a greater responsibility to moderate their language and be as scrupulous with the facts as they are able. This responsibility flows from the fact that they have positions of national trust. The reckless charges made by Gore and Kennedy gave license to others who are distant from the chambers of government, who do not have their access to information, and who are dependent on them for guidance. To launch a verbal war within the war, instead of showing restraint (not agreement) as a loyal opposition, is politically reckless and morally unconscionable.

When *The New York Times* runs stories about the mishandling of prisoners at Abu Ghraib on its front pages for more than 60 days, humiliating America's forces in Iraq and disorienting America's allies, and when Ted Kennedy compares America's prisons in Iraq to Saddam Hussein's torture-chambers, that is more effective than any enemy propaganda. It can only serve to demoralize Americans and undermine their will to resist an enemy who is as ruthless as any we have ever faced. Imam al-Sistani, the Shi'ite leader in Iraq, said nothing about the matters at Abu Ghraib because, unlike *The Times'* left-wing editors, he wanted America's liberating forces to win.

If things go badly in Iraq, *The New York Times* and the Democratic Party leadership must shoulder a significant part of the blame. Since Howard Dean and his supporters stampeded the Democratic Party into the anti-war camp, the administration has had to fight the war with one hand tied behind its back. To point this out, to say that this degree of distortion at the very center of America's political debate and this volume of attack at the highest national levels gets Americans killed, should be obvious. To make the observation is appropriate criticism of an opposition that is out of control. And it is very different from saying that *any* criticism of the war is tantamount to treason, or that all "anti-war folks" are in the enemy camp.

The bipartisan principle in the national debate on matters of war and peace was honored by both parties during the Cold War, and up to the moment Al Gore and Jimmy Carter decided to throw it overboard in the fall of 2002. When Ronald Reagan was president of the United States, liberals hated him with ill-concealed passion. But no Democratic leader accused Reagan of betraying the American people on issues of war and peace, let alone of lying to put American troops in harm's way, as the current Democratic leadership has done in regard to President Bush. The anti-war *left* has obviously never operated under such constraints. "Hey, hey LBJ, how many kids did you kill today?" was one of its characteristic "anti-war" cries.[7] But even Democrats like Eugene McCarthy and Bobby Kennedy, who finally broke with the Vietnam War, never spoke about Lyndon Johnson in the ugly accents employed by the present Democratic Party leadership. Their decorum symbolized the bonds shared as Americans and made the country strong.

The closest any congressional figure came to the kind of poisonous rhetoric that has recently become commonplace was when radical congressman Ron Dellums told a "Stop the Draft" protest in Berkeley that "Washington, D.C. is a very evil place." This remark was made during the Soviet invasion of Afghanistan, the first time the Red Army had crossed an international border since 1945. Dellums dismissed the Soviet threat in these words: "From my vantage point, as your representative, I believe we are at a very dangerous moment. Washington, D.C. is a very evil place. While Mr. Zbigniew Brzezinski [the president's national security advisor] professes to see the arc of crisis in Southeast Asia as the Balkan tinderbox of World War III, well Ron Dellums sees the only arc of crisis being the one that runs between the basement of the West Wing of the White House and the war room of the Pentagon."[8]

Ron Dellums is a charter member of the anti-American left, a pro-Castro radical who colluded with the Marxist dictatorship in Grenada to deceive his own government about an airstrip Cuba was building on the island to accommodate Soviet nuclear bombers. But while Dellums denounced Jimmy Carter and his administration as evil and a threat to the peace, the Democrats

---

[7]http://www.psywarrior.com/nviet4.html

[8]Speech to Berkeley students at an anti-war demonstration in 1980; cited in a speech by David Horowitz, "The 'Peace' Movement," to the Conference of the Law and National Security Committee of the ABA, Washington, D.C., January 31, 1991, http://discoverthenetworks.org/Articles/The% 20Peace% 20Movement.htm

made him chairman of the subcommittee on Military Installations (worldwide) and then elevated him to chair of the House Armed Services Committee. When Dellums eventually retired during the Clinton administration, he was awarded the highest civilian honor for "service to his country" that the Pentagon can bestow.[9] This is what makes it difficult to draw the necessary distinctions between loyal and disloyal opposition on the Democratic side of the debate. It is also why Democrats have a large credibility problem on issues of national defense, which was a key factor in deciding the 2004 presidential election.

That election result, on the other hand, has begun to stimulate some second thoughts in liberal circles. Peter Beinart is the editor of *The New Republic,* a magazine that, thanks to its publisher Martin Peretz, has generally taken a strong anti-Communist/anti-totalitarian position on matters of national defense. The December 13 issue of *The New Republic* contained an essay by Beinart which was self-described as "An Argument for a New Liberalism" and specifically for an "anti-totalitarian liberalism."[10]

According to Beinart, the problem was that while Democrats had a "fairly hawkish foreign policy establishment" at the top of the party, "below this small elite sits a ... grassroots that views America's new struggle [the War on Terror] as a distraction if not a mirage." Beinart calls the members of this grassroots "softs," and believes that the Democratic Party has a dim electoral future if it continues to allow them to shape its policy. He recalls the days of the early Cold War, when the Democratic Party was riddled with Communists and their sympathizers who thought the struggle against Stalin and the Soviet empire was also a distraction and a mirage. The remedy liberals eventually arrived at was to condemn

---

[9]Congressional Record, V. 144, Part 1, January 27, 1998 to February 13, 1998, p. 622, http://books.google.com/books?id=3HAUh5DS_WwC&printsec=frontcover&source=gbs_ge_summary_r&cad=0#v=onepage&q&f=false

[10]Peter Beinart, "A Fighting Faith," *The New Republic,* December 13, 2004, http://www.tnr.com/article/politics/fighting-faith#

the Communists and fellow travelers (who called themselves "progressives" then as now), and expel them from their organizations. These precursors of what Beinart calls the "softs" on totalitarian Islam were the followers of former Vice President Henry Wallace, who allowed himself to become the presidential candidate of the Communist-controlled Progressive Party and condemn the Cold War. As current symbols of "Wallacism" in the Democratic Party, Beinart identifies the filmmaker Michael Moore and the political website MoveOn.org:

> Moore views totalitarian Islam the way Wallace viewed Communism: As a phantom, a ruse employed by the only enemies that matter, those on the right. Saudi extremists may have brought down the Twin Towers, but the real menace is the Carlyle Group. Today, most liberals naively consider Moore a useful ally, a bomb-thrower against a right-wing that deserves to be torched. What they do not understand is that his real casualties are on the decent left. When Moore opposes the war against the Taliban, he casts doubt on the sincerity of liberals who say they opposed the Iraq war because they wanted to win in Afghanistan first. When Moore says terrorism should be no greater a national concern than car accidents or pneumonia, he makes it harder for liberals to claim that their beliefs in civil liberties does not imply a diminished vigilance against al Qaeda.

Beinart is absolutely right about this, and it is encouraging to hear him say that the time has come for liberals—the decent left—to take back their movement. He takes as his model the purging of Communists from the CIO and other organizations by socialists like Walter Reuther and liberals like Hubert Humphrey and Harry Truman. "Liberals ... must first take back their movement from the softs. We will know such an effort has begun when dissension breaks out within America's key liberal institutions."

I hope this happens, but I am not as sanguine as Beinart that it will. In the first place, I think Beinart underestimates the opposition that decent leftists like him face in purging the "communists" from their ranks. The left—the hard, indecent left—is much more powerful today than it was in the heyday of communism. In the second place, the Michael Moores are not merely "softs" as Beinart describes them. ("The softs ... were not necessarily Communists themselves. But they refused to make anti-Communism their guiding principle.") There were, and are, softs like this. But Michael Moore and the leaders of the "anti-war" movement are more analogous to the Communists of the Cold War themselves. They are Marxist activists who believe not that there is *no* enemy, but that *we* are the enemy. The fact that people like this are entrenched in major institutions of the Democratic Party—such as MoveOn.org, the George Soros-inspired 527s, and the government unions that are the funding base of the Democratic Party—is unprecedented, and will make this battle much more difficult.[11]

The most important aspect of Beinart's challenge to the left is that it reminds us that liberals like Beinart, and my friend Sherman Alexie, share a common agenda with conservatives when it comes to defending this country and its liberties from the totalitarian enemy. This is the bond that makes us a nation, and it must stand before all others in matters of war and peace.

[11]http://www.discoverthenetworks.org/viewSubCategory.asp?id=1237

4

The McGovern Syndrome

On Christmas Day, former U.S. senator and Democratic presidential candidate George McGovern wrote a letter to the editor of the *Los Angeles Times* calling for an American surrender in Iraq. George McGovern has not been in the headlines for three decades, and his name consequently may be unfamiliar to many. But no one has had a greater or more baleful impact on the Democratic Party and its electoral fortunes than this progressive product of the South Dakota plains. The leftward slide of the Democratic Party, which has made it an uncertain trumpet in matters of war and peace, may be said to have begun with the McGovern presidential campaign of 1972, whose slogan was "America Come Home"—as though America were the problem, not the Communist aggressors. The McGovern campaign drew on the rank-and-file of the anti-Vietnam left, much as the Henry Wallace Progressive Party campaign of 1948 had drawn on the anti-Cold-War communist left, and as the Howard Dean campaign of 2004 would draw on the anti-war radicals opposed to the war against Saddam Hussein. McGovern was himself a veteran of the Wallace campaign; and virtually all the leaders of the anti-Iraq movement, including most of the Democratic Party leaders who supported it, are veterans of the anti-Vietnam campaign.

I have lived this history as both spectator and actor. My parents were Communists, and my first political march was a Communist

---

December 27, 2004, http://archive.frontpagemag.com/Printable.aspx?ArtId=10111

Party May Day parade in 1948 supporting the Wallace campaign against the Cold War; that is, against America's effort to contain communism and prevent Stalin from expanding his empire into Western Europe. Our chant was this: "One, two, three, four, we don't want another war/Five, six, seven, eight, win with Wallace in '48." The Wallace campaign marked an exodus of the anti-American left from the party; the movement of anti-Vietnam radicals into the McGovern campaign marked its return. The organizers of the movement against the war in Vietnam were activists who thought the Communists were liberating Vietnam, in the same way Michael Moore thinks Abu Musab al-Zarqawi is liberating Iraq. In 1968, Tom Hayden and the anti-war Left organized a riot at the Democratic Party convention which effectively ended the presidential hopes of its pro-war candidate Hubert Humphrey. This paved the way for George McGovern's failed presidential run against the war in 1972.

The following year, President Nixon signed a truce in Vietnam and withdrew American troops. His goal was "peace with honor," which meant denying a Communist victory in South Vietnam. The truce was an uneasy one, depending on a credible American threat to resume hostilities if the Communists violated the truce. Three years earlier, Nixon had signaled an end to the draft, and the massive national anti-war demonstrations had drawn to a halt. But a radical vanguard continued the war against America's support for the anti-communist regime in South Vietnam. Among its leaders were John Kerry, Jane Fonda and Tom Hayden. They held a war-crimes tribunal to condemn American troops as war criminals, and successfully persuaded congressional Democrats to cut off all aid to the South and to Cambodia, opening the door for a Communist conquest. When Nixon was forced to resign after Watergate, the Democratic congress cut off the aid as their first legislative act. They did this in January 1975. In April, the Cambodian and South Vietnamese regimes fell.

The events that followed this retreat in Indochina have been all but forgotten by the left, which has never learned the lessons of

Vietnam but instead has invoked the disastrous retreat as an inspiration for opposing the war in Iraq. Along with leading Democrats like party chairman Terry McAuliffe, McGovern called for an American retreat from Iraq even before a government could be established to assure the country would not fall prey to the Islamic jihadists: "I did not want any Americans to risk their lives in Iraq. We should bring home those who are there." Explained McGovern: "Once we left Vietnam and quit bombing its people, they became friends and trading partners."[1] Actually, that is not what happened in Vietnam. Four months after the Democrats cut off aid to Cambodia and Vietnam in January 1975, both regimes fell to the Communist armies. Within three years, the Communist victors had slaughtered two-and-a-half million peasants in Indochina to pave the way for their socialist paradise. The blood of those victims is on the hands of the Americans who forced this withdrawal: John Kerry, Ted Kennedy, Howard Dean, George McGovern—and anti-war activists like myself. It is true that Vietnam eventually became a trading partner with the United States ("friend" is another matter). But it was not true that this occurred "once we left and quit bombing its people." Before that, the slaughter took place, and then a Republican president confronted the Soviet Union in Europe and Afghanistan and forced the collapse of the Soviet empire. It was only after their Soviet Communist backers had been defeated that the North Vietnamese Communists accommodated themselves to co-existence with the United States.

The "blame America first" mentality so manifest in this ignorant McGovern statement is endemic to the appeasement mentality he personifies. "Iraq," he continues, "has been nestled along the Tigris and Euphrates for 6,000 years. It will be there 6,000 more whether we stay or leave, as earlier conquerors learned." In McGovern's Alice-in-Wonderland history, Iraq did not invade two

[1]George McGovern, "Rumsfeld In, G.I.'s Out," *The New York Times*, December 25, 2004, http://www.nytimes.com/ 2004/12/ 25/opinion/l 25mcgovern.html

countries, use chemical weapons on its Kurdish population, attempt to assassinate a U.S. president, spend tens of billions of dollars on banned weapons programs, aid and abet Islamic terrorists bent on destroying the West, and defy 17 UN Security Council resolutions requiring it to disarm, open its borders to UN inspectors, and adhere to the terms of the truce it had signed when its aggression in Kuwait was thwarted.

During the battle over Vietnam policy 30 years ago, President Nixon warned the anti-war left about the consequences that would follow if their campaign was successful. If the United States were to retreat from the field of battle, the Communists would engineer a "bloodbath" of revenge and complete their totalitarian agendas. McGovern, Kerry and other activists dismissed these warnings out of hand, regarding them as unfounded attempts to justify an imperial aggression. Time proved Nixon's opponents to be catastrophically wrong. But they have never had the decency to admit it. If the United States were to leave the battlefield in Iraq now before the peace is secured, there would be a bloodbath along the Tigris and Euphrates just as there was in the earlier war. The jihadists would slaughter our friends, our allies, and all of the Iraqis who have struggled for their freedom. Given the nature of the war we find ourselves in, this bloodbath would also flow into the streets of Washington and New York and potentially every American city. The *jihadists* have sworn to kill and subjugate us as infidels. People who think America is not vulnerable, that America can just leave the field of this battle and thereby gain peace, do not begin to understand the world we live in.

Or *if* they do understand it, they have transferred their allegiance to the other side. McGovern's phrase, "as earlier conquerors learned," speaks volumes about the perverse moral calculus of the progressive left. To McGovern we are conquerors, which makes the al-Zarqawi terrorists "liberators" or, as Michael Moore has called them, "patriots." The left that wants America to throw in the towel in Iraq is hypersensitive when its loyalties are questioned but at the same time can casually refer to our presence in

Iraq as an "invasion and occupation." It wants to use the language of morality, but it only wants the moral standard to apply in one direction. There is no one-dimensional standard, and a politics of surrender is not a politics of peace.

5

Unholy Alliance

Last fall, I published a book called *Unholy Alliance: Radical Islam and the American Left.* In it, I argued that the progressive left in the West has entered into a *de facto* alliance with the Islamic jihadists; that this alliance developed out of the left's support for the campaign of Palestinian jihadists against the Jews of Israel, and also out of its "anti-globalization campaign," which is the way it describes its global assault on world capitalism.

With the support of *Frontpagemag.com,* talk radio, and the conservative press, the book has done pretty well. There are 50,000 copies in print and most of them have been sold. On the other hand, *Unholy Alliance* went unnoticed by the mainstream press except for *The New York Times.* There it received a dismissive treatment, noted in passing in a review of five books—the other four being exclusively about Islam. The reviewer was an Islamist-friendly NYU professor, Noah Feldman, who scoffed at it as the work of a "relic."[1,2] Who but David Horowitz would think that there were still Communists around, or people who thought like them?

May 31, 2005, http://archive.frontpagemag.com/Printable.aspx?ArtId=8448

[1]Noah Feldman, "Political Islam: Global Warning," *New York Times,* February 6, 2005, http://www.nytimes.com/ 2005/02/06/books/review/06FELDMAN.html?pagewanted=print&position=&_r=0

[2]Letter to the Editor, David Horowitz, "'Unholy Alliance,'" *New York Times,* March 6, 2005, http://query.nytimes.com/gst/fullpage.html?res=9401EEDF143DF935A35750C0A9639C8B63

The fact is that many people like Feldman refuse to acknowledge that there is even a left in the West—let alone an activist one determined to undermine American institutions, sabotage our nation's war on terror, and help our enemies prevail. To enlighten such deniers, I created a website at discoverthenetworks.org that documented the links between radical Islam and American progressives. These links are organizational but also forged by their shared agendas—opposition to the Patriot Act and the instruments it created to secure the homeland; provision of legal and political support for the terrorists incarcerated in Guantanamo; and so on. Just as *Unholy Alliance* was scoffed at by *The Times* and ignored by the rest of the progressive culture, the website I created was ridiculed and attacked by leftists all over the Web. How absurd to think that American radicals and their progressive allies had any connection whatsoever to the forces arrayed against us, even though a million of them marched in the streets to prevent the removal of Saddam Hussein and then went on to obstruct the administration's war to overthrow his monster regime.

Or consider the assault on the terrorist incarceration center in Guantanamo Bay. This is a holding pen for keeping captured terrorists from returning to the field of battle, which potentially includes planting dirty nuclear bombs in large American cities. According to *The New York Times*, elite "white-shoe" law firms have been mobilized to provide legal support to the Guantanamo inmates by Michael Ratner, a well-known anti-American radical and lifelong advocate of Communist causes.[3] According to *The Times*, Ratner is "coordinating the assigning of lawyers to prisoners." *The Times* doesn't mention that Ratner is a former president of the National Lawyers Guild, created as a Soviet front and still wedded to its Communist heritage; or that he is the current head of the Center for Constitutional Rights, which was launched by

[3]Neil A. Lewis, "In Rising Numbers, Lawyers Head for Guantánamo Bay," *The New York Times*, May 30, 2005, http://www.nytimes.com/2005/05/30/politics/30detain.html?hp&ex=1117425600&en=6541be69d71b4357&ei=5094&partner=homepage

William Kunstler and Arthur Kinoy in lieu of the Communist Party they had originally planned to create. I was approached personally by Arthur Kinoy with the plan when I was an editor of the radical magazine *Ramparts* in the early 70s.

The Center for Constitutional Rights has dedicated itself to defending terrorist states like Castro's Cuba and the Communist guerilla armies in Central America during the 1980s. It represents the terrorist army Hamas, whose charter calls for the destruction of the state of Israel and its Jews. One of its legal stars is the convicted and unrepentant terrorist Lynne Stewart. Ratner and his fifth-column friends are also spearheading the anti-Patriot Act movement and the successful effort to get hundreds of municipal governments to refuse to cooperate with the Department of Homeland Security.

All this information is readily available and deliberately ignored by *The Times.* The silence fosters the impression that the unholy alliance we have documented in detail is somehow a figment of the imagination. No one actually reading the profiles posted at DiscovertheNetworks.org could reasonably reach such a conclusion. Laziness and denial are important if unappreciated factors in human affairs. But there is also willful perversity. The other day I received an email referring me to an Iraq News Network interview with British Labourite George Galloway, Saddam ally and hero of such websites as Counterpunch.org and CommonDreams.org, who embraces the idea of a progressive alliance with the jihadists:

> Mohammad Basirul Haq Sinha: You often call for uniting Muslim and progressive forces globally. How far is it possible under current situation?
>
> George Galloway: Not only do I think it's possible but I think it is vitally necessary and I think it is happening already. It is possible because the progressive movement around the world and the Muslims have the same enemies. Their enemies are the Zionist occupation, American occupation, British occupation of poor countries mainly Muslim countries. They have the same interest

> in opposing savage capitalist globalization which is intent upon homogenizing the entire world turning us basically into factory chickens which can be forced fed the American diet of everything from food to Coca-Cola to movies and TV culture. And whose only role in life is to consume the things produced endlessly by the multinational corporations. And the progressive organizations & movements agree on that with the Muslims.
> Otherwise we believe that we should all have to speak as Texans and eat McDonalds and be ruled by Bush and Blair. So on the very grave big issues of the day - issues of war, occupation, justice, opposition to globalization - the Muslims and the progressives are on the same side.[4]

Galloway is a celebrated member of the anti-war coalition, and represents its more radical element. Yet while his political views differ from those of its more moderate members, their own critiques of the Bush administration and the war in Iraq are generally so extreme, and so often parallel to Galloway's outlook, that it is difficult to see how they oppose his agenda. They are merely more discreet about it. The broad spectrum of the left supports the "Palestinian cause," which means the cause of Hamas and the PLO, two terrorist parties that supported Saddam Hussein and embrace the *jihad*. The disinterest of *The New York Times* in Michael Ratner's radical profile is the editorial behavior of a political ally, not a neutral journalism.

An anti-war academic like Todd Gitlin would be appalled by Galloway's call. Gitlin has criticized Bolshevik groups like International ANSWER, and his work is welcomed in liberal venues like *The New Republic* and *The New York Times*. But when Gitlin's corpus of writings about patriotism and the War on Terror are examined, as they are in *Unholy Alliance*, there is little to distinguish their disgust with America—not just in this war but from

---

[4]http://ww8.iraq-news.de/ This link is now dead, but identical Galloway views are reported by Richard Cravatts, "George Galloway and the Left's Unholy Alliance," http://hnn.us/node/122985

its origins—from the views of the left he claims to despise. If liberals want the respect of conservatives, they need to reset their priorities. The first target on their agenda should not be the Bush administration but the jihadist enemy and its fifth-column supporters here at home.

6

The London Bombings

Everyone will take from the Islamist bombings in London the "lessons" they are already seeking. According to the left, the bombings show the war in Iraq is actually producing the terror instead of fighting it; as though concern for Muslims is what inspires the *jihad* rather than hatred for non-Muslims and the West. In fact, Saddam and the terrorists have killed a hundred times more Muslims than American forces. Moreover, American forces have saved millions of Muslim lives in Bosnia, Kosovo, Somalia, Afghanistan and, yes, in Iraq. This is not a war about America's treatment of Muslims, and never was.

The left never understood the Iraq war in the first place, so it can't really be expected to understand the violence in Europe now. The Islamic *jihad* against the West, in which Iraq is but one—albeit very important—battlefield, did not begin in 2003 with the toppling of Saddam. It is rooted in a radical movement that began in Egypt in the 1920s, and is the creation of the Muslim Brotherhood, whose little red book is the Koran as interpreted by Hassan al-Banna, Sayyid Qutb and the Ayatollah Ruhollah Khomeini, leader of the first revolutionary Islamic state. The *jihad* began in earnest in November 1979 with the ayatollahs' Islamic revolution in Iran, which climaxed in the taking of American hostages and the materialization of a million fanatics in the streets of Teheran chanting "Death to America." One of the takers of those hostages

---

July 11, 2005, http://archive.frontpagemag.com/Printable.aspx?ArtId=7998

and leaders of those chants is the newly elected president of Iran, Mahmoud Ahmadinejad. No surprise that this week they were chanting "Death to America" again. The Islamic government of Iran is the creator of Hezbollah or "Party of God," the terrorist organization that blew up the Marine barracks in Beirut in 1983, which was—after the seizure of the American embassy in Teheran—the first terrorist attack of the *jihad* directed at us.

One can concede the left's argument that the American-supported war to liberate Afghanistan from the Soviet occupation was another proving ground for the Islamic *jihad.* As it happens, the Soviet invasion of Afghanistan was launched in December 1979 and, as leftists like to point out, was the training war for Osama bin Laden and many of the Palestinians who went on to create al-Qaeda, Hamas and other Islamic terrorist groups. The war against the Soviets in Afghanistan also led, however, to the liberation of hundreds of millions of captive peoples from the Soviet empire, a fact the left would prefer to forget. The left isn't interested in history, except to pluck out isolated facts that it can stick in America's eye. Thus, the left uses its Osama "fact" to claim that America *created* bin Laden, and that we are responsible for the attacks on our homeland. Inevitably, whatever the alleged facts it is interpreting, the left ends up demonstrating that it is at war with America. (Of course, watch it scream "foul" when anyone points out this obvious truth. Are you questioning our *patriotism?*)

The left's Afghanistan twist is several lies in one, but there is no need to disentangle them here. Leftists are uninterested in the history of our proxy-war against the Soviet invaders of Afghanistan because their sympathies lay with the invading Soviets. Just as radicals today like to think of themselves as "anti-anti-Saddam," so at that time they were "anti-anti-Communist." In practice, this meant they were the mainstay in the West for the Soviet empire and its expansion into vulnerable nations on its periphery, like Afghanistan. The United States provided training and arms for the Muslim *mujahideen* in Afghanistan because its conscience was roused by the Soviet invaders, whose scorched-earth policies had killed a million defenseless Afghan civilians before the resistance, with America's help, was able to stop them. Leftists don't wish to look at the momentous historical fact that the victory of the *mujahideen* triggered the chain of events that led to the fall of the Marxist empire. In other words, America's support for the Palestinian, Egyptian and Saudi terrorists (Osama among them) who flocked to the cause was a somewhat bad deed in the service of a very great good one.

When the left blames the bombing of London on America's intervention in Iraq, it ignores the statements of the *jihadists* themselves. In a *fatwa* last year, al-Qaeda leader Zarqawi explained that America is the enemy "as the bearer of the cross," not (as leftists would have it) as the aggressor in Iraq. The left forgets all the attacks on us that preceded the war in Iraq: Mogadishu, the World Trade Center 1993, the barracks in Saudi Arabia, the US embassies in Africa, the USS Cole, and the World Trade Center 2001; not to mention all the failed strikes, from those planned on the Lincoln and Holland Tunnels to the millennium plot, which were designed to kill hundreds of thousands. The left's argument about Iraq also contradicts the argument it was making before London: that the war in Iraq was a *distraction* from the War on Terror, not its cause.

The Islamic *jihad* is not a response to the intervention in Iraq or any particular actions of the West; it is a religious war against the *infidels* of the West. Its armies began forming in 1979 in Iran and Afghanistan and in the West Bank and Gaza. Because the *jihad* is not about Iraq, its ambitions (which the left never bothers itself about) will not be satisfied by an American withdrawal from Iraq or Afghanistan, or an Israeli withdrawal from the West Bank or Gaza. Instead, it will be *incited* by them just as Arafat and the al-Aqsa murderers' brigade were incited by the weakness shown by Clinton and Ehud Barak in offering concessions to people who want—literally—the world. The radical Islamists see their *jihad* as an Armageddon with the non-Muslim world, and there is no way out of the war for us but to win it.

The bombings in London show the folly of well-meaning liberals who think that the display of tolerance towards an avowed enemy will persuade him to change his mind. The Islamic community in London houses more than one mosque of hate preaching war against Britain. The British tolerated the haters, which led to disaster. The war in Iraq is an excuse for radicalism, not its cause, just as the war in Vietnam was an excuse for radicals to conduct a war against America they were already determined to fight. The radicals' war over Vietnam has not only continued into the present; it has morphed into a massive effort to support a *jihadist* designed to kill us. An expert on suicide bombings analyzed 71 terrorist attacks between 1995 and 2004, and concluded from the pattern that the immediate military goal of the *jihadists* was "to compel the United States and its Western allies to withdraw combat forces from the Arabian peninsula and other Muslim countries."[1] This is precisely what the left is demanding. It has opened a political front behind our lines. But America's surrender is not what the Iraqi people are demanding; it is not what the people of Afghanistan are demanding; it is not what the Saudis or the Lebanese are demanding. It is what the terrorists are demanding.

The left preaches surrender to the Islamists on all fronts: retreat from Iraq; retreat from Afghanistan; retreat from the territories in Gaza and the West Bank in absence of a peace. The retreats are called for in the name of ending the violence. But America and Israel are not the causes of the violence. Therefore the retreats will only produce more bloodshed, both abroad and at home. Why? Because Americans and Israelis are tolerant and the enemy is not; because we are compassionate and the enemy is savage; because we are merciful and the enemy is ruthless. The retreats the left is calling for will produce slaughters that will make 9/11 look tame.

---

[1]Robert A. Pape, "Al Qaeda's Smart Bombs," *New York Times*, July 9, 2005, http://www.nytimes.com/ 2005/07/09/opinion/09pape.html

The real lesson of London, therefore, is to take seriously what our enemies say. For years Britain has tolerated imams in its midst who are calling for war. Not because they don't like this particular Tony Blair policy or another, but because they hate the secular and Christian and Jewish West. In their religious imaginations, the West is *Dar al-Harb,* the world of the unbelievers, of the infidel and the damned. *Dar al-Harb* is literally "the realm of war." Leftists, who have no patience for Christians, are blind to the religious mentality of Islamic fanatics whose crusades they are abetting. The lesson of London is that tolerance can kill you.

It is time for the West to begin to set limits to the suicidal softness it considers its soul. We can no longer afford to tolerate hate directed against us, particularly the hate that emanates from religious pulpits and preaches murder in God's name. We can no longer tolerate hate that is directed at us by thinking that we are powerful and the hate can't hurt us. The lesson of London is that it can.

The imams of hate, their followers, and their secular defenders in the West, are self-declared enemies who need to be watched closely by all of us and confronted from now on. They need to be watched in their mosques, in the civil-liberties fronts they have formed to secure the release of their captured, and in the political groups that identify us as the enemy and them as the victims. When these domestic enemies step over the line, they need to be prosecuted. If they are non-citizens who hate us, they need to be deported.

A lesson of London for the British is that they need a British Patriot Act. Their frontline protectors are as hamstrung as ours before 9/11. The Patriot Act criminalizes not only terror but "material support for terror." It allows the FBI to surveil not only groups that have actually committed a crime against us, but groups that have demonstrated the *passion* and the *will* to commit crimes against us. The Patriot Act allows law enforcement to monitor the threats that come from our enemies within. That is why the left is up in arms against the Patriot Act. They want to strike down the provisions that allow us to keep an eye on them and their friends.

The stakes are high. These homemade London bombs, apparently not the work of professionals, killed more than 50 people and injured more than 700. A dirty nuclear bomb in an American city is not something we will be able to take in stride. Our own internal problem from those who hate us is as big as Britain's, perhaps even bigger. I am weary of watching American apologists for Islamic terror and opponents of our defenses treated as "liberals," as though the most important thing for the rest of us to do is avert our eyes from the malice in their hearts and pretend that it's politics as usual. We are trained in complacency by the genius of our democratic political system. Though passions run high, the stakes in our elections are remarkably low. One side loses an election. No one dies. No one goes to jail. In America, politics can seem like a game.

Friday night I was watching Alan Colmes, a decent leftist who doesn't understand this war. His guest on "Hannity & Colmes" was Kevin Danaher, husband of Medea Benjamin and a leader of the indecent left, which unlike Colmes wants us to lose the wars in Iraq and Afghanistan and deliver the Jews in Israel to their enemies who want to destroy them. Danaher and his wife are leaders of Global Exchange, Code Pink and Iraq Occupation Watch, which is the campaign to dissuade American youngsters from serving our country. They are at work day and night to cripple our lines of homeland defense, to deprive us of the protections afforded by the Patriot Act, and to disarm the military, which is keeping our enemies at bay. The discussion on "Hannity & Colmes" was about the violence of the radicals with whom Danaher is associated raining rocks on the recent G8 meeting in Scotland, which the bombs planted by the terrorists were designed to disrupt. In other words, they were both working with different weapons to the same end. Danaher, a leader of the global anti-capitalist left that staged the attacks, would not condemn the rock-throwers but was cynical and shrewd enough to disapprove violence in the abstract—or, as he put it, the violence of "both sides." It was his people who were attacking, but both sides were at fault.

Colmes was frustrated because he understood that Danaher's position, as argued, was suspect; but since Danaher was against the war in Iraq—a view Colmes shared—he attempted to coach him to do better. "Look," Colmes began, "I agree with your agendas, but ..." In fact Colmes doesn't agree with Danaher's true agendas, which Colmes—like many other so-called liberals—refuses to confront. Alan Colmes doesn't have the foggiest notion of who Kevin Danaher is or what his malicious intentions towards his country really are. Liberals like Colmes have up to now protected the anti-American left by pretending that it is all a game. In their eyes, people who denounce the president as Adolf Hitler and America as Hitler's Germany are "foolish" and aren't really aware of what they are saying. Well, actually some are not so foolish and they are. This is the lesson of London: Take the hostile force within your country and your political coalitions seriously. It's not a game anymore.

One thing I learned in my years on the left is that, all too often, people mean what they say. Those who talk revolution and war against our country are quite capable of acting on their talk, and of abetting those who are already at war and want to kill us. When the day comes that they step over the line and translate their words into action, they will do it with the best of intentions: to make the world a better place. That is precisely the reason they are so dangerous. Like Mohammed Atta and the 9/11 attackers who did it for Allah, they will do it for a noble cause.

Understand this, and you will understand that people who use the language of war need to be isolated and regarded with care. Understand this, and you will understand that those who describe America as Hitler's Germany can be dangerous, and need to be watched. These may be disturbing thoughts to any American, as they are to me. But, in the aftermath of London, it would be foolish to deny that precautions are necessary. The notorious professor, Ward Churchill, began by describing the victims of 9/11 as "little Eichmanns."[2] He has already moved on to inciting military personnel to kill their officers, while encouraging college students to applaud those who do. As a matter of progressive duty, mind you. Can anyone be confident that there are no Ward Churchill disciples who might take his words seriously and put them into practice? Ideas have consequences.

Nazi Germany is a symbol of evil. There is not a "progressive" who does not also think of himself as someone who would fight evil if given the chance. The purpose of identifying America with Nazi Germany is to identify America as evil, and to justify hating us. And that hatred will lead to action. Yes, we have rights in this country that guarantee to radicals the privilege of expressing their hatred openly. But this does not deprive the rest of us of the right to defend ourselves. The beginning of this defense is to take their words seriously, to remember London, and to understand that this is no longer a game.

[2]Ward Churchill, "Ward Churchill Statement," *Common Dreams,* February 1, 2005, http://www.commondreams.org/headlines05/0201-05.htm; et. seq. Ward Churchill, "'Some People Push Back': On the Justice of Roosting Chickens," http://www.kersplebedeb.com/mystuff/s11/churchill.html; et. seq. Marlena Gangi, "Little Eichmanns & 9/11: Ward Churchill Revisited," An Interview with Ward Churchill, September 29, 2008, http://wardchurchill.net/archived/a8_MarlenaGangi.pdf

7

Whose Side Are You On?

In war, the first order of business is to know whose side you are on, and who is on yours. In the case of the war to defeat the terrorists and establish a democratic government in Iraq, the answer is not always easy to come by. Take the American press. Take, in particular, the *Los Angeles Times*. On Wednesday, October 26, 2005, the main headline spread across two columns of the *Times* was, "U.S. Death Toll in Iraq Hits 2,000."[1] The sub-headline began: "Anti-war protesters plan demonstrations...." Two photos centered at the top of the front page showed President Bush declaring that "Iraq has made incredible political progress from tyranny to liberation to national elections;" and an "anti-war" activist lighting 2,000 candles for the dead. Underneath the two photos, a three-column story headlined "A Deadly Surge" began: "A year and a half ago, at the first anniversary of the U.S. occupation of Iraq, the death rate for American troops accelerated. Since then, none of the political milestones or military strategies proclaimed by U.S. officials have succeeded in slowing the death toll."

The article on the death toll continues into a full two-page spread inside the paper, with further details of the body count,

---

October 27, 2005, http://archive.frontpagemag.com/Printable.aspx?ArtId=6795

[1]Richard Boudreaux, Louise Roug and Paul Richter, "U.S. Death Toll in Iraq Hits 2,000," *Los Angeles Times*, October 26, 2005, http://articles.latimes.com/ 2005/oct/ 26/world/fg-deaths 26

including a half-page chart of the dying and a map of the United States showing where each of the dead soldiers lived. In other words, *let's bring the war home.* Facing the charts and continuing the front-page story, the headline reads, "Fallouja Marks Divide." The "divide," as the *Times* editors see it, is not the battle of Fallouja, which destroyed the main and only terrorist stronghold in Iraq and paved the way for democratic elections; it is the "fact" that the death toll of American soldiers has only "accumulated" since Fallouja. As if this were odd for a war, or this numbing repetition of a single fact which in itself has no significance wasn't enough, the *Times* devoted another full page to continuing the "Deadly Surge" story (new headline: "US At Grim Milestone In Iraq War: 2000 Dead") and a human-interest column ("A Life Back in Flower When It Was Lost") on one of the casualties. In all, the *Times* devoted 23 newspaper columns to a death toll which has no significance in itself and which is smaller in two years than the number of Americans who died in ten minutes on 9/11.

Buried by the *Times* editors in a three-column story on page 6 is the following item: "Iraq Charter Ratified by Big Margin in Final Tally."[2] What's this? On the same day as an American volunteer was killed in Iraq (and became part of the front page package of stories designed to turn Americans against the war), the final tallies of the vote on the new Iraq constitution were counted. Here's the news the *Los Angeles Times* worked so diligently to bury and subvert: Nearly 70 percent of the Iraqi people voted to endorse the most democratic constitution in the entire Muslim world—and in the entire 1,300-year history of Islam itself.

The margin of victory for the new constitution was 4-to-1. Moreover, the majority of Sunnis who had boycotted the previous election voted this time. This is (or should be) momentous news. Front page. Under the Saddam tyranny, the Sunnis had oppressed

[2]Richard Boudreaux, "Iraq Charter Ratified by Big Margin in Final Tally," *Los Angeles Times,* October 26, 2005, http://articles.latimes.com/2005/oct/ 26/world/fg-constitution 26

the Shi'ites and Kurds for the previous 40 years. But now they were voting in an election sponsored by the "occupiers"—*us.* In other words, the news is (or should have been) that, in a country that every naysayer on the left has proclaimed incapable of supporting a democracy and resentful of our "occupation," the majority has now joined the political community we have created. Yes, the Sunnis rejected the constitution. But by voting they agreed to debate and haggle over its details—over the details of their new democracy—in elections to come. In other words, this was a victory for freedom in Iraq, a defeat for our terrorist opponents, and a great boost for the security of Americans here at home. Yet in reporting the events of October 26, the editors of the *Los Angeles Times* (and—to be fair—*The New York Times* and the rest of the American mainstream media) did their best to obscure these momentous facts and to spin them in the opposite direction.

In two years, with less loss of life than we suffered on 9/11, America has liberated 25 million Iraqis, ended the most heinous tyranny of the 21st century, inflicted terrible defeats on our terrorist enemies, and created the first democracy in the history of Islam. But with no support for these victories from the American press. The words of the president mocked by the *Los Angeles Times* are 100 percent correct: "Iraq has made incredible political progress from tyranny to liberation to national elections." By contrast, the *Los Angeles Times* edition of October 26, 2005 is designed to make a mockery of his leadership and his words, and to turn Americans against the war for Iraqi freedom. What a shame. What a disgrace. What a tragedy for our nation.

PART V

Confronting the Enemy

(12/5/2005—5/2/2011)

I

Enemy Press

This is a war. You can be unhappy about it and sit it out, and that's okay. That's what a democracy is about—your right to dissent. You can criticize the war and vote for another government that promises to leave the field of battle. That's okay too. That's also what a democracy is about. But the young men and women an elected government sends into battle are embroiled with a ruthless enemy in the field. You can't attempt to cripple their efforts or do the work of the enemy side and expect the rest of us not to regard you as a saboteur, a Judas, an enemy within.

These thoughts are provoked by the lead story in Saturday's *Los Angeles Times*, and then by a missing lead in the paper the next day. On Saturday, the lead headline on the front page of the *Times* was, "Bomb Kills 10 Marines at Fallouja."[1] My first question is: what kind of a lead story is this? We're at war. What's the big news that ten soldiers have died? And by one roadside bomb? It could happen any day—even on the last day of a war before a peace. There is no story. This is not news, certainly not front-page headline news. It's like running a headline that today 110 people were killed in car accidents. That is probably an actual fact, since 55,000 Americans die every year in car wrecks. But no one writes head-

December 05, 2005, http://archive.frontpagemag.com/Printable.aspx?ArtId=6378

[1]Richard Boudreaux, "Bomb Kills 10 Marines at Fallouja," *Los Angeles Times*, December 3, 2005, http://articles.latimes.com/2005/dec/03/world/fg-marines3

lines about it because it's not news. It's life as we know it. As long as there are millions of cars on the roads, there are going to be accidents and deaths. So too with war.

The only reason the *Times* ran a front-page feature about the commonplace death of a few soldiers in war (a regular occurrence in our media during this war) is that its editors want to make the war seem like nothing more than a senseless killing-field. They know that this will serve to drain public support from the war and cause America to cut and run from the battlefield. So they are conducting their own psychological-warfare campaign against the war. It's immaterial whether we call this sabotage treason or not. Undeniably it is psychological warfare, which the terrorists would conduct themselves if they had the means to do it.

Terror is about inflicting enough pain on free societies so that they will surrender without a fight. If America's pain threshold is lowered enough, the terrorists will win in Iraq by default. And then they will come after Americans here at home with Iraq's oil billions behind them, and with the chemical and biological and eventually nuclear weapons they are now desperately seeking. Is this what the *Times* wants? Or perhaps the *Times* editors are so delusional they think, like John Kerry, that *we* are responsible for creating the terrorists—that they wouldn't exist if we weren't in their faces. But of course we weren't in their faces when they attacked us on 9/11.

On Sunday, the *Los Angeles Times* lead story was again about Iraq: "Private Security Guards in Iraq Operate With Little Supervision."[2] This was not a big story either, but it was also a negative one and so it was the *Times* editors' choice for the lead. It would further undermine Americans' will to continue the fight. But there was another Iraq story on Sunday that the *Times* editors pushed to the inside pages. The headline for this story was: "Senior Leader of

---

[2]T. Christian Miller, "Private Security Guards in Iraq Operate With Little Supervision," *Los Angeles Times,* December 4, 2005, http://articles.latimes.com/ 2005/dec/04/world/fg-guards4

Al-Qaeda Is Killed in Blast."[3] Actually it was the number three al-Qaeda leader after bin Laden and Zawahiri. This was big news—or should have been big news for people who think that the war in Iraq is a distraction from the War on Terror. And of course it *was* big news for them. That is why the *Times* editors kept it off the front page. Because, in addition to opposing an American war for freedom, the *Times* editors are dishonest journalists; they relentlessly subordinate the facts to the service of their political agendas.

No sooner had the *Times* story about the killing of al-Qaeda's number three laid out the details of the event than it sought to diminish the significance of that event. "[Unnamed] experts cautioned that the killing was likely to have a limited effect because al-Qaeda is less a hierarchical organization and more a movement that can carry out missions without directions from top leaders." Oh, like 9/11. What this malicious subterfuge is designed to conceal is the fact that while the *Los Angeles Times* and the leadership of the Democratic Party were busily sabotaging the American War on Terror, the Bush-Cheney-Rumsfeld team was destroying al-Qaeda as we knew it. Today al-Qaeda may be more decentralized, as the *Times* claims, but that is because America has taken the offensive, killed many of al-Qaeda's leaders and driven them into hiding, destroyed much of its infrastructure and reduced its capabilities so dramatically that the United States has been safe from terrorist attack for more than four years. Thanks for this should go to the much-maligned George Bush, Dick Cheney, Donald Rumsfeld and the thousands of men and women under arms who have had to fight a war against a ruthless enemy with half the country either on the sidelines or actively stabbing them in the back.

---

[3]Paul Watson and Ken Silverstein, "Senior Leader of Al Qaeda Is Killed in Blast," *Los Angeles Times,* December 4, 2005, http://articles.latimes.com/ 2005/dec/04/world/fg-terror4

2

Al Gore's Assault on Reason

When he was in office and responsible for protecting us, Al Gore was absent from the war on terror. As vice president, he was part of an administration that failed to respond to the first attack on the World Trade Center in 1993; that cut and ran when al-Qaeda ambushed U.S. army rangers in Mogadishu; that called for regime change in Iraq when Saddam expelled the UN weapons inspectors but then failed to remove Saddam or to persuade him to allow the UN inspectors back in; that failed to respond to the murder of U.S. troops in Saudi Arabia or the attack on an American warship in Yemen; that reacted to the blowing up of two U.S. embassies in Africa by firing missiles at an aspirin factory in the Sudan and empty tents in Afghanistan; that refused to kill or capture Osama bin Laden when it had a dozen chances to do so; and that did not put in place simple airport security measures, recommended by its own task force, which would have prevented 9/11.

In short, to every act of war against the United States during the 1990s, the Clinton-Gore response was limp-wristed and supine. And worse. By refusing to concede a lost presidential election, thereby breaking a hundred-year tradition of electoral concessions, Gore delayed the transition to a new administration that would have to deal with the terrorist threat. As a result of the two-month delay, the comprehensive anti-terror plan that Bush ordered on taking office (the Clinton-Gore team had none) arrived on his desk only the day before the 9/11 attack.

June 29, 2007, http://archive.frontpagemag.com/Printable.aspx?ArtId=27199

Yet it is characteristic of Gore's myopic arrogance that he would wag his finger at the Bush administration for *its* failure to anticipate the 9/11 attack: "It is useful and important to examine the warnings the administration ignored," Gore writes in a new screed, *The Assault on Reason,* which turns out to be self-referential.[1] As if to underscore his own hypocrisy, he adds: "not to 'point the finger of blame' ..." Of course not. Like his Democratic colleagues, Gore sees himself as a restorer of "reason" to an America that is on its way to perdition, thanks to the Republican serpent in the Rose Garden. According to Gore, Bush *is* the arch deceiver: "Five years after President Bush made his case for an invasion of Iraq, it is now clear that virtually all the arguments he made were based on falsehoods."

The first big Bush falsehood, according to Gore, is that the Bush administration went to war to remove Saddam Hussein's WMDs—or, as he puts it: "The first rationale presented for the war was to destroy Iraq's weapons of mass destruction." This familiar Democratic claim is itself probably the biggest falsehood of the Iraq War. In fact, the first—and last—rationale presented for the war by the Bush administration *in every formal government statement about the war* was not the destruction of WMDs but the removal of Saddam Hussein, or regime change. This regime change was necessary because Saddam was an international outlaw. He had violated the 1991 Gulf War truce and all the arms-control agreements it embodied, including UN resolutions 687, 688 and 689, and the 14 subsequent UN resolutions designed to enforce them.[2] The last of these, UN Security Council Resolution 1441,[3] was itself a war ultimatum to Saddam, giving him "one final opportunity" to dis-

[1]Al Gore, "The Assault On Reason," Penguin, 2007

[2]http://en.wikipedia.org/wiki/United_Nations_Security_Council_Resolution_687; http://en.wikipedia.org/wiki/United_Nations_Security_Council_Resolution_688; http://en.wikipedia.org/wiki/United_Nations_Security_Council_Resolution_689

[3]United Nations Security Council Resolution 1441, November 8, 2002, http://en.wikipedia.org/wiki/United_Nations_Security_Council_Resolution_1441

arm, or else. The ultimatum expired on December 7, 2002, and America went to war three months later.

Contrary to everything that Al Gore and other Democrats have said for the last four years, Saddam's violation of the arms control agreements that made up the Gulf War truce—and not the alleged existence of Iraqi WMDs—was the legal, moral and actual basis for sending American troops to Iraq. Al Gore and Bill Clinton themselves had called for the removal of Saddam by force when he expelled the UN weapons inspectors in 1998, in a clear violation of the Gulf War truce. This was the reason Clinton and Gore sent an "Iraqi Liberation Act" to Congress that year; it is why the congressional Democrats voted in October 2002 to authorize the president to use force to remove the regime; and it is the reason the entire Clinton-Gore national security team, including the Secretary of State, the Secretary of Defense and the Director of Central Intelligence, supported Bush when he sent American troops into Iraq in March 2003.

The "Authorization for the Use of Force"[4] legislation—passed by majorities of both parties in the Senate—is the legal basis for the president's war, which Democrats have since betrayed along with the troops they sent to the battlefield. The authorization bill begins with 23 "whereas" clauses justifying the war. Contrary to Gore and the Democratic critics of the Bush administration, only two of these clauses refer to stockpiles of WMDs. On the other hand, *twelve* of the reasons for going to war refer to UN resolutions violated by Saddam Hussein.

Even if these indisputable facts were not staring Gore in the face, the destruction of WMDs could not have been the "first rationale" for the war in Iraq for this simple reason. On the very eve of the war, the president gave Iraq an option to avoid a conflict with American forces. On March 17, two days before the invasion,

---

[4]Authorization For Use Of Military Force Against Iraq Resolution Of 2002, Page 116 STAT. 1498, Public Law 107- 243, 107th Congress, Joint Resolution, http://www.gpo.gov/fdsys/pkg/PLAW-107publ243/html/PLAW-107publ 243.htm

Bush issued an eleventh-hour ultimatum to Saddam: leave the country or face war. In other words, if Saddam had agreed to leave Iraq, there would have been no American invasion. It is one of the most revealing features of the Democrats' crusade against George Bush that they blame the war on him, not on Saddam.

If Bush's offer had been accepted, he would have left in place a regime run by the Ba'athist Party, headed by Foreign Minister Tariq Aziz or some comparable figure from the old regime, along with any WMDs that existed. The idea behind the offer was that, without Saddam, even such a bad regime would honor the truce accords of 1991 and UN Resolution 1441. This would have led to Iraq's cooperation with the UN inspectors and the destruction of any WMDs or WMD programs that Saddam might have had—without a war.

Ignoring—and willfully distorting—the facts about how and why his country went to war, Gore repeats the slanders against the president, and therefore his country, that have become an all-too-familiar aspect of our political life. The charges are transparently designed to destroy the authority of America's commander-in-chief, and to do so while his troops are in harm's way. The use of these charges has been an unprecedented campaign to sabotage a war-in-progress by a major political party. In the course of repeating these false charges, Gore reiterates another false claim—that Bush manipulated the facts about Iraq in order to serve a hidden agenda: "It was as if the Bush White House had adopted Walter Lippmann's recommendation to decide in advance what policies it wanted to follow and then to construct a propagandistic mass persuasion campaign to 'manufacture' the consent of the people to do what the 'specialized governing class' had already made up its mind to do."[5]

Of course, Walter Lippmann never recommended any such thing. This gross misrepresentation of a Lippmann argument can be traced to Noam Chomsky and his Marxist tract, *Manufacturing*

---

[5]Al Gore, "The Assault On Reason," Penguin, 2007

Consent. According to Chomsky, the term "manufactured consent" refers to a conspiracy of the ruling class to snooker Americans into war. But this is a typically malicious Chomsky misreading of Lippmann's text. In his book *Public Opinion,* Lippmann observed that modern society had become so complex that only specialized experts were in a position to understand the implications of a given national policy. Because of this complexity, informed policy debates could not be conducted by the voting public but necessarily took place between specialized experts who were then supported by constituencies on both sides of the argument. In other words, Lippmann was already recognizing the role of what we now call "special interest" and "public interest" groups in shaping the national policy debate. It was in this sense that Lippmann wrote that democratic consent was inevitably "manufactured." Lippmann never recommended that rulers organize a "propagandistic mass persuasion campaign" to deceive the public and manipulate the result. This is Chomsky's perversion of Lippmann's idea, which Gore plagiarizes.

Even so, the argument that Bush manipulated the facts about Iraqi WMDs to pursue a war policy that was aggressive and unfounded is yet another easily disposed of falsehood. Bush acted on the consensus of every major intelligence agency—including the British, the French, the Russian, the German and the Jordanian—all of whom believed that Saddam had WMDs. In other words, he cannot reasonably be accused of inventing the existence of Saddam's WMDs, although that is precisely what Gore and other demagogues on the left do on an almost daily basis. Since every Democratic senator who voted for the war was provided by the administration with a copy of the intelligence data on Saddam's WMDs, the charge made by Gore and other Democrats—that they were deceived—is cynical and hypocritical as well as untrue.

Gore's charges continue: "We were told by the President that war was his last choice, when it was his first preference."[6] Was it?

---

[6]Al Gore, "The Assault On Reason," Penguin, 2007

That depends on what one means by "first preference." If what Gore means is that the president prepared for war with Saddam long before the war began, well, of course he did. It was his responsibility to do so. It is the Pentagon's motto—and a fundamental doctrine of every strategist from Sun Tzu to Clausewitz—that if you want peace, prepare for war. By 2001, when Bush took up residence in the Oval Office, Saddam had already broken the Gulf War truce many times over. American pilots were engaged in a low-intensity armed conflict with the Iraqi military over the "no-fly zones" the truce had created. Clinton and Gore had allowed Saddam to get away with breaking the truce he had signed for two reasons: first, because they were preoccupied with the fallout from Clinton's sexual affair in the White House; second and more importantly, because ever since Vietnam the Democrats had shown no interest in deploying American troops to protect the nation's interests (and thus had opposed the first Gulf War).

In 1998, Saddam expelled the UN inspectors from Iraq. Why would he do so if it were not his intention to do mischief as well? Specifically, why would he do so if it was not his intention to develop the weapons programs—the WMD programs—that the Gulf truce outlawed and that the UN inspectors were there to stop? The terrorist attacks of 9/11 showed that Saddam's mischief could have serious consequences—not because Saddam had a role in 9/11, but because Saddam celebrated and endorsed the attacks, had attempted to assassinate an American president, and had hosted terrorist organizations and gatherings engaged in a holy war against the West.

The only reason Saddam allowed the UN inspectors to return to Iraq in the fall of 2002 was that Bush placed 200,000 U.S. troops on his borders. It would have been irresponsible of Bush to put those troops on the border of a country that was violating international law unless he meant to enforce the law. But the troops were there to go to war only if Saddam Hussein failed to honor the 1991 truce, not—as America's enemies and Al Gore maintain—to satisfy the aggressive appetites of the president. Saddam's offer to allow the UN inspectors to return to Iraq coincided with Bush's appearance at the UN in September 2002. His message to the UN was that it needed to enforce its resolutions or become irrelevant. If the UN did not enforce the resolutions that Saddam had violated, the United States would do so in its stead. Jimmy Carter and Al Gore marked the occasion by publicly attacking their own president for putting such pressure on Saddam Hussein. This was the beginning of the Democratic campaign to sabotage an American war in progress, a campaign which has continued without letup ever since.

As a result of Bush's appeal, the UN Security Council voted unanimously to present Saddam with an ultimatum whose 30-day deadline was set to expire on December 7, 2002. By that date he was to honor the truce and destroy his illegal weapons programs or "serious consequences would follow." The ultimatum was UN Resolution 1441—the 17th attempt to secure the truce in the Gulf War of 1991. The deadline came and went without Saddam's compliance. Saddam knew that his military suppliers and political allies—Russia and France—would never authorize its enforcement by arms. This is the reason the United States and Britain went to war without UN approval, not because George Bush preferred unilateral measures, which is simply another Democratic falsehood.

Since war was not the president's preference—first, last or otherwise—the United States did not immediately attack. Instead, the White House spent three months after the December 7 deadline trying by diplomatic means to persuade the French and Russians and Chinese to back the UN resolution they had voted for, and to force Saddam to open his country to full inspections. In other words, to honor the terms of the Gulf War truce that they—as Security Council members—had ratified and promised to enforce.

Virtually all of the claims that make up the core of the Democrats' attacks on Bush's decision to go to war—that he manipulated data on aluminum tubes to present them as elements of an Iraqi nuclear program, or that he lied about an Iraqi attempt to buy yellowcake uranium—were never part of the administration's rationale for the use of force, and were not mentioned in the Authorization for the Use of Force congressional legislation. They were *political* attempts to persuade the reluctant and double-dealing Europeans to enforce the UN ultimatum and international law. Even then, by offering Saddam an escape-clause if he would agree to leave the country, Bush provided an alternative to war. If Saddam would re-settle in Russia or some other friendly state, the United States would not invade.

Another Democratic lie regurgitated by Gore is the famous accusation about the 16 words Bush used in the State of the Union address on the eve of the war. According to Gore, Bush claimed "that he had documentary proof" Saddam Hussein had attempted to buy fissionable uranium from the African state of Niger. According to Gore, the "documentary proof" was revealed to be an Italian forgery for which Bush failed to apologize. According to Gore, there was no inquiry into how this happened. According to Gore, the Niger claim was one of the key falsehoods on which Bush based the "rationale" for the war. Every one of these assertions is either a distortion of the facts or simply false.

First, the Niger claim was not part of the rationale for the war. It is not mentioned in the Authorization for the Use of Force legislation or in UN Security Council ultimatum 1441, which constitute the actual reasons the United States and Britain went to war in Iraq. In his State of the Union address, the president did *not* say he had "documentary proof" of an Iraqi mission to obtain uranium in Niger. He said: "The British government has learned that Saddam Hussein recently sought significant quantities of uranium from Africa." Those 16 words were all he spoke. Every one of them was true then and remains true today. The British did report that Saddam "had sought significant quantities of uranium from Africa," and they have stuck by their report, which—contrary to Gore's malicious assertion—has indeed been investigated by a Senate intelligence committee, and has not been found to be false as Gore and legions of unprincipled Bush critics have falsely claimed. Moreover, the Italian document—which was not mentioned in the

State of the Union address, as Gore falsely suggested—was quickly acknowledged by the Bush White House to be a forgery.

The Niger claim, along with the administration's claims about aluminum tubes and Colin Powell's February speech to the UN, which are falsely presented by administration critics as rationales for the war, were all made more than a month after Saddam defied the December 7 deadline. They were not rationales for the war but were strictly for the benefit of the appeasement parties in Britain and France. They were put forward as part of an attempt to secure a second Security Council resolution to reinforce the 1441 ultimatum. This was requested by British Prime Minister Tony Blair, even though a second Security Council resolution would have been redundant. It was needed by Blair to respond to the attacks he was under from Britain's anti-American left.

In January, weeks before Powell's speech, 800,000 Britons—mainly Labourites—had descended on London to protest the war. This would have been equivalent to four million Republicans descending on Washington to protest Bush's decision to go to war. If Powell's UN speech was a "manipulation" of the facts to hoodwink the public, it failed miserably. It certainly did not persuade any of the leftists who had poured into the streets of London in Saddam's defense; and it did not persuade the French or Russian allies of Saddam to desert him. In America, the majority support for the war had long been in place, and for them Powell's speech was superfluous.

For Gore and the president's Democratic critics, all these facts count for nothing. In their place is the malevolent George Bush. According to Gore and the Democrats, America went to war for reasons that are either illegitimate or immoral or both. According to Gore, the sending of American troops to Iraq was an imperial aggression, orchestrated by the president and his advisors who manipulated the evidence, deceived the people and ignored the UN to carry out their malign intent: "The pursuit of 'dominance' in foreign policy led the Bush administration to ignore the United Nations," writes Gore, showing his utter contempt for the facts.[7]

Unlike Gore's president, who in going to war in Bosnia did ignore the UN, Bush secured a unanimous Security Council ultimatum to deliver to Saddam Hussein. Bush eventually did ignore France, which had built Saddam's nuclear reactor, collaborated with Saddam's theft of the "Oil for Food" billions, and made clear it would veto any attempt to enforce the UN ultimatum. Bush also ignored Russia, which had supplied two-thirds of Saddam's weapons, helped him sabotage the UN sanctions, and refused to enforce the UN ultimatum. What Bush did not ignore were the 17 UN resolutions designed to keep the Middle East peace and protect the world from the consequences of its failure. It was Al Gore who did that.[8]

---

[7]Al Gore, "The Assault On Reason," Penguin, 2007

[8]For a sense of the surreal political climate at the time, here is a summary passage from Michiko Kakutani's sycophantic review of Gore's book in *The New York Times,* May 22, 2007: "And yet for all its sharply voiced opinions, *The Assault on Reason* turns out to be less a partisan, election-cycle harangue than a fiercely argued brief about the current Bush White House that is grounded in copiously footnoted citations from newspaper articles, Congressional testimony and commission reports — a brief that is as powerful in making its points about the implications of this administration's policies as the author's 2006 book, 'An Inconvenient Truth,' was in making its points about the fallout of global warming." Michiko Kakutani, "Al Gore Speaks of a Nation in Danger," *New York Times,* May 22, 2007, http://www.nytimes.com/2007/05/22/books/ 22kaku.html?_r=0

3

Does the Left Know Who the Enemy Is?

Does anyone wonder where the Tom Hayden-Jane Fonda SDS radicals went? The ones who chanted, "Hey, hey LBJ, how many kids did you kill today?"[1] and cheered on the Communists in Vietnam, and went into the streets to demand America's withdrawal from Vietnam and became suddenly silent when our troops were pulled and the Communists proceeded to slaughter two-and-a-half million Cambodians and Vietnamese? Well, today they are the heart and soul of the Democratic Party, calling for a capitulation in the war in Iraq and casually referring to George Bush as a liar and worse, while insisting that America's war in Iraq is a mask for conquest and imperial ambitions.

These aging New Leftists are also busy digging graves for the Jews in the Middle East by pretending that thc gcnocidal Muslims in the Palestinian territories are really victims of Israeli oppression and only express genocidal desires because they're reduced to desperation by American-backed Israeli power. These leftists are grouped around magazines like *The Nation* and *The American Prospect* and websites like *Daily Kos* and *Common Dreams;* their organizations are embedded in the Netroots and Democratic Party caucuses like the "Campaign for America's Future," which are now mandatory stations on the road to the White House for the current crop of Democratic presidential candidates.

August 17, 2007, http://archive.frontpagemag.com/Printable.aspx?ArtId=27797

[1]http://www.psywarrior.com/nviet4.html

These observations are inspired by an email I received recently from one of them, an academic with an undeserved reputation for moderation named Rick Perlstein. His email read: "Couldn't find your *jihad* vid on YouTube as promised in your email today. What's the YouTube url?—RP." Of course, I knew who Rick Perlstein was, and the lack of a hello in his email, or any indication of civility, which even a political opponent could be expected to muster, was not a good sign. On past occasions, Perlstein had attacked me pretty viciously; this email was not a response to anything I had actually written but to a newsletter that my staff had put out over my signature. But telling him to get lost or just ignoring his email is not the way I normally deal with people who solicit my help. Moreover, I can never give up the hope that political disagreements, which are so sharp and divisive these days, will turn into dialogues and actual exchanges of ideas. So I responded thus: "Dear Rick, I'm not sure which of our three videos you're referring to. You can access all three at www.terrorismawareness.org. . . ." To which he replied: "Your e-newsletter says *What Every American Needs to Know About Jihad* is on YouTube, which I'd like to embed on my site." By this time, I had a pretty good idea that whatever he was going to do with the video was not going to be pleasant; but I went along with the program anyway. "I'm happy to be collaborating on something with you. I'll have to pass this question on to my technical people . . ."

Perlstein did "embed" the video on his website—a section of the History News Network, a gathering place for academic historians, but not to make others aware of the *jihadist* threat. This was his commentary:

> August 15, 2007—12:57pm.
>
> The right's preeminent shrieking harpy—no, not Ann Coulter; even worse than Ann Coulter—importunes me with an "e-newsletter" about the latest goings-on at his David Horowitz Freedom Center. A tidbit that caught my eye:

One strong measurement of the effect we're having (and the need for what we do) came in the form of request from the head of the FBI-California Highway Patrol Joint Counter-terrorism Task Force who called this week to ask if their group could use our flash video 'What Every American Needs to Know About Jihad' as a training film.

See *What Every American Needs to Know About Jihad* for yourself, and let the California Highway Patrol know if you think this is productive use of their officers' time, and a useful contribution to California's public safety [. . .][2]

The four-minute video runs through 25 major terrorist attacks, from the 1983 bombing of the barracks in Lebanon through the London bombings of 2005, with graphic photographs of their human toll; it quotes Islamists like Ahmadinejad and bin Laden about their goals; and it finally shows their supporters in Europe and America calling for death to the infidels who insult Islam. Perlstein's reason for posting the video was not to help us alert Americans to the fact that the *jihadists* are planning our destruction, or even to engage us in a debate about whether our film accurately portrayed the threat. It was to mobilize a campaign of other leftist academics to harass individuals from the Los Angeles Joint Counter-terrorism Task Force and pressure them to rescind their decision to use the video as a training film. They succeeded. Hyper-sensitive law enforcement officials dropped the film, rather than risk public controversy.

Reading Perlstein's appeal and the comments that followed was revealing. I have written an entire book—*Unholy Alliance: Radical Islam and the American Left*—to explain how the hatred felt by many American leftists towards their country and their fellow citizens (whom some of them regard as "little Eichmanns") has led them into tacit alliances with religious zealots who want

[2]"Rick Perlstein vs. David Horowitz: Who the Enemy Is," *History News Network*, August 15, 2007 and August 17, 2007, http://hnn.us/roundup/entries/41959.html

to destroy us. Yet, even though I have explained this convergence at great length, I continually find myself unprepared for the actual intensity of the hatred, which—when one considers that they themselves will be regarded as infidels by the terrorists—is suicidal. So, while I knew Perlstein was up to something, I was not really prepared for the fact that he would consider this little video, rather than its subject, to be the menace.

Consider the following comments, taken from Perlstein's "Campaign for America's Future" website. This is an audience, remember, which Hillary Clinton, Barack Obama and the other Democratic aspirants to the presidency think it is necessary to woo:

> "Now David Horowitz seems to be trying to fill the shoes of both Goebbels and Leni Riefenstahl.... Bragging that the Joint Counter-terrorism Task Force is using his 'film' is like bragging that the Nazi's are buying his Swastikas.[3] The JTTF has a track record that marks it as a political unit designed to target Bush administration opponents —Citizen Steve."

Is this the company Rick Perlstein keeps? People who think the CHP and the FBI are Nazis?

Here's one from someone who wrote the CHP:

> "I looked at the video, and it is, indeed, right-wing garbage. I then clicked on the link for the California Highway Patrol, and filled out the form for a citizen complaint. As a California resident, I am deeply concerned that the CHP would even consider using such garbage as a training film. There's no 'training' in the film whatsoever, only hysteria raising." —farbie

And here's one from one of the many leftists who were on the wrong side in the Cold War:

---

[3]http://www.sourcewatch.org/index.php?title=FBI's_Joint_Terrorism_Task_Force#California. Sourcewatch is a left-wing database.

"New Graphics, Old Shtick
"Hot damn! substitute the word 'communist' and you have a classic 1950's 'global domination' classroom propaganda flick. every day, the corporo-military right gets more desperate and determined to keep the cattle 'on message.'"
Submitted by billykidd on August 16, 2007—1:07pm.

And then there's this one in response to the photos we showed of demonstrations in Chicago and Los Angeles, supporting Hezbollah, and displaying signs with Israeli flags defaced with swastikas:

Jihadists in Chicago and Los Angeles!!!
Aug 15th, 2007 by oldmancoyote
Rick Perlstein notes that the California Highway Patrol, apparently, are interested in using it as a training video. I'm not sure what the training would be for other than profiling Muslims.
Posted in Conservative Craziness, PR

In other words, it is right-wing hysteria to regard as dangerous the *jihadists* who have carried out 9,000 terrorist attacks since 9/11, who have sworn our destruction, who could very well possess biological, chemical and nuclear weapons, who want to die so they can get to heaven, who believe in the mass slaughter of innocents, and who have allies across this country, including those who don't take the threat seriously and/or regard those who do so as the real threat. To do so is to be a "shrieking harpy," a Goebbels incarnate, a right-wing corporo-military fascist, and an Islamophobic racist. To such a pass we have come.

4

The Democrats and the War

Most conversations about the coming elections focus on the question of which candidate is most suited to lead the nation as it confronts the challenges and threats ahead. A better question would be to ask whether there is one party which has demonstrated in word and deed that it is unfit to lead the nation in war at all. Criticism of government policy is essential to a democracy. But in the last five years, the Democratic Party has crossed the line from criticism of war policy to sabotage of the war, a position no major political party has taken until now. Starting in July 2003, just three months into the war in Iraq, the Democratic National Committee ran a national TV ad whose message was: "Read his lips: President Bush Deceives the American People." This was the beginning of a relentless five-year campaign to persuade Americans and their allies that "Bush lied, people died," that the war was "unnecessary" and "Iraq was no threat." In other words, for five years, the leaders of the Democratic Party have been telling Americans, America's allies and America's enemies that their country is an aggressor nation, has violated international law, and was in effect the "bad guy" in the conflict with the Saddam regime.

The first principle of psychological-warfare campaigns is to destroy the moral character of the opposing commander-in-chief and discredit his nation's cause, which is a perfect summary of the

---

June 4, 2008, http://archive.frontpagemag.com/Printable.aspx?ArtId=31214

campaign that has been waged for the length of this war by the Democratic Party leadership—Joe Lieberman being the honorable exception, and he was driven out of his party as a result. The one saving grace for Democrats would be if their charges were true—if they were deceived into supporting the war, and if they had turned against it only because they realized their mistake. But this charge is demonstrably false.

In fact, the claim that Bush lied in order to dupe Democrats into supporting the war is itself the biggest lie of the war. Every Democratic senator who voted for the war had on his or her desk before the vote a 100-page report, called "The National Intelligence Estimate," which summarized all America's intelligence on Iraq that was used to justify the war.[1] We live in a democracy; consequently, the opposition party has access to all our secrets. Democrats sit on the Senate Intelligence Committee, which oversees all of America's intelligence agencies. If any Democrat on that committee, including Senator John Kerry, had requested any intelligence information on Iraq, he or she would have had that information on his or her desk within 24 hours. The self-justifying claim that Bush lied to hoodwink the Democrats is a fraudulent charge with no factual support. The Democrats who had supported the use of force changed their views on the war in Iraq for one reason and one reason alone: in June 2003, three months into the war, a far-left Democrat named Howard Dean was poised to win the Democratic Party presidential nomination by running against the war and promising that he would get us out.

The Democrats' other principal charge, that Iraq was no threat, is also false. In his recent book *The Assault on Reason,* Al Gore claims that "Iraq posed no threat" because it was a "fragile and unstable" nation. But if that were true, the same argument would apply to Afghanistan on September 10, 2001. Afghanistan is half

---

[1]National Intelligence Estimate [From October 2002 NIE], Congressional Record: July 21, 2003, Pages E1545-E1546, http://www.fas.org/irp/congress/ 2003_cr/h072103.html

the size of Iraq and a much poorer and more unstable nation; it is not a principal energy source for Europe, and its government did not invade two countries or use chemical weapons on its own citizens as Saddam did. Yet, by providing a safe harbor for al-Qaeda, Afghanistan made possible the murder of 3,000 Americans in half an hour and allowed Osama bin Laden to do what the Germans and the Japanese had failed to accomplish in six years of the Second World War: to kill Americans on American soil. That is why in February 2002, a year before the war in Iraq, Al Gore was saying that "Iraq is a virulent threat in a class by itself" and that President Bush should "push the limit" to do what was necessary to deal with Saddam Hussein.[2]

But the most self-serving and deceptive of the lies told by the Democratic leadership is this: you can support the troops and not support the war. No, you can't. You can't tell a 19-year old, who is risking his young life in Fallujah and is surrounded by terrorists who want to kill him, that he shouldn't be there in the first place; that he's with the "bad guys," the aggressors, the occupiers who have no moral right to be in Iraq. You can't do that and *not* threaten his morale, encourage his enemies, deprive him of allies and put him in danger. And that is exactly what the Democrats have done—and all the Democrats have done—for five years of America's war to deny the terrorists victory in Iraq.

---

[2]Adam Nagourney, "Gore, Championing Bush, Calls For a 'Final Reckoning' With Iraq," *The New York Times,* February 13, 2002, *http://www.nytimes.com/ 2002/02/13/world/nation-challenged-democrat-gore-championing-bush-calls-for-final-reckoning-with.html*

5

Fort Hood: Our Brain-Dead Country

A Muslim fanatic kills 13 unarmed soldiers at Fort Hood and wounds 32 others. The shooter, who has an Internet site praising Islamic suicide bombers, is a major in the U.S. army, with access to military intelligence and lethal weaponry.[1] How did this happen?

It's not as though the army didn't know that he was a Muslim fanatic and supporter of the Islamic *jihad* against the West. He was under investigation for six months prior to the massacre because authorities were aware of his anti-American, *jihadist* rantings. He did not want to be deployed as an American officer to Afghanistan because that would mean killing fellow Muslims instead of infidels like us. He wanted to be discharged. But despite his known identification with America's enemies, the army kept him in its officer corps and promoted him from Captain to Major. How was this possible?

After identifying America as the "aggressor" in Afghanistan and Iraq, this *jihadist* picked up an armful of semi-automatic weapons and headed for the center at Fort Hood where unarmed

---

November 9, 2009, http://frontpagemag.com/ 2009/david-horowitz/our-brain-dead-country-by-david-horowitz/

[1]David Forsmark, "To MSNBC the Least Important Thing about Killer Army Doctor Is He Was a Muslim Who Lauded Suicide Bombers: Meltdown with Keith Olbermann Part 14," *Newsrealblog.com*, November 5 2009, http://www.newsrealblog.com/ 2009/11/05/to-msnbc-the-least-important-thing-about-killer-army-doctor-is-he-was-a-muslim-who-compared-suicide-bombers-to-soldiers-who-throw-themselves-on-grenades-to-protect-others-meltdown-with-keith-olberma/

soldiers were in the process of being deployed to fight his fellow *jihadists* in Afghanistan intending to kill as many as possible. This morning, the Fox News Channel chyron says: "Investigators search for a motive in the Fort Hood killings." Is everybody in government out of their minds?

The Fort Hood killings are the chickens of the left coming home to roost. Already, the chief political correspondent of *The Nation* has decried anyone who might refer to the fact that the killer, Nidal Hasan, is a Palestinian Muslim.[2] According to *The Nation,* to merely mention that fact is "Islamophobia." *The Nation*'s transparent attempt to protect America's enemies continues its 60-year tradition as a fifth-column collaborator with America's enemies—defender of the Rosenbergs, defender of Hiss, defender of their boss Stalin, defender of Mao, defender of Castro and now defender of Islamic *jihadists,* providing them with the camouflage they need to keep America asleep.

The Nation's response is only the tip of an iceberg. The fifth column of the unholy alliance between radical Islam and the American left is now so entrenched in our government that its influence is sufficient to make even our military captive in matters such as the Fort Hood attack. This is the first successful manifestation of the preventable atrocities some of us have been warning about since 9/11. We are facing an *internal* threat posed by this fifth column whose Muslim Brotherhood network reaches into our universities, our government and our military. But it is "politically incorrect" to mention or take notice of this fact. For talking about it, one can be barred, as I have been, from speaking on university campuses (in particular the Jesuit school, St. Louis University). This embargo puts every American at risk. Hasan had semi-automatic weapons, but not nuclear devices. That possibility is not too far off unless we undergo a sea change in our attitudes,

---

[2]John Nichols, "Horror at Fort Hood Inspires Horribly Predictable Islamophobia," *The Nation,* November 5, 2009, http://www.thenation.com/blog/horror-fort-hood-inspires-horribly-predictable-islamophobia

and marshal the intelligence and the courage to recognize the threat.

[Postscript: As of 2013, the Obama administration officially describes the *jihadist* attack at Fort Hood as "workplace violence" and has refused to award purple hearts to the more than thirty soldiers who were wounded by the assailant.]

6

How Embarrassing to Be a Liberal in the Middle of a Holy War

Why is it that, whenever a so-called liberal opens his mouth about the Fort Hood massacre by a Muslim *jihadist,* I know that I'm going to feel less safe? The Democratic mayor of Chicago blames the shooting of 39 soldiers ready to be deployed in the war against Muslim *jihadists* in Afghanistan on the "fact" that "America loves guns."[1] Actually the American soldiers were not allowed to have guns on the base. (How is that possible?) Nor did the armed traitor Nidal Hasan particularly love guns. What he loved was the Islamic war against the West, and what he hated was America and its infidel citizens. Because there were no guns permitted on the Fort Hood base, his soldier-victims were defenseless and unarmed, which is why no one shot him dead after his first blast. What is wrong with American liberals that they proudly and publicly reveal themselves to be brain-dead when it comes to the Muslim holy war that has been declared against us?

The *New York Times* website devoted a whole article to summarizing the debate on the motives of the traitor, as though this was a mystery. The article included a sampling from a blog on "the

---

November 11, 2009, http://frontpagemag.com/ 2009/11/11/liberal-idiocy-on-fort-hood-by-david-horowitz/

[1]Andrew Marcus, "Chicago Mayor Daley Blames Fort Hood On America's Love Of Guns!," *Breitbart,* November 10, 2009, http://www.breitbart.com/Big-Government/ 2009/11/10/Chicago-Mayor-Daley-Blames-Fort-Hood-On-America—-s-Love-Of-Guns

meaning of Fort Hood,"[2] which provides a good picture of the mush that the brains of such respected left-wing commentators as *The Atlantic*'s James Fallows have been reduced to. Fallows is the author of a column on the attack entitled "The Meaninglessness of the Shootings."[3] Veteran leftist Michael Tomasky writes in *The Guardian:* "So if Hasan was indeed an America-hating extremist, what are we to make of it?"[4] And he concludes: nothing.

"America-hating extremist" would be an accurate description of some of Tomasky's friends at *The Village Voice,* where he once worked. But from the evidence already in hand, it is hardly an adequate description of Nidal Hasan. Hasan thought of himself as a soldier in a global army that has declared war in the name of Islam, first on Americans and Jews, and then on all infidels. That lends a somewhat different shade to his disposition than "America-hating extremist," which could easily describe Michael Moore. This Muslim radical declared to an audience of doctors at a military university that those who do not believe in Islam should be beheaded, and boiling oil should be poured down their throats.[5] Are liberals too sensitive about religious tolerance to notice details like this? Would they be so blind if the speaker were a Christian and his targets were Jews?

In fact, it is not sensitive that they are, but in denial. And why is that? Well, it is the same denial that progressives maintained

---

[2]Eric Etheridge, "The Meaning of Fort Hood," *The New York Times,* November 9, 2009, http://opinionator.blogs.nytimes.com/ 2009/11/09/ the-meaning-of-fort-hood/

[3]James Fallows, "The Meaninglessness of Shootings," *The Atlantic,* November 5, 2009, http://www.theatlantic.com/technology/archive/ 2009/11/the-meaninglessness-of-shootings/ 29723/

[4]Michael Tomasky, "More on Hasan, " *The Guardian,* November 9, 2009, http://www.guardian.co.uk/commentisfree/michaeltomasky/2009/nov/ 09/nidal-hassan-fort-hood-shootings

[5]Nick Allen, "Fort Hood Gunman Had Told US Military Colleagues that Infidels Should Have Their Throats Cut," *The Telegraph,* November 8, 2009, http://www.telegraph.co.uk/news/worldnews/northamerica/usa/ 6526030/Fort-Hood-gunman-had-told-US-military-colleagues-that-infidels-should-have-their-throats-cut.html

through 70 years of the Communist nightmare: denial that mass slaughters were being conducted by socialists, that socialist states were vast prison camps, and that a similar fate awaited us in the West if we didn't wage a cold war against their expansionist ambitions. The only mystery is why progressives like Tomasky and Fallows should bend over backwards to protect medieval zealots who idolize Osama bin Laden, Hamas and Hezbollah and embrace their genocidal agendas. There is only one possible answer to this question: to one degree or another, progressives also regard America as the Great Satan (and Israel as the Little Satan); and they believe that the policies of these two countries are the real cause of the Muslim violence that is directed against the West.

7

Why I Am Not a Neo-Conservative

When George Bush launched the military campaign to remove Saddam Hussein and enforce Security Council Resolution 1441 (along with sixteen other Security Council resolutions Iraq had defied), I supported it. I support it today. It was a necessary war and a just war. By toppling a monster who had flouted international order and was an obvious threat, Bush did the right thing. When he named the campaign Operation Iraqi Freedom, I was also an enthusiast. It put the Democratic Party, which quickly betrayed the war it had supported, and the political left, which instinctively opposes any war America is engaged in, on the defensive. When the president said he was going to create a democracy in Iraq, I almost believed him. And that seemed to put me in the camp of the neo-conservatives, for whom democracy in Iraq was not only an aspiration but an agenda. In any case, people labeled me that way—not least because I am a Jew, and "neo-conservative" functions for the ominously expanding anti-Semitic left as a code for allegedly self-serving Jews who want to sacrifice American lives for Israel.

But whatever I wrote about the war in support of the neo-conservative agenda, I was never a 100-percent believer in the idea that democracy could be so easily implanted in so hostile a soil. I wanted to see Saddam toppled and a non-terrorist-supporting government in its place. I would have settled for that, and for a large

---

March 23, 2011, http://frontpagemag.com/2011/03/23/why-i-am-not-a-neo-conservative/

U.S. military base as well. But I allowed myself to be swept up in the Bush-led enthusiasm for a democratic revolution in the Middle East—in part, as I have already said, to hoist the left on its own petard. I remained on board the democracy movement until the Beirut spring began to wane; I got off when election results in Gaza came in and put an Islamic Nazi party into power. That was the end of my neo-conservative illusions.

It looks as if we are headed for the same result in Egypt, where the Muslim Brotherhood is poised to win the September elections. The reality is that a totalitarian Islam is the increasingly dominant movement in the Arab world. Any elections likely to take place will be on the order of one man, one vote, one time. For their part, neo-conservatives are now cheering on the Obama administration's reckless intervention in Libya, as though the past ten years have taught them nothing. The nation-building effort in Iraq led to a squandering of American resources and a weakening of American power. Putting a man who is hostile to American power in the White House is not the least aspect of this American decline. Because of these nation-building delusions, we are still mired in Afghanistan—now the longest war in American history. And now we have plunged into the Middle Eastern maelstrom with no clear agenda or objective.

In my view, the Obama administration is the most radical and therefore the most dangerous administration in American history. Conservatives need to be very clear about the limits and objectives of American power, so that they can lead the battle to restore our government to health. To accomplish this, neo-conservatives need to admit they were wrong and go back to the drawing board. They should give up the "neo" and become conservatives again.

8

Bin Laden Is History, the Jihad Is Not

The now deceased Osama bin Laden was a symbol of the Islamic *jihad.* After 9/11, surveys by Al Jazeera and other sources indicated that between 10 and 50 percent of Muslims regarded him as a hero. That is somewhere between 150 million and 750 million people. Osama bin Laden was the symbol of their aspirations. Symbols are important, and the death of this one is important. But the *jihad* will go on.

The fact that bin Laden was killed in a mansion near Islamabad (fitting name) is a mark of the support he had from regimes in the Muslim world. But by the time our forces penetrated his hiding place ten years after 9/11, the center of the *jihad* had long passed from the caves of Waziristan in Asia to its spawning grounds in the Middle East—the Islamic Republic of Iran, its proxies Hezbollah in Lebanon and Hamas in Gaza, and to the fount of the Islamic crusade against the West, the Muslim Brotherhood in Egypt.

Obama will take an earned credit for the death of al-Qaeda's leader, and for the aggressive strikes he has conducted in Pakistan in particular. This is a forward strategy that provoked the wrath of the "liberal" establishment against Nixon over Vietnam, Reagan over Libya and Bush over Iraq. Unfortunately, this is only the right hand of Obama's strategy towards the *jihad.* The left hand is

---

May 2, 2011, frontpagemag.com/ 2011/05/02/osama-bin-laden-is-history-the-jihad-is-not- 2/

simultaneously stoking the fires of Islamic aggression in its Middle Eastern heartland, while obscuring the identity of the enemy.

In his speech tonight, Obama talked as though the war is exclusively a conflict with al-Qaeda, even though al-Qaeda has played a diminishing role in the 17,000-plus Islamic terrorist attacks that have been perpetrated since 9/11. After 9/11, Bush swore that the United States would not tolerate terrorist regimes that threatened the democracies of the West. You are either for us or against us, he said then to the dismay of the appeasement left. But since he spoke those words Islamic terrorist regimes have been created in Lebanon and the West Bank, Gaza and Somalia; the Taliban has been resurgent in Afghanistan; and the Muslim Brotherhood has emerged as a dominant force in Egypt. The storm clouds that are gathering, not least because of the feckless actions of the Obama administration itself, will not be dispelled by one man's death.

There are many clouds of grief and suffering on the horizon. As President Bush so rightly said in the days after 9/11, this will be a long, hard war that is likely to last our lifetimes.

9

The Great Betrayal

Four years ago, I co-authored a book with Ben Johnson called *Party of Defeat: How Democrats and Radicals Sabotaged the War in Iraq*. In it, we documented the Democrats' bad faith in supporting the decision to go to war and only four months later, to turn their backs on the war, while American troops were still engaged in battle. For the next five years, Democrats conducted an unprecedented campaign against the war, describing it as an illegal aggression, both unnecessary and immoral. They accused America's commander-in-chief of lying to them in particular and to the American people in general, in order to manipulate support for a war that should never have taken place.

As we pointed out, the Democrats' charge that "Bush lied, people died" was itself the biggest lie of the war. Senate Democrats John Kerry, Jay Rockefeller and Dianne Feinstein sat on the Intelligence Oversight Committee. They had access to every piece of intelligence data that was available to President Bush. If they had any cause to doubt the reliability of the information provided to justify the use of force, they could have summoned the director of intelligence, George Tenet, a Clinton administration appointee, and asked for clarification or additional data. The reason Senate Democrats supported the decision to remove Saddam Hussein was that doing so was a necessity, regardless of whether Saddam

---

Originally written as an introduction to *The Great Betrayal: Obama's Wars and the War in Iraq* by Daniel Greenfield, July 2012, http://frontpagemag.com/upload/pamphlets/great-betrayal.pdf

possessed WMDs or not, and had been recognized as such by Democrats themselves. The issue was always the character and therefore the intentions of Saddam Hussein—a ruler who had launched two aggressive wars in the Middle East, violated the Gulf War truce, defied 16 UN Security Council resolutions, massacred more than 300,000 Iraqis, used poison gas on the Kurds, was determined to build WMDs and was denying UN inspectors access to his weapons facilities. For these reasons, regime- change in Iraq had been an official American policy since 1998, when President Bill Clinton signed the "Iraqi Liberation Act"[1] into law.

Democrats lied about why they changed their minds in regard to Iraq because the truth was too damning. The reason they turned against the war had nothing to do with the war itself, or the rationale for undertaking it, or misinformation fed to them by George Bush. It was a presidential primary season for Democrats, and they turned against the war for purely political reasons. An anti-war candidate from the left named Howard Dean had surged ahead in the polls among Democratic primary voters and was running away with the nomination. It was the desire to win a primary election that caused John Kerry and John Edwards to reverse their positions on the war, to turn their support into opposition and mount reckless attacks on their own government and the party in power. Once Kerry and Edwards reversed their position on the war, they gained the support of the primary voters, overtook Dean, and became the nominees on the Democratic ticket. Until this turn in the Democratic primary, opposition to the war had been the political cause of the radical left. But it now became the official position of the Democratic Party.

The Democrats could not admit the truth; namely, that they had turned their backs on troops they had only months before sent into harm's way because they wanted to win an election. So they said—and had to say—*Bush lied.* There were honorable exceptions

---

[1]Iraq Liberation Act of 1998, http://en.wikipedia.org/wiki/Iraq_Liberation_Act

to this disgraceful assault, like Joe Lieberman and Dick Gephardt, who sacrificed their presidential ambitions for the good of their country. But the majority of the Democratic Party leadership was now set on a path of unconditional, no-holds-barred attacks on the war, whatever the cost. Opposition to the war was the central theme of the Democrats' general campaign during the 2004 presidential election. In a debate with Bush, the Democrats' standard-bearer John Kerry declared Iraq to be "the wrong war in the wrong place at the wrong time."[2] This demoralizing attack on a war in progress was made by the same John Kerry who, only months earlier, had given an eloquent speech on the floor of the Senate in support of the use of force.

Despite the Democrats' betrayal, however, neither the Bush administration nor Republican leaders held them accountable. For the next five years, the Democrats continued their attacks on the war, while Republicans treated their sedition as though it were a normal contribution to a foreign policy debate. In fact, it was not normal; it was unprecedented. Ever since the onset of the Cold War, bipartisanship in foreign policy had been the rule, with both parties observing the principle that "politics stops at the water's edge." The debate over Vietnam was not really an exception. It did not begin until there was bipartisan agreement that America should withdraw its forces. The debate itself was over *how* to withdraw, not whether America was an aggressor nation that had violated international law and was conducting an indefensible and immoral war against a country that was "no threat." The Democrats' unrestrained and unprecedented attacks on the Iraq War led to a bitter polarization on the home-front from which the country has yet to recover. The divisions crippled the effectiveness of the commander-in-chief, and prevented America from dealing with Saddam's allies in Syria and Iran. This failure has had incalculable

[2]Patricia Wilson, "Kerry on Iraq: 'Wrong War, Wrong Place, Wrong Time,'" *Common Dreams*, September 6, 2004, http://www.commondreams.org/headlines04/0906–02.htm

consequences for the politics of the Middle East, and also for the security of the United States.

Because of these developments, I was anxious that the book Ben Johnson and I had written should have the widest possible audience. Consequently, I sent the galleys of *Party of Defeat* to prominent conservatives, receiving endorsements from national figures such as former senator Rick Santorum, former U.N. ambassador John Bolton, former Clinton CIA director James Woolsey and Fox TV anchor Sean Hannity, who called it "an eye-opening account of one of the greatest betrayals in American history." To make sure that the book and its argument were taken seriously, I also sent copies of the galleys and requests for endorsements to senators and congressmen, including the chairs or ranking members of the armed services, intelligence, homeland security and judiciary committees. The argument laid out in *Party of Defeat* was endorsed by 18 legislators including senators Jeff Sessions, Jon Kyl, James Inhofe and Tom Coburn, and representatives David Dreier, Mike Pence, Peter Hoekstra, Peter King, Howard "Buck" McKeon, Lamar Smith, John Shadegg, Ed Royce, Ginny Brown-Waite and Tom Tancredo, all of whom signed this statement: "*Party of Defeat* is a well-documented and disturbing account of the unprecedented attacks by leaders of the Democratic Party on a war they supported and then turned against. In a democracy like ours, criticism of war policy is legitimate and necessary. But deliberate undermining of a war policy, the authors of this book argue, is a different matter. Every American concerned about the future of their country in the war on terror should consider the arguments in this book."[3]

When *Party of Defeat* was published in the spring of 2008, I was anxious to see the reaction. But there was none. Despite the endorsements from senior Republican legislators responsible for overseeing foreign policy, intelligence and national security mat-

---

[3]http://www.amazon.com/Party-Defeat-David-Horowitz/dp/product-description/1890626740/ref=dp_proddesc_0?ie=UTF8&n=283155&s=books

ters, the book was greeted with a deafening silence. Except for the web magazine I myself published at Frontpagemag.com, not a single review of the book appeared either in print or on the Internet. I was used to the blackout from the "liberal" press, and expected it. What I was not prepared for was the silence from conservative reviewers.

I'm not quite sure how to explain this, given the fact that 18 senior Republicans in congress had endorsed the book. But I think it is fair to say that, ever since the early days of the Cold War, conservatives and Republicans have been generally skittish when it comes to noticing the uncertain loyalties frequently displayed by people on the left in regard to matters of national security. During the Iraq War, for example, *The New York Times* leaked a number of classified secrets, thereby destroying at least three national-security programs designed to protect Americans from terrorist attacks. To embarrass their president and their country, *The Times* also ran stories about the scandal at Abu Ghraib prison on its front page for 32 straight days and 60 all told, which was more than two-and-a—half times the total number of stories *The Times* ran on the Holocaust and more than ten times its front-page features on the Holocaust in the course of the entire Second World War.[4]

Democrats, by contrast, had no such compunction about questioning their political adversaries' patriotism. Referring to President Bush, former vice president Al Gore—who had initially supported the use of force—now reversed himself, screaming "He betrayed us!"[5] in a speech before the left-wing organization MoveOn.org. Senator Edward Kennedy called the war "a fraud concocted in Texas" to make money for Bush's friends.[6] These

---

[4]"*New York Times* Streak of Page One Stories on Abu Ghraib Ends at 32 Days!," June 2, 2004, http://www.freerepublic.com/focus/f-news/1145998/posts

[5]Katharine Q. Seelye, "Gore Says Bush Betrayed the U.S. by Using 9/11 as a Reason for War in Iraq," *New York Times,* February 9, 2004, http://www.nytimes.com/ 2004/02/09/politics/campaign/09GORE.html

[6]Sean Loughlin, "Kennedy Stands by Criticism of Bush on Iraq," *CNN.com,* September 19, 2003, http://www.cnn.com/ 2003/ALLPOLITICS/09/19/kennedy.iraq/

attacks on the moral character of America's commander-in-chief were a gift to America's Islamist enemies around the world. Attacks on the moral character of the leader of the *enemy's* forces are, in fact, prescribed as the first order of business in psychological-warfare manuals. Yet Republicans refused to respond in kind, or in a manner appropriate to the offense Democrats were committing. Not a single Republican legislator or spokesperson rose to characterize the Democrats' attacks as the betrayals or sabotage they were. None even suggested that dividing the home-front and conducting a propaganda campaign worthy of the enemy was to risk the lives of American men and women in the field. Yet, when one publicity-seeking preacher burned a Koran in Florida during the Obama administration's war in Afghanistan, Democrats and Republicans were quick to condemn him for precisely that reason.

The failure of *Party of Defeat* to gain an audience effectively closed the book on the case we had made. There was little that was personal in the frustration I felt over this situation. I have written many books, and whether one is successful or not is of no great moment. But the fate of *Party of Defeat* was a different matter. I made one additional effort to draw attention to it by inviting leading critics of the Iraq War, like *Newsweek*'s Michael Isikoff and Brookings' security expert Lawrence Korb, to respond to our argument. I published the debates in Frontpage magazine.[7] But the exercise proved to be futile. All of the six war critics I invited chose to duck the issue of the Democrats' false claim that Bush had lied, and went on to rehash their original critiques.

My personal frustration at the failure of our argument to gain an audience was nothing compared to my frustration when the long-term consequences of the Democrats' "anti-war" campaign began to unfold. Because of the severity of the attacks on the war in Iraq, and the fact that the Democratic Party was their chief carrier, the Bush administration was unable to pursue Saddam's flee-

[7]David Swindle, "Revisiting Party of Defeat," *FrontPage Magazine*, March 4, 2010, http://frontpagemag.com/2010/03/04/the-sledgehammer-comes-down-on-the-party-of-defeat/

ing generals and shipments of weapons into Syria, or to punish Iran for supplying the IEDs that killed most of our troops on the battlefield. This national paralysis was a direct result of the divided home-front; it was soon followed by the destruction of Lebanon by Syria and the installation of the terrorist army Hezbollah as a regime within the regime. It also emboldened the regime in Iran to go forward with its nuclear program and to step up its war against the state of Israel by supporting the terrorist organization Hamas. Indeed, the Islamist upheaval that is now transforming the Middle East and empowering the jihadists was greatly encouraged by the Democrats' success in blackening America's reputation, defaming American policies and crippling the Bush administration's War on Terror—a war that Obama has officially declared over.[8]

When the policies of the new Obama administration began to unfold in Afghanistan and Iraq—the theaters of war that Democrats had previously attacked—and when Obama then undertook a new war in Libya, which violated every principle the Democrats had invoked to condemn Bush's intervention in Iraq, I felt the need to re-open the discussion, and saw an opportunity to do so. In these wars Obama was daily exposing each of the lies Democrats had used to sabotage the War on Terror. They had attacked Bush for conducting an aggressive war, for detaining suspected terrorists without trial, and for causing civilian casualties. Now Obama was invading a country, Libya, that was "no threat," blowing up whole families in a non-combatant nation, Pakistan, and using drones to assassinate suspected terrorists without trial. And he was committing all these acts with Democratic approval. I asked Daniel Greenfield, a talented and insightful writer, to look at these wars Obama was now conducting, and to place them against the back-

---

[8]Toby Harnden, "Barack Obama Declares the 'War on Terror' Is Over," *The Telegraph*, May 27, 2010, http://www.telegraph.co.uk/news/worldnews/barackobama/7772598/Barack-Obama-declares-the-War-on-Terror-is-over.html

drop of Bush's war in Iraq and the Democrats' unbridled opposition to that war; I asked him to call it *The Great Betrayal.*[9]

[9]Available as an ebook on Kindle or from the David Horowitz Freedom Center in Los Angeles, https://secure.donationreport.com/productlist.html?key=5DGIXYHTRFJI

Index